Old Ideas, New Practices: When Religion Is for Relationships

Old Ideas, New Practices: When Religion Is for Relationships

A Handbook of Instructional Strategies for Teachers and Parents

Bernard Lawrence Potvin

RESOURCE *Publications* • Eugene, Oregon

OLD IDEAS, NEW PRACTICES: WHEN RELIGION IS FOR RELATIONSHIPS
A Handbook of Instructional Strategies for Teachers and Parents

Copyright © 2021 Bernard Lawrence Potvin. All rights reserved. Except for brief quotations in critical publications or reviews, no part of this book may be reproduced in any manner without prior written permission from the publisher. Write: Permissions, Wipf and Stock Publishers, 199 W. 8th Ave., Suite 3, Eugene, OR 97401.

Resource Publications
An Imprint of Wipf and Stock Publishers
199 W. 8th Ave., Suite 3
Eugene, OR 97401

www.wipfandstock.com

PAPERBACK ISBN: 978-1-7252-8466-1
HARDCOVER ISBN: 978-1-7252-8467-8
EBOOK ISBN: 978-1-7252-8468-5

03/11/21

Contents

Abstract | vii
Preface | xiii
Acknowledgements | xix
Prologue | xxi

SECTION I: THE RATIONALE | 1
    1. The Kingdom of God | 3
    2. Jesus's Big Idea; Now What? So What? | 11
    3. Paradigm Shifts | 22

SECTION II: THE PROGRAM OF STUDIES | 45
    4. Early and Middle Childhood: Ages 4–13 | 48
    5. Middle Years: 13 to 17 Years of Age | 90
    6. Later Adolescence: 19 to 22 Years of Age | 125
    7. Young Adults: 21 to 24 Years of Age | 147

STUDY GUIDE | 161
    Session 1 | 165
    Session 2 | 167
    Session 3 | 171
    Session 4 | 174
    Session 5 | 177
    Session 6 | 179
    Session 7 | 182
    Session 8 | 184

Glossary | 187
Bibliography | 209
Index | 213

Abstract

THIS HANDBOOK IS FOR teachers. Maybe not for all teachers and for sure not just for any teacher. This handbook is for teachers who suspect that teaching young people can be, and should be, more than some elaborate form of delivery of words. This book is for that teacher who wants to know more about designing learning experiences so that young people's learning experiences are a 'lived experience', tinged with wonder, silence, presence, imagination, inquiry and magic, memory building and perhaps even a bit of wildness. For these teachers, this handbook may be just the permission you need to stop looking for new results by relying on old teaching practices, ones that have amounted to little more than brokering in abstractions to young people. This handbook addresses the deep suspicion of a thoughtful teacher that we can do better, to look for more from their teaching than what seems to have been a transmission of ideas, like Plato's cave, "a parade of shadows that we take for the real world."[1]

This book is designed around a big idea, an essential concept, that the goal of teaching young people is for them to develop right relationships. Not all at once, but experiences of successive approximations of right relationships, with the Creator, others, themselves, and the created and natural order. Right relationships? The word 'right', in the context of this book means 'suitable, desirable, as they should be.' Relationships that indeed are suitable and desirable work to produce certain evidences and not others. These evidences are the indictment that right relationships are being experienced, that the lived experience of a young person has been and is being desirable and suitable. It is the evidences, not a teachers'

---

1. John O'Donohue, *Anam Cara: A Book of Celtic Wisdom*, 1st ed. (New York: Harper Perennial, 1998), x; His was a voice speaking from a place of his own spiritual wonder and mysticism.

good intentions, that reveal that teachers, along with their learners, are getting somewhere important towards ways of being in the world that come from and produce desirable relationships. Desirable means that the connections young persons are experiencing are with 'what is,' call it reality if you like, but with what Chesterton called 'the most important truth, what is. Desirable teaching does not start or end not with a teacher's transmission of abstractions, insistence on following Plato's parade of shadows, or expecting young people to turn out okay by their just understanding words, including words in the Bible. It is a minds-on engagement with ways of being in the world that come about through being in right relationships.

Connecting is another word we could use to mean learning; learning is connecting with the Creator of everything, other people, the created and natural order, and self. *Freedom* is one evidence that connecting is working as it could be-freedom to learn ways to be a true self, freedom to not hurt others, freedom to not be afraid to be 'taken out' of ruts and grooves of unhealthy thoughts; to develop generous thoughts, freed up in relationships that help young people find that sweet spot where what makes them happy meets up with what could make the world happy. Another evidence is *balance*, instead of either/or ways being in the world, is; as are finding real *world spaces* that bring joy and not fear, awakening young people to a world that is a mystery to be taken up, not an issue to be resolved. Another evidence is *forgetting* what needs to be forgotten. To forget includes forgetting to be perfect. Besides being the most interesting people, broken people have cracks that allow the light in. Not too big a crack however, because the bigger the crevice the more that wonder and imagination might escape. Forgetting is letting go questions, issues and problems that keep us comfortably in non-living, in self-preoccupations, fear, false self and worry.

And of course, *Loving*, learning in approximations how to love and give in to the experience of 'love.' Love is the flagship of evidences. This evidence is not some abstraction like young people hearing over and over that 'God loves you' or 'you should love yourself.' The evidence is in and in favor that you are doing things right educationally, when young people 'want to want' what is best in and for their relationships. That is what love means. The verdict is in-success' is when teachers see young people pioneering on to look closely at the data of their lives to see their places to practice love. They are not settling for love's camouflages and disguises, like some moralistic rules when it comes to love. Learning to love may be the most convincing evidence that teaching is being effective. Love has its successive approximations worth learning include practicing kindness, giving into, and taking up a cause that would result in *justice* for neighbors and neighborhoods, '... *treating inequality 'unequally*,'[2] as Mortimer Adler (1981) described justice.

What do I mean by relationships? Merriam-Webster nails it for us- '*the state of being connected.*' I should probably use a different word than relationships-like relationship-ing or relating. Relationships are verbs, not nouns. Being connected is not static. It is not a destination, a final state, a noun, like arriving once and for all to Pittsburgh or to the corner grocery store. It is dynamic. It has a unique characteristic of needing to be learned to be right. A desirable relationship does not just happen. It is a way of being in the world that develops over time and in certain conditions, not others.

This handbook includes over one hundred strategies, tactics, logistics and relationship-builders, practical ones that have been tried sometime, somewhere, over my fifty years of teaching. This handbook is a guide for teachers who want to lead young people on their journey into knowing their true selves, and into practices of friendship with the Creator of everything. The handbook includes practical suggestions for guiding young people into ways of being in their world that include kindness and empathy for others and for the created and social order, to learn to keep justice for all a lifetime goal.

This book includes a section titled *Paradigm Shifts*, a journey back in time to old ideas and practices in teaching young people. This is the regeneration section of the book-to take an old teaching idea and practice at different times in history and then consider if the old idea has any inherent worth, any value if it were to be restored with a regenerative agenda, a breathing of new life into an old practices in teaching.

This book also includes eight lesson plans (now there is an old idea that needs regeneration) that a teacher of teachers and parent might consider implementing, as part of a mentoring program of guiding or leading teachers out into better, more effective and dare I say appropriate teaching approaches.

---

2. Mortimer Jerome Adler, *Six Great Ideas* (New York: Macmillan, 1981); He edited the Encyclopedia Britannica in all his spare time.

Abstract

Welcome Home

I hope that this book will feel like coming home. Maybe for you this book will be what you have been looking for, so that you can say, back home again for the first time.

The Irish proverb is an appropriate word picture for this book as well. *It is in the shelter of each other that we live.* Two years ago, I invited a Syrian friend, Talal, to speak to my university class about his experiences of war in Syria, being a refugee and coming to Canada. He and his wife were just one more refugee family, one more nameless couple among the 60 million refugees and internally displaced people in the world. They were victims of horrors in Syria, ones that included napalm type bombs being dropped on children in school playgrounds and hospitals being bombed by Syrian forces, as a warning to towns and cities about helping the opposition. He and his wife spent two years living in refugee camps, one failed attempt to cross the Mediterranean to Europe, loss of family members. His wife watched their home explode under a bomb and fall on her mother, grandmother, and sister. He and his wife lost their career as engineers, their evenings and holy days picnicking in parks dotted with olive trees and any sense of a safe and wonderful world. They won the lottery by being picked to come to Canada and I helped a group of good people in our local neighborhood arrange for them to come to Canada, an experience that included finding housing, car, shopping places and more for them and their newly born baby.

Talal tells a story of arriving in Canada, to the Calgary airport, he, and his wife, both full of apprehension, uncertainty, and depression. The first Canadian he met was a customs officer at the airport. Talal described him as someone with 'muscles on his muscles.' You could have heard a pin drop in my university class as Talal went on to tell that the customs officer walked up to him and asked him if they were the family from Syria. He as reading off an official looking piece of paper and not making any eye contact. Talal said, "Yes." The customs officer held out his hand and said two words, 'Welcome home.'

There were not too many dry eyes in my university class that moment. Those words were the scaffold for a new life, for a nameless couple to have and hear their names spoken- Talal and Areej-to be connected in real ways to a new possibility, a new imagination. But they were far more than mere words, shadows, and abstractions. Those wonderful words, welcome home, were shelters, permitting them to escape into imagination of new possibilities, new futures, and the birth of hope.

This book is my attempt to invite you into new practices of teaching, to reimagine new possibilities of ways of being with young people, to awaken and regenerate some old ideas about teaching young people. I hope that you enjoy the journey.

Preface

In Frederick Buechner's *Final Beast* (1965) a young man in a crisis of faith bolts from a church and ends up in a field, there crying out for Jesus to come. A friend looks for and finds him, hears from him despair spilling out in a cry for Jesus to come to him. The friend chooses a moment to ask the man if he hears a noise, which turns out to be nothing more than the click clack of leaves rustling in the wind. The friend asks the man this question, that if the life of faith that we live were a dance, and this was its only music, could you dance to it? "If we saw anymore of the dance than we do it would kill us for sure."[1]

I cannot imagine my relationship with God as if it were a dance. After all, a dance is intimate and close, real, and visceral. My experience of God has rarely if ever resembled a dance. Except for a few brief encounters I have experienced God as distant and a bit angry. It has been easy for most of my life to either ignore God or making choices in life that I hoped would keep the spiritual scorecard going in my favor. Faith's only music has a been for me not much more than that, the click-clack of leaves in the wind.

But I like to dance. I am not very good at it but enjoy the actual experience of the rhythm and creativity, the touch and embrace of a dance. The lived experience of dancing is full of contradictions needing resolving. Dancing is like life. Freedom and dependencies are rolled into both, as is trying to be in the moment while thinking of new possibilities. Dancing with my wife includes trying to impress her but focusing on how underwhelming I probably look.

If the life of faith that we lived were a dance. If I was ever on God's dance card, I guess I just did not know it? Perhaps God came to me in

---

1. Frederick Buechner, *The Final Beast* (New York: Atheneum Books, 1965), 378; A Buechner example of writing about raw and authentic people and events.

a different disguise, perhaps disguised as my life as Paula D'Arcy put it. I think so.

Here is the story of at least one disguise God used to came to me.

In June 1974, I left Canada for an adventure of a lifetime. I said goodbye to family, friends, and a teaching job in small farming community in Alberta. flew off to Zambia to teach in a school deep in the bush, in a military outpost on the borders of Mozambique and Zimbabwe. I was going to change the world. That was what I told people. That was what I told myself. When you are 24 years old, male, and still operating your life with a teen age brain that makes you think that you can change the world. You know just about everything there is to know. You can do just about anything too. Solving the mid-east crisis is easy, just ask me how. Survive crazy 40-foot dives off cliffs into water? What is the problem?

However, the truth was that I was less interested in saving the world then I was with needing to save myself. I knew that I was an angry, insecure, an addicted overachiever. I was not doing a very good job at saving myself. To borrow a Thomas Merton notion, I had been putting my ladder up against life's wrong wall and finding out that there was nothing up there. That wall would be an international hero to everybody back in Canada. Being a hero would save me. I needed to put my ladder up against a different wall. My adventure of a lifetime was about to go horribly wrong.

Fourteen months later, on August 12th to be exact, I stood at the front door at some place called the Mayflower Family Centre in east London, England. I had contracted filariasis and my big African adventure came to an end. A routine blood test in Zambia showed high levels of filaria. I was sick, confused, and panicky. I wanted out. A colleague told me that the best place to get treated for tropical diseases was in London, England, at The Centre for Tropical Diseases and Medicine. And that she had heard of a place in east London called the Mayflower Family Centre where I might be able to stay temporarily while being treated. I had an airplane ticket in my pocket, about fifty pounds in my wallet and that feeling that we all get from time to time that we are in a 'twilight zone' movie, playing out some weird script made just for me.

This was 1975 and the internet and email had not been invented yet. I wrote two letters while packing my suitcases and getting ready to leave Zambia. One was to the Centre for Tropical Diseases and Medicine, asking for an appointment. The second was to the Mayflower Family Centre, asking if I could stay there for a few days during the time of my appointment. The medical center never received my letter. But the Mayflower Family Centre did.

When I arrived at Heathrow airport, I looked like 'death warmed over' an expression my mother was fond of saying. I weighed 118 pounds, had not shaved, or washed for days. I had one suitcase, a hundred pounds in my pocket and a piece of paper with the name and address of the Mayflower Family Centre. I stepped up into the taxi line and told the first driver where I wanted to go. He looked at me and said, are you sure? East London? I said yes. The trip ended up costing me nearly all the money I had. Now, in addition to everything else gone wrong, I was financially broke.

I remember two things about that night. On the long taxi ride through London I prayed. Sort of. Jesus, please get me out of this train wreck, this adventure gone wrong. On that long ride I do not recall any inspiration, any visions of Jesus on a billboard with 'it is going to be alright' written under his picture. Nothing, silence and just a long taxi ride to who knew where and what?

What I thought about God and Jesus in those days is still a little embarrassing to me. Who was this Jesus anyway? I had shown him how smart I was to choose him over my addictions and, frankly, over hell? I grew up as a Catholic. Being a Catholic for me was like rubbing the magic rabbit's foot, do it the right way and presto, you can get what you want. God was for me like your evil math teacher though; you had better get the equations right or would need to do them all over again. You get zero. That is why purgatory made good sense to me. A back door if I needed it, and I really did need it. I did not look forward all that much to meeting Jesus's Dad until I had said more than enough Hail Mary's and Our Father's. My concept of God for years has had little to do with any concept of love. And this train wreck of an adventure was doing nothing at all to change my concept.

Until four words would set in motion an experience that would change my life.

The taxi driver dropped me off at Mayflower Family Centre. It was 2:00 a.m. in the morning, raining and cold. I knocked on the door and I will never forget the first words out of Jenny Sainsbury's mouth, 'You must be Bernie.'

You Must Be Bernie

The Mayflower Family Centre was a church of England run mission in the heart of Canning Town, in East London. This was still Dicken's London in so many ways. Cockney markets, kids growing up tough and old people growing old lonely. Young people grew up never seeing a tree or blade of grass. At the time I came there were over thirty young men and women, some on gap years others just wanting to be a means of grace (the most common expression used around the dinner table) to people in the neighborhood. A few others were like me, in transition and needing fixing. Everyone there had to find work in the neighborhood or in the Mayflower Family Centre. Roger and Jenny Sainsbury were the Rectors and leaders of the mission. The dining room table was our altar. You would not been able to have enough buckets to hold all the fun and laughter we had telling our stories of working with the youth at nights in 'youth club,' or the senior folks living in the tenements. Knowing the right stuff was not important. Loving people we worked alongside was. Justice and love trumped ought to(s), should(s), and have to(s).

After a few days I tore up my airplane ticket to Canada and ended up staying for six months. An African hero adventure was about to be replaced with a different kind of adventure. The medical people gave me a clean bill of health. My experience at the Mayflower was about to give me something more important-a head start to a new identity. As is the case with most 'experiences,' this one would reveal its meaning later, in surprising ways, in new possibilities I took up over the next four decades, possibilities that followed along the ruts and grooves laid down in my mind, in my concepts about just about everything. God came did come to me alright, disguised as an adventure that I would never have chosen, a new future that was never planned for.

I wanted to replicate the experience in Canada. I have had some spectacular failures in trying to recreate my Mayflower experience. I took a teaching position immediately upon arriving back in Canada, in northern Alberta. I moved into an abandoned farmhouse a few miles outside of town. The house had no running water, wood stove for heating and power had been cut off for years. I had a .22 rifle that I was going to use to hunt rabbits for food (never even saw a rabbit during my six months there). Thank God for the Safeway in town. I hired on as the town's one and only Pastor, part time, and became a wired-up zealot for 'living in community' and a recruiter for my new mission. No one joined me in a replicated Mayflower experience. I guess living in an abandoned farmhouse had little appeal.

At the end of my teaching contract I snuck out of town in my 1964 Chevy and have never gone back.

I have had some remarkable successes too. In 1984 my wife and I bought a rambling 7-bedroom house in Highlands, Edmonton, that had been built in 1912. Over sixty people lived with us, many for three or four years. I loved every moment of this experience and know that bought some good into lots of young lives.

In 1997 we moved to Calgary. In 2004, we met up with a couple who were to play a leading part in an initiative called '40 days to community.' I recall the Sunday afternoon sitting across from six other couples from the neighborhood. Each couple had shown up, largely out of curiosity I think, to discuss this notion of 'doing life together.'

Seventeen years later four couples are still at it. Other couples have come and gone. 'Group' as we affectionately call it has morphed and does not look much like the original vision. I think it is better looking to be honest. We have continued to use the acronym SERVICE as our manifesto, our mission statement of what we do and how we want to be known. We continue to engage in book studies and spiritual formation, to practices 'extending' hospitality, doing recreation together, helping each other with our respective volunteering activities, and either supporting or going on international justice related missions. We extend compassion to our neighbors and care to each other.

I have learned much in in each experience about living into a relationship based Christian life.

I write about my lessons learned in this book. Thank God for His disguises.

Acknowledgements

FIRST, I WANT TO thank my three grown up children who have taught me about life, teaching, and being in the world in authentic ways. I love them and want them to know how much they mean to me. I want to thank the editors who have weighed into this book and given me honest and helpful feedback. Noah Harms, Christine Jacob and Glendon Frank, thank you. Above all I thank Lesley Perry who once again has shown her gift with words and ability to tell the writing truth. I thank Dr. Joyce Chan, a faculty member at Carey and a continuing support for me and my work as a teacher. Thank you. To Jim Paul for the idea of misdirection. I thank hundreds of university students who challenged and caused me to continue to think more deeply than I think is possible

Above all I thank my wife and life partner Ann. She is the smartest person I know and I love her deeply.

Prologue

What Is the Meaning of Life?

I WAS DRIVING MY thirteen-year-old son home from his hockey practice late one winter evening. After some minutes of silence, he asked me, 'Dad, what's the point of life?' Now what kind of question is that from a thirteen-year-old? Ask me again where do babies come from? We had had 'the talk' some time ago. I guess he did not want to hear that story again.

I recall much from that question from the back seat. What is the point of life? I did not know how to respond. Adequately enough anyway? I pulled up the God talk script into the work room of my mind. Love God. Believe in Jesus. Do good. I had the Christian propositions, all there, ready to go. I remember thinking at least this would buy me some time. He had asked me an important question, a real question, an authentic question. He had given me some information in asking the question. But what was it? What was he really telling me? Wisely, I think, I put the God talk script back down into long-term storage and did not preach at my son. In those days I was quick to make it all about Jesus talk. I was like the boy in the catechism class when shown a picture of a steam engine and asked by his teacher, "What is this?" The boy replies, 'Well, it looks like a steam engine, but it must be Jesus.' My son needed a different conversation that night.

For my son, I think given his big question, life must have been looking like a mystery, a puzzle, maybe a dilemma, a double bind that felt unsolvable (something wrong with him? something wrong with life)? Maybe a big cosmic joke. Jesus would not have been the answer that night. One day, yes. But not then. I put that tactic back down where it belonged. Perhaps another day.

But the question hung in the air. I am a professor. We are notorious questions askers ourselves. "What do you think?" The thought crossed my mind to pull that one out of my bag of teaching tactics and ask him. That would provide some much-needed relief.

I knew that I needed to at least dignify the question. I said 'let us talk about this later. Maybe this book is the later. He would learn more from me that evening from how I would take up the question than what content I loaded up into my answer. I saw ahead of me a curriculum in the making, or as Ted Aoki my former Chair at the University of Alberta, called it a *curriculum of being*.

Later in the book I will tell you what I ended up saying that evening. I will tell you this much now. My son spent the next ten years living in quiet desperation I was to find out later. His quiet desperation lurked in the corners of that question. For years he wandered around it while dealing with bullying, learning to fly fish, developing guitar playing skills and spending hours walking in the woods behind our house.

The answer for him came later, much later. What is the point of life? It came in the woods behind our house. It came with my son taking up a right relationship with the natural order. And just maybe that experience disguised a right relationship with the Creator, him, and others. Maybe Elizabeth Browning was right, earth is crammed with heaven.

SECTION I

The Rationale

1

The Kingdom of God

The aim of education is to teach a few powerful ideas that explain and encompass everything.

—A.N. WHITEHEAD[1]

IN JESUS WE HAVE a living illustration of how to be in the world. Unfortunately, his biggest and most powerful messages of how to be in the world, of intimacy and depth, of being and belonging, of love and connectedness to what already is, have been hijacked and replaced with grubby and small moralistic counterfeits, religious nonsenses that do nothing to stir the imagination or to set humans up to be poised for new possibilities. What we have instead is a set of ought-to(s), should(s) and have-to(s), and moralistic and narrow ideas regarding who is in and going to heaven and how, and who is not. The transaction is a quid pro quo, or so it seems. You pray some sort of formulaic prayer and presto, you are in. It seems that Jesus's death and resurrection, around which history spins, trumps his life, his big idea, his core message. Maybe it should. But then again, maybe Jesus's big teaching idea of right relationships has been under promoted. Or maybe it just feels too real, too demanding, and not spiritual enough.

Jesus taught a powerful idea that explained and encompassed everything—not only for his followers, for their time, but also for everybody,

---

1. Whitehead, *Aims of Education and Other Essays*.

for all time, for good. He taught that the kingdom of God is a way of being in the world that comes about through right relationships with God, others, self, and the created and natural order. When we take up and practice Jesus's teachings, right relationships are produced.

Jesus referred to this concept of the kingdom of God at least sixty times. You can find at least another twenty references to the kingdom of God in the letters in the New Testament and another twenty references to this concept in the Jewish scriptures—the Old Testament. No other concept, big idea, or theme gets as much airtime in the Bible.

However, there are problems with this concept. It has been overused and often misunderstood. Kingdoms are places or jurisdictions where someone is a king, a ruler. Using the definite article 'the' when referring to the kingdom of God does not help either. The logical deduction given the definite article is that the kingdom is exclusive and can be found over there somewhere. It is understood, it seems by many to be a place.

When the kingdom is referred to in the Scriptures, it is more often in language that raises more questions than answers. The kingdom is within you. It is like a mustard seed. Jesus compared it to leaven and to a tree. He gave us clear marching orders to seek it first. Odd and difficult metaphors to understand, and hard to know what to seek, exactly. Nothing seems to give it all away in the descriptions. No pattern. Hardly a theme to lay hold of. Or so it seems.

To make matters worse, history seems to be that long story of many shifts in how people understood the kingdom of God. No need to look any further than denominational expressions of Christianity today in the world. How in the world did that happen, from Jesus's message of a way of being in the world that comes about through right relationships, to over one hundred different Christian denominations, each with its own road map into truth and heaven. And that does not even include hundreds more different expressions of people's desire to find and know what indeed is true about everything.

But here is the real problem. The kingdom of God does not exist until it does. You will not find it over there, in a building, in the Bible, in a country, in some sacred building in some corner of the world. It is not inert. It is not a place, or a religious system. It is not in nature (though creation is full of hints and guesses of what might be—of new possibilities, new futures). Jesus's kingdom of God comes into existence only through right relationships. Until it does, it does not exist. This is the big idea of this book—that religion, that the uniquely human pursuit of religious answers to the meaning of everything, is explained and encompassed by right relationships.

Perhaps we need to pay attention to the concept of the kingdom of God, again for the first time, but this time do so as a metaphor. A metaphor is usually bigger than the thing it represents and, when it comes to the kingdom of God, that is a good idea. The reality is that the kingdom is not exclusive, small, and does not need to be confined to a mere concept. Teachers and parents may need to reconsider what and how we teach our young people about the kingdom of God as our biggest idea, most essential of all concepts. This first section is a set of reconsiderations for exactly that. Given Jesus's teaching about the kingdom of God, what should we teach young people and how should we teach them? What are the frames of reference necessary for teachers to understand the concept of the kingdom of God?

What to Teach

The *what* part of the question will be addressed in this book by an idea and practice in teaching called backward design. This book describes ways to be effective architects of learning experiences with young people, for parents who are intentional about teaching and not just reacting to their young people, and for teachers who are paid to be serious about being architects and implementers of learning experiences. One big idea of this book is for teachers and parents to have an end in mind when teaching and that end is right relationships. This desired end of teaching young people might not seem to be enough. I think it is. You decide after reading this book.

The visible expressions of learning, the intended learning outcomes of your teaching, may be quite different than what you or I likely experienced. Maybe the intended outcome of your teachers and parents was a decision by you for Jesus. C.S. Lewis puts it poignantly that should we 'choose to choose' God as an alternative to hell, that will be accepted by Him as uncomplimentary as that might be.[2] My own learning experiences were laced with performing, to demonstrate behaviors would add up to some plus side of a spiritual ledger. I am sure today that it had to be hardly flattering to the Creator that I would choose any negative reinforcer such as threats, fear, worry, or guilt to guide my life. Back then,

---

2. Lewis, *Problem of Pain*.

I practiced guilt like it was an art and science. By my early twenties, my one remaining spiritual friend would broker two these two well-worn abstractions, God loves you and you need to love God. Both were meaningless to me by my early twenties. Besides, by that time, I was already well on my way out into practicing anything but God to make me happy.

I am convinced now that it can be different for young people. If anything, the desired ends you design should be for guiding young people into taking up personally chosen ethical actions, modeling virtuous decisions, and affirming moral behaviors. You become an architect, a designer of experiences for young people to take up, ones that will guide them developmentally and iteratively into freedom to engage with all of life, guided with compasses of prayer, observance, discipline, thought and action7 Your intended outcome, the desired end of your teaching needs to be stated as an action. If your desired outcomes end in *ing*, perhaps you just already might be in the right game of teaching for right relationships and being in the world in particular ways

The how part of the question will be addressed by a pedagogy of being—the art, science and craft of teaching and learning that rises and falls on practicing right relationships. The *how* is a verb, always a verb. Parents and teachers should be guides of young people, leading them to be inquirers, to unpack whatever meaning they are developmentally able to understand, from their actions and seeing the results of their actions. Guidance includes pouring meaning into possible solutions to relationship problems, thinking about ways to address relationship issues, providing authentic answers to real questions that arise from practicing relationships good ones and not so good ones. That is teaching at its best; that is the minds-on teaching that can make a difference.

The content part of your mission as a teacher is Jesus's big idea, it is the end you should have in mind, the big goal you should intend for young people. Your guiding question should be, "How does this my teaching and choices of resources serve the interests of guiding young people into being in the world in particular ways, into right relationships? Does what and how I am teaching guide my students into that way of being in the world that comes about through right relationships?

One way to determine if you are on point regarding an outcome of right relationships is to ask yourself what interests are being served by what you do with your young people. Is the interest being served by you and your teaching right relationships or right ideas? If right ideas trump right relationships, quite likely this book will be disruptive and trouble you. If right relationships, you may discover as I have that in and through the practice of right relationships, right ideas do emerge and are clarified. We do act our ways into new ways of thinking as Parker Palmer suggests.

How to Teach

The activities or how part of your mission includes making choices of strategies, tactics, logistics and relationship-builders that serve the interests of young people developing successive approximations of right relationships-with the Creator, others, self and the created and natural order. What I am proposing is modest, simple but not easy. Why? There are anchorages we all experience. Perhaps the interests of a church, or just keeping young people busy and entertained. I personally must confess to being more concerned about my children's behavior and how that made me look than I was with their behavior. Now that was some anchor. Maybe an anchor for you is thousands of dollars of curricular materials sitting on your shelf, lots of worksheets and coloring books that you are not sure what to do with, if teaching is just all about right relationships? Or maybe your anchor is more of a mindset notion, like ones I have had to interrogate in my own teaching. Is the key to teaching young people dare to discipline? What about memorizing scripture? Youth group? Or is the key to teaching far more profoundly simple-modeling and teaching right relationships.

This book is intended for learning focused teachers. That includes parents who want to understand more about how best to guide and teach young persons along the direction of their predispositions, personality, and interests. This book is for parents who have grown suspicious of simplistic answers to what and how they should teach, to simple answers to complex questions of young people's psychological, spiritual, and social development. I have tried to honor and affirm the intelligence of parents by offering both practical teaching ideas as well as academic and research-based support for the teaching ideas proposed in this book.

This book will also be welcomed by professional schoolteachers, who have known, at least intuitively from their earliest days of their work with young people, that their teaching effectiveness rises and falls on their relationships with their students. If you are this teacher and have wanted to learn more about how to form and nurture those relationships, this book is for you. Finally, this book is for men and women who have a teaching role in church, but suspect something is wrong, as young people continue to vote with their feet. More adolescents and young adults than ever are leaving church.[3] I am convinced today that we teachers can effectively address this real problem, not through words but through right relationships

This book is for teachers who have deduced that the word *right* in *right relationships* is an essential word, a big idea that will need lots of meaning poured into it. Perhaps you are one of those teachers who has heard it all before. Right relationships, of course! I get it that you might have some difficulty suspending any disbelief in a book that promotes right relationships and not right ideas as the *big idea* of what Jesus taught us and therefore should be our one standard for teaching. Please read on.

The big idea in right relationship with God is friendship. The Creator made us to be a friend- to be for us, not against us. Friendship is characterized by hanging out with the Creator, expressed differently at different developmental phases of life. Young children need a foundation of hanging out with God by giving in to the wonder and the mystery of it all, while being trained in the virtues and guided by teachers who inquire into real questions, issues, and problems that arise in their day to day living. Young adults need a curriculum of hanging out with God, of friendship with their Creator by giving into the fact that God created them for friendship, and not so much so that they should initiate and work hard on maintaining that friendship (a good idea but not the main point) but so that God could love them, be friends with them. Given the concreteness of young person's thinking, friendship with someone they cannot see is best taught from a scaffold of friendship they have seen and experienced. Small friendship first, before big friendship can be understood and practiced. Small and personal exodus taught first before the story of Exodus can be understood fully; encouraging small, daily practices of *worrying in order* before inviting students to take up not worrying about big issues.

The big idea in right relationship with oneself is identity. We are created to find our true self, or as Dolly Parton put it, "Find out who you are and do it on purpose."[4] Identity is characterized by developmental life crises, or turning points, and the resolving of a life crisis determines the outcome, the resolution of one's identity. Young children need to resolve the identity issue of competency or inferiority. Children need to get good

---

3. Barna, *Trends: The Truth About a Post Truth Society*. Remains the best source of research on trends in American religion and church life.

4. Parton, "Dolly Parton Quote."

at things, lots of things or just one or two, does not matter. Children will carry competency or inferiority forward into their next crisis and into all subsequent identity crises. Young adults need a curriculum of intimacy vs isolation, of being intimate with at least one other person, and that can include sexual intimacy. They will carry into this new identity crisis the quality and essence of their competency development developed far back in their childhood years. Intimacy with other persons, will always influenced by their early identify formation and early experiences.

The big idea in right relationships with each other is love. We are created to love, to be loved, to want what is best for us and others. Our significance and security in life, for all our lives, is based on learning to want what is best for me and for others. That is the best definition for love that I can offer here. Learning to love, over time, and without selling out to unhealthy relationships to do so, works for the best of those who learn how to serve. It is a pragmatic thing as well as an altruistic thing. Love for those with young children is characterized by concrete thinking, self-serving and egocentric generosity-based actions. All good and developmentally normal characteristics of love for four to thirteen-year old children. These and many other psychological and developmental needs described later in this book are going to be accommodated by young adults into new expressions of love characterized by mutuality, justice, freedom, and truly wanting what is best for the other person.

The big idea in right relationships with the created and natural order (culture and nature) is justice, learning to treat inequality unequally.[5] We are created to be partners with the Creator and with others in trying out, exploring new possibilities, new futures in equity-gender, poverty, education, sharing our resources. Children are naturals here; they are genuinely altruistic and express *that is not fair* almost as if it is their prime directive. They have deep sentiments and a passion for justice, for fairness, and for wanting a world to live in for themselves and others that is far different than the world we see emerging today. They get it when you tell them the Irish proverb that when you have been given an abundance it is time to build longer tables not higher walls. The intention of this book is to provide you with the tactics, and strategies that not only preserve this way of being with young people, but nurtures and develops it into a lifestyle of seeking justice for all, the freedom for all people to be fully alive, for nature to thrive and to continue to inspire us into thankfulness and awe.

5. Adler, *Six Great Ideas*. Adler complied and edited the Encyclopedia Britannica, I guess in all his spare time.

In between early childhood and young adulthood are four distinct, but not separate, developmental phases described in this book, each with a set of teaching tactics and strategies that I have tried and found to be true, effective and fun for teachers to use. You need to wait for it. Let us start at the beginning.

2

Jesus's Big Idea; Now What? So What?

Purpose First

I HAVE BEEN GETTING ahead of myself. Purpose first. Everything in education rises and falls on purpose. Why bother with old ideas, new practices? Why is the most effective teaching method dependent on right relationships? Purpose trumps everything. Get the purpose right and everything we teachers do could make sense. Back to the kingdom of God for a few moments. What is the purpose, the rationale, the reasons why we all need to reconsider old ideas into new practices and the kingdom of God? Before looking more closely at old ideas, new practices, we need to look closely at why bother with the kingdom of God, with backward design, paying attention to how we teach perhaps more closely than what we teach?

So, what is the reason, the purpose to introduce a new way of teaching old ideas? Let us start with the big idea of Jesus's kingdom of God. The purpose of this book, like the kingdom of God, is waiting to unfold in the presence of the right conditions. If you would spend just a few minutes reading the next sections to understand the kingdom of God from an educator's, and not a theologian's point of view, pass judgement on what you read and perhaps test what you conclude here against your own lived experience, I think you'll get the purpose of this book.

Good News, Bad News

There is good news and there is bad news about the big idea of Jesus's the kingdom of God concept. Jesus's idea was a metaphor. The bad news is that we have a theological landscape littered with books, sermons, and essays about this metaphor. I bet that your eyes even glazed over when you read kingdom of God.

Yes, it does appear that the metaphor has been tapped out, overused and worse, often communicated in very difficult to understand terms. One very vague notion must be that the kingdom is already but not yet. Huh? Not very helpful, right? Certainly not useful for teachers and parents as a goal or purpose for teaching. No wonder that the metaphor has lost its appeal. Let us take a more analytical look at this big idea of Jesus.

Anomalies and Paradigm Shifts

Jesus's big idea was an anomaly. It did not fit the times, culture, or zeitgeist. It does not today either. It has little to do with building higher walls to keep people out. The bad news is Jesus's big idea in his era also had very little to do with the times, including what had been a part of the Jewish program of studies. The lived experience of rabbinical educational practices was complex and rigorous. The hidden curriculum of Jewish education must have been experienced as ways and means to play an impress God contest.

However, for Jesus, the point of it all was different. He did not champion keeping a spiritual scorecard. He was not promoting some sort of requirement for people to keep a checklist of spiritual accomplishments. There was not going be a multiple-choice test we need to pass to get through the pearly gates, no cosmic examination at the end of life to see if people had nailed down the correct religious ideas. For Jesus, life was not a worthiness contest, a spiritual walk on a tightrope or a legal system of dos and don'ts. Jesus's big idea called into question complex legal systems and complicated theologies for the how and why of living. In one of his more edgy teachings, he told us, in pretty clear terms, that a deep, passionate, one-on-one relationship with the Creator is going to prove to have trumped mighty works and saying all the right things. "I never knew you" might not be what you or I will want to hear one day (Matthew 7:23).

The Kingdom within Us

From Jesus's teachings we were left with the sobering idea that this kingdom is not out there, somewhere, but starts with us, within us. We are responsible to the kingdom by being responsible for the kingdom. Any engagement with the Jesus way of being in the world is up to us. According to Jesus, the new way of being, the kingdom of God, was to be found in the most unlikely of places—in you and me. Maybe we need to pour much more meaning into Jesus's cryptic messages about the kingdom being like a mustard seed, being within you (Luke 17:21) and a way of being-not a matter of eating and drinking, but of righteousness and peace and joy (Romans 14:17).

Leo Nikolayevich Tolstoy in his book *The Kingdom of God is Within You*, (2006), translated by Constance Garnett, described the quietness, anticipation and hopefulness that lived in the kingdom within him when he wrote, "In the midst of winter, I find within me the invisible summer." His writing reveals something of the inwardness of the people's journey of kingdom.

Bernard Lonergan, in his book *Method in Theology*, (1990) described bed the destination of this hopeful, quiet journey, another important piece of the particular way of being in the world he named insight, something that lays compacted, amorphous within us, waiting to unfold in the presence of conditions that could best be described as pedagogy; paying attention to the data of our lives, understanding at some level the meaning of that data, passing judgement on what it all means and acting on it, with careful attention to the iterative nature of coming to insight, wisdom and the particular way of being in the world. Engaging with our personal aging, alienation or illness are obvious examples of how this pedagogy is quite organic and natural.

Upside Down Kingdom

The theme of Donald Kraybill's book, *The Upside-Down Kingdom* is noisier and more outward than either Tolstoy or Lonergan.[1] He suggests that if you were to take the most accepted, paradigmatic idea and turn it over on its head, there you would find a description of the kingdom of God. Those who would be great must be servants. Jesus described

---

1. Kraybill, *Upside-Down Kingdom*; Tolstoy, *Kingdom of God Is Within You*; Lonergan, *Method in Theology*.

the peacemakers, those poor in spirit, the humble as getting it right. Do not worry about anything. Pray. One reason that we need old ideas, new practices is that we cannot expect new and better outcomes from our educational practices if we continue the same, tired, old educational practices. Einstein called this insanity. We practice our collective insanity as teachers when we expect new results from old practices. If old practices of teaching were producing peacemakers, joy-filled and worry-free people, then why bother changing anything? We would have no need for new practices, right? Need I say more here?

Never Really Wanted

GK Chesterton pointed something important about the action part of the kingdom, that the Christian ideal has not been tried and found wanting, it has simply been left untried because it has never really been wanted.[2] The same could be said for Jesus's big idea he taught, the kingdom of God. Another reason for old ideas, new practices is that it appears to me, at least, that some parents and teachers may have settled for a curriculum of comfort rather than one of truth. Why do I say this? In my nearly fifty years in education I hear the metaphor most often that our teaching job is to greenhouse kids; protect them and keep them safe. I get it. But C.S. Lewis might have put it best as a corrective worth considering by teachers when he suggests that should we look for truth, we may find comfort in the end; but to set out first looking for comfort we will get neither comfort not truth, only wishful thinking that ends in despair.[3] For a long, long time, my own educational practices were designed far more to entertain and amuse, placate, and minimize other parent complaints than to learn how to be in right relationships. Far easier for me was to have a curriculum of abstractions, of rules and regulations as a curricular focus, then go with a curriculum of nurturing right relationships. I am embarrassed to admit this, but confession is good for the soul, right?

The Emperor Has No Clothes

I have had a long history of academic and professional experience with current practices and have come to the conclusion that our ultimate goal

---

2. Chesterton, *What's Wrong With the World*.
3. Lewis, *Mere Christianity*.

in education seems to resemble comfort (for teachers as well as for young people) rather than the rough and tumble relationship-based principles and practices of the kingdom of God. My suspicion that what has been going on in Christian religious education, including claims for its grand outcomes, simply have not been true. Today, still, we are being sold a bill of goods regarding the value of Christian schools, efficaciousness of church programs, and the importance of dare to discipline approaches to raising children. Later in this book I will draw your attention to the research that does not paint a rosy picture of what is going on with far too many of our young people. For now, let me be personal and describe an anomaly that began the paradigm shift for me, from a performance-based teacher to a relationship based one.

My personal paradigm shift to this notion of right relationships began with PhD studies at the University of Alberta.[4] The Experience of Christian Religious Education: An Interpretation included courses at Boston College, leading me to some surprising insights. The Christian schooling emperor indeed had no clothes. Young people were experiencing a far different lived curriculum than what was intended for them. And most upsetting to me was that far too many young people were experiencing a hidden curriculum that was far more developmentally influential then anything that could be found written down in a curriculum document.

The Hidden Curriculum

Ask my children what they learned in Christian schools, or any school for that matter, and they will tell you nothing. But, when you ask my son what he really learned, he will tell you that he learned that other people hurt you, and he learned how to hide the hurt. He was bullied for all his years at a Christian school. Down deep he still hurts. Ask my daughter what she learned in a Christian school and she will say she learned that some people say they know the answers when they really do not. She

---

4. PhD studies at the University of Alberta (1983–1987). My dissertation title was "The meaning of Christian religious education: An interpretation." My academic interest was in the lived experience of young people in their Christian religious education, and how language expressed this experience. I was surprised as I engaged in an ethnographic study with two fifteen-year old young people as well as three years of study of religious education experiences found in case studies and research. My research themes included young people's expression of the importance of personal growth guiding their learning agenda, their acknowledged need for community, and their desire for meaningful learning experiences.

would add that she learned that it pays to give people the answers they want rather than the answer that she was struggling with. She remains skeptical about anything overtly Christian to this day, while being an example to me of a loving, justice-seeking, and truthful woman. Ask my other daughter what she learned in her brief less than one-year experience in a Christian school and she will say, she learned that it is far safer, less risky existentially to be quiet in the midst of doubts, issues, and real questions that live in her world. Only later as adult does she feel free enough it appears to search for answers to the real questions, seek real ways to address real issues and solve real problems that live in my world. Enough said. I just get sad all over again thinking about what my three children experienced in Christian education, school, church, and home.

Subsequently, my three years as a superintendent of a Christian school added yet another confirmation that it is not what it all seems to be. I have been a pastor, a Dean of Education at a Lutheran University and an eager reader of both history and practices of Christian education. I have lived in intentional community, taken a few just and unjust hits by Christians (we all have, haven't we?) and studied with or talked with some of the flagship theologians in the world, including R.C. Sproul, J.I. Packer[5], and Thomas Groome. I have been called out in public by Paulo Freire for my naivety in claiming that the problem starts and ends in the human heart. He told me that I was naïve. His gentle correction was one more alignment of my thinking, my mindset that the kingdom is a way of being, inclusive of thinking and behaving but far, far more profound, and inclusive, more ontological, and important.

Another corrective in my thinking was listening to R.C. Sproul tell a young inquirer, a college-aged, fresh faced young man who asked what happens to aborted babies, that, we all deserve hell and it is only through God's mercy will some people get into heaven.[6] In other words, given the premises of reformed theology, some aborted babies could very well end

---

5. J. I. Packer (1926–2020) was once named by Time magazine as one of the top 25 evangelicals in America. His book *Knowing God* is considered a classic.

6. Sproul, *Holiness of God Video Series*; Sproul (1939–2017) was the founder of Ligonier Ministries, and an author and apologist for the concept of the holiness of God. He was a proponent for reformed theology. In my D Min studies at Reformed Theological Seminary (unfinished), I would listen in on conversations he would have with truth-seeking students. To a student who asked him, "Where do aborted babies go?" he responded with the traditional reformed line that we all deserve God's punishment, but some people will receive God's mercy and get to heaven. That statement from Sproul was the beginning of a theological turning point for me.

up in hell. My reformed theological pursuits came to a crashing end that afternoon, and I have never looked back.

My conclusion after nearly fifty years in the practice of teaching and learning is that indeed the kingdom of God, rising and falling on right relationships, has never really been wanted. Religion yes. Theology, even bad theology, for sure. But friendship with the Creator? Pursuit of one's true self? Justice? Love? Hardly ever, it seems to me.

Paradigm Shifts Have a High Cost

Why has the simple but big idea of the kingdom never really caught on? Because paradigms do not shift easily. The Protestant Reformation was a paradigm shift. However, the shift had a high cost. The Reformation opened-up divisions and fractions and legitimized a pattern of thinking and behaving that remains alive and well to this day-of reforming and reshaping spiritual thinking and practices. Up until recently, our various religious expressions of Christianity have certainly appeared to be far less grand and transcendent, less actionable (a way of being) and more stagnant. Maybe over the last twenty or so centuries the paradigm shifts have resulted in our inability to preserve or conserve a resultant regenerative idea from Jesus's teachings. A Protestant Reformation was set in motion by an anomaly that called everything into question. Somehow, mysteriously, we do not need to do perform but simply accept what has been offered. Luther led us to see that it was grace, not works, that saved us. But it came at a high cost.

Something Other Than God

There is no need for right relationships, once a formalized religion has been created, accompanied by its tightened down theology, denominational distinctives being the hills to die on, and each denomination having an idea that they have the right way to interpret scripture. It would appear to be so if history teachers use anything at all, it is that, human history sure looks like the long, terrible story of man trying to find something other than God which will make them happy.[7] Why bother with a right relationship with the Creator or with anyone else, for that matter

---

7. Lewis, *Mere Christianity*. The big ideas and logic of his apologetic sealed the deal for me as I gave in and admitted that the Jesus story was true.

if a far easier way of rules and regulations, a list of have to(s) has been designed for me. Something other than God will make me happy and feel like I am doing okay. Rule- following will do that.

History is also a story of paradigms, of ideas and practices that characterized a period of time, sometimes a long period of time as we see with the Reformation and the prevailing idea within much of evangelical Christianity that the "just shall live by faith." It is through grace that we are saved. Saved from what to what remains debatable and debated. Other paradigms have been shorter lived, as was the case with the catechumenate, a complex induction system used to bring people systematically into the church and faith.

Later in this book I identify some highlights of some time periods, paradigms that offered up a distinct idea of what right relationships meant and should look like. And in a few cases I will propose considering one or two ideas from that time that just might have some regenerative potential, an old idea that might be reconceptualized into a new practice.

The Intolerable Compliment

A right relationship with this God, the Creator, characterized by friendship, is one essential message of this book; how to recognize it, take it up and live into it. The challenge has always been to have a right relationship with a God we cannot see and have been told all kinds of things about. We have settled for Jesus, as the picture of God and we do so with good reason. Jesus once said, ". . . anyone who has seen me, has seen the Father . . ." (John 14:9 NIV) We have also been given some clear marching orders for what this right relationship could look like. Trust seems big, not worrying too much about anything because this God sometimes seems moved by prayer, and not moved by prayer, and it does not matter. From Jesus we are left with the intolerable compliment that the Creator is personable, a real being who appears to love us and wants what is best for us. What is best for us is to be in right relationships with the Creator, each other, ourselves, and the created and natural order. These ends, these relationship ways of being, trump everything else, even including getting our prayers answered.

Also fascinating for those of us who are students of good teaching is the simple brilliance of Jesus's teaching about the Creator and right relationships. We have clear marching orders—simply to follow Jesus and

His teachings. Fifty times in the Gospels alone, as a matter of fact, we are instructed to simply act into a way of being in the world. There is a real pedagogic reason for these orders, based on the intimate relationship between behaviors and the development of our brains. We do act our way into new ways of thinking. Why? Well just maybe that is the way we have been created. The brain is an adaptive system; it responds and does not lead.

Again, to use teacher language, Jesus's program of studies was largely descriptive first, not prescriptive. Where Jesus appears to be prescriptive, i.e., telling people what they should do, read the context of the prescription; it is always descriptive, the true state-of-affairs that characterize the kingdom. The section of the gospels known as the beatitudes is a good example of a set of descriptions of what result will be for a person choosing to be a peace maker, poor in spirit, meek and given to God's friendship. Take up and practice the idea that the divine is for us, always.

Perhaps the kingdom is simply too good to be true. It really cannot all be that simple can it? That beautiful and liberating?

Brilliant Art, Science, and Craft

Jesus describes what right relationships look like not only with the Creator but with others, self, and the created and natural order. Throughout the stories of Jesus's life, we get glimpses of a master teacher, practicing the art, science, and craft of teaching. Jesus was a brilliant teacher. He differentiated instruction, depending on his audience, by sometimes using parables, and at other times using direct instruction, coaching techniques, and nurturing (primarily to a bunch of misfits). At other times, given his audience, he laid out a challenge with an edge, describing to people where God can be found (fascinating really to think that Jesus said God is found with and in the poor, homeless, hungry). Again, do not take my word for it. Read Matthew 25.

Jesus's teaching was political when it was needed (some of us don't like to hear that) and far more about justice and social reform for people than it was about our fixation with moral issues that were current then and are current hot items today. When all was said and done, he gave us a curriculum of new possibilities, options for a new future and new ways of being through seeking right relationships. The adjective *right* will be the most important word in this book.

Noun, Verb, Adverb, Adjective

Something goes sideways, I think, maybe even horribly wrong, when we continue to use Christian as an adjective. When the word Christian is put in front of anything, watch for nonsense that usually follows. My friend and philosopher, Gary Colwell, used to put it this way, Lets go Christian ice-fishing, then go for a Christian doughnut and Christian coffee? The idea of a Christian wall to keep people out is really a lot of nonsense regardless of where you put the word Christian.

What is the role and place of Christian as a noun then? Of knowing the right stuff—what the theorists call domain specific declarative or semantic knowledge? Or what is the role and place of Christian as a verb? What is the role and place of actions, behaviors and doing in Christianity? The educationists call this domain specific procedural knowledge—knowledge expressed through the hands. What about executive control functioning? Identity issues of false self vs true self? The point here is that

What about language and how it not only communicates understandings but shapes it, contributing to our conceptual frameworks and schemata? The kingdom is ontological, a way of being that does not yet exist until it does. It is a verb, an action first and foremost.

The Problem with Concepts

We should not be surprised that we have lost our way and ended up with a very small Christianity when we make it out to be about right concepts. Any concept, including *the kingdom of God*, is limited to a frame of reference, a mindset. Gregory of Nyssa once wrote that "Concepts create idols; only wonder comprehends anything. People kill one another over idols. Wonder makes us fall to our knees."[8] Thinking about the kingdom as a metaphor is better. A metaphor is less literal and more poetic, more wonder-producing and offering new futures, newer possibilities. Metaphors are always bigger or smaller than the thing they represent. The smaller our understanding of the kingdom, the bigger the influence of alternatives. People will choose anything but God to make them happy. The banal does have appeal. Jogging helps us lose weight and money in our pockets makes us forget that we are not getting out of this thing called life alive. We forget that the leading cause of death has always been birth. The problem has

---

8. Gregory of Nyssa, "Quote by Gregory of Nyssa."

rarely been with an understanding of the kingdom that is too big. Maybe I protest too much, and we just need to all live, eat and be merry.

Or just maybe we need old ideas, new practices because our young people deserve it.

3

Paradigm Shifts

Regenerating Memories

IN THIS CHAPTER I take you through a snapshot look at ten old ideas about nurturing right relationships in people, from children through to adulthood, and how those ideas were evident in visible expressions that, at the time, made sense politically, economically, and sociologically. But, as you will read, the seeds of fragmentation, the wearing away at the edges of Jesus's original big idea were already planted, not only within a hundred years of Jesus's death and resurrection, but throughout the next two thousand years. The kingdom of God through right relationships, and not through right religion, never really had much of a chance to change people or the world.

This section is a reclamation project. The section presents eleven big ideas, old ideas that were at one time paradigmatic, accepted and acceptable within Christian practices, but today have either been lost, partially or fully, along the landscape of history, or so set in to be impossible to change. The result? Jesus's big idea remains just that, a big idea. Each of the eleven paradigmatic ideas presents us with an image from the past. A snapshot. A subversive memory. Maybe, just maybe, a memory that could be regenerated, life breathed into it or expressed into a new practice. Here is a good starting place for our journey into old ideas-new practices.

Try first to imagine how each image, each old idea you will read in this section is subversive, in the sense that the image or idea calls into question current understandings and practices in teaching young people. Yet, at the same time, imagine how each image confirms suspicions that many of us feel we need to reclaim something, anything, because what we are doing today with young people in teaching and learning is not working out all that well. If it were, we would not have the exodus from churches that we are experiencing. Young people are voting with their feet. Perhaps, like me, you would like to at least consider an old idea, regenerated to fit today's culture, and attach a new instructional practice to it.

You may accuse me of begging the question, but what has been lost from each *old idea* has been something to do with right relationships as the organizing principle, the big idea of Jesus. The further along we go, from Jesus to the twenty-first century, the greater the loss, the more profound has been the movement away from Jesus's proposal for a new possibility, a new future for people designed for right relationships, a way of being that explains and encompass everything.

The Usefulness of the Notion of Paradigms

A paradigm can be an example or an illustration. The more common understanding of a paradigm is a system of thoughts and behaviors that constitute what is normal, for example, in the rules and practices of science. Thomas Kuhn drew our attention to something called paradigm shifts in science in his book. For Kuhn (1962) a paradigm is an entire constellation of beliefs, values, techniques shared by a given community.[1]

Einstein's theories of general and specific relativity challenged the prevailing paradigm, His remarkable insights were the anomalies that did not fit the normal rules and practices of the science community in his day. The anomaly was that time and space were relative and not absolute as had been thought or been the paradigm. That upside- down idea could not be explained by the current rules and practices of science at the time. Either Einstein was wrong, or the current practices and rules of science were wrong. Turns out he was right. His ground-breaking theories regarding relatively, both general and specific, were anomalies that changed virtually everything considered normal in science.

Jesus's big idea was another anomaly, that the kingdom of God is a "particular" way of being in the world that comes about through right relationships. Philosophically, this idea did not align with current taken for granted assumptions and expectations, ideas about what were true and important. His big idea did not align with educational practices of his

---

1. Kuhn, *Structure of Scientific Revolution*.

day, expectations of what people were to learn and understand. Religion was supposed to be about ought to(s) and should(s), rules and regulations, and for sure what the Messiah was supposed to do and accomplish. He disappointed most of them. But not all of them.

Jesus's big idea was going to have short shelf life on one hand; on the other hand his essential concept, his message has obviously remained attractive enough, compelling and perceived to be important enough for people's well-being that expressions of the kingdom idea have continued to show up in smaller expressions along history's highway. Anomalies moved these smaller expressions through changes and modifications, adaptations and at times strange visible expressions of the kingdom (e.g., church denominations). This section of the book is a look at ten smaller expressions of Jesus's big idea, the anomalies that moved people's thinking and visible expressions of Jesus's big idea into smaller expressions, and what we educators might reclaim and regenerate into new practices with young people today.

Paradigms and Theology

The theory of paradigms and paradigm shifts has been widely applied to theology. Jürgen Moltmann[2], Edward Shillebeeckx[3], Martin Marty and Hans Küng applied the theory of paradigm shifts to Christian theology and practices. Hans Kung in particular, applied the theory of paradigm shifts to theology and theology's prevailing practices and rules during epochs of time periods. The combination of shifts in thinking and new knowledge, as well as new ways of knowing (epistemology) slowly and incrementally changed. According to Kung, theology has been characterized by six paradigms: Jewish Christian apocalyptic; Hellenistic Byzantine; Roman Catholic; Reformation Protestantism; Enlightenment

---

2. Jürgen Moltmann (1926 to present) is a theologian and writer who wrote "Theology of Hope" and other books to express his view that God suffers with us as well as rejoices with us when we suffer and rejoice. He was influenced by Hegel and the notion of the dialectic yet remained strongly reformed in his theology. He was also strongly oriented toward liberation theology. His personal background is quite fascinating. It includes joining the German army in 1944, surrendering to the first British soldier he saw then spending the rest of the war in prison. He remained deeply troubled by Auschwitz and Germany's treatment of Jews and others, as evidenced in his writing.

3. Edward Schillebeeckx (1914–2009) was a Dominican priest and was influential in Vatican 2. He was also a controversial theologian, particularly for his views on the literal resurrection of Jesus.

modern; and Contemporary ecumenical.[4] Each paradigm constituted what was normal, taken-for-granted thought and practices in Christendom. The paradigm was a collective mindset, an idea that explained everything, and could be used to understand everything.

The influence of a paradigm should not be underestimated. Even very early practices and understandings in science, well before Einstein, were limited and constrained by the theological paradigm. Until Copernicus and Galileo, the prevailing idea, the paradigm in science, was that the earth was the center of the universe. The Bible's ideas could be construed to neatly fit into the current scientific paradigm. Prevailing Christian paradigms strongly influenced rules and practices in economics as well. Sharing wealth was an accepted paradigm for the early Jesus's followers. They had all things in common we are told in Acts. Yet, it all changed. Who today lives in community with all things in common?

Shifts in paradigms can be discontinuous and disruptive. The Copernican revolution is an example. The change was quick and upsetting and led to a reexamination of everything, including taken-for-granted ideas about the earth and its place in the universe. Paradigm shifts can be slow and continuous.[5] Doubts of faith, convictions, conversion experiences, and cognitive dissonance produce events that contribute to gradual shift of a paradigm. The Protestant Reformation is an example of such a continuous shift, one that arguably is still going on.

Sometimes syncretism is the result of a paradigm shift, a fusing of ideas and practices, a confluence of ideas and practices. Common today are expressions of church that advertise themselves as churches for people who do not fit church.

Whether we are in a twenty-first century swamp of syncretic merging of rules and practices in theology, or an actual paradigm shift is debatable. But something is going on. Rules and norms of being a Jesus follower are changing. Practices are changing. Church attendance in evangelical, as well as in mainline Protestant and Catholic churches, is dwindling (Barna, 1995, Thiessen, 2017, Bibby, 2010). How many of us today would nail ninety-five theses to the door anywhere to protest

---

4. Küng, *Christianity Essence, History and Future*. Kung (1928 to present) is a Swiss born theologian, Catholic and controversial writer who regularly called into question papal infallibility, clergy abuse, commonalities in world religions and death with dignity.

5. Das, "Enquiry into the Paradigm Shifts"; Das's paper offers a perspective on paradigm shifts from an eastern worldview perspective.

anything? Stand for anything? What constitutes normal practice and shared common ideas about anything theological is difficult.

What practices might be possible by being next to what is already operational educating young people? What can a new future, a new educational possibility, by creatively modifying or accommodating what is already in place? Most sports are possibilities that emerged next to an original sport. Pickleball from tennis; tin can cricket from baseball; football from rugby. No throwing out the proverbial baby with the bath water unless it is time to do so. Our western culture has families, and they will not go away entirely. Families, however, can be accommodated, can change and do so to accommodate new futures, new possibilities. Maybe neighborhood cohorts will emerge as the next possibility to the current practice of family. This possibility is for all of us to rethink the emphasis in western Christianity on the nuclear family of mom and dad and a couple of kids and a dog. Scriptures talk far more about community, about the church, about ecclesia (the gathering of people called out around a big idea) than about little families. Families are designed to disintegrate. Kids grow up and move out. The reality is that families are disintegrating today far too early and far too often. No wonder, the nuclear family simply cannot stand up under the pressures of contemporary culture. However, neighborhoods can, the church which evidences persons in right relationships can as well. The church is a good idea.

Through my experience, and study, I have come to question our western emphasis, particularly in evangelical Christianity, on a paradigm in which a focus on the family is emphasized. It should be noted that the little nuclear family is hardly talked about at all in the Scriptures. When it is, it is not always in very flattering terms. Jesus even calls us out into a mindset change, to leave our fathers and mothers and follow him (Luke 14:26). The bigger emphasis throughout all the Scriptures is clearly on people, groups, tribes, and church as a community of believers. And maybe it should have been? Children's development, psychologically and spiritually, needs more than mom and dad, brother, and sister, maybe a dog or two. The odds are stacked against this little family unit ever being able to withstand the pressures of twenty-first century life.

We have denominations, religious practices, public and private schools, and a prosperous and long-lived population. There may be no immediate need to jettison entirely any of the above (especially long-lived old people, of which I am a part). There may be a need, however, to assimilate old ideas, reclaimed and regenerated from the past, into what is already in practice.

One important and last reminder; patterns of continuous change follow a predictable course, one that has both sociological, as well as psychological, logic. Robert Bellah's notion of the double bind (1967)[6] may or may not be resolved for you by reading this book. We may start off thinking that because there is nothing wrong with God, creation, and the natural order, and others, there is no need for this book. If there is something wrong, there just may be something wrong with me. Or maybe, there is nothing wrong with me, so there must be lots wrong with God, the Creator (if God even exists), others, and the created or natural order. The messages I interpret from others often leads me into the double bind, either I confirm one or the other, nothing wrong me, or lots wrong with me. Maybe we should not be too quick to try to resolve the double bind, particularly if we have not come to the insight that everything good, right, and true comes about through right relationships.

I can choose to remain in a revolving door of circular reasoning, assimilating and accommodating my ideas to a much smaller way of being than that of right relationships, so I can maintain some sort of cognitive balance in my life, to avoid any cognitive dissonance. Like shopping in a supermarket, I can pick and choose which concepts to buy into. I carefully select only those concepts that do not upset my sense of significance and meaning making. When I claim that Jesus was more political than philosophical, more concerned with people doing justice than understanding it, my fundamentalist friends do simple mental gymnastics work. They go back down their food chain of knowledge representations, to their current frames of reference, scripts and right down to macro-propositions (simple noun-verb relationship statements like God is just, or sinners in the hands of an angry God) that can be safely confirmed so as to preserve their sense of security. I too pick my favorite macro proposition, scripture, and use it to disprove any idea I find upsetting or prove an idea I am committed to. The end is often an entrenchment of bad ideas. Church is a building. The ticket into the exclusive club of the saved is deciding for Jesus and Christianity. And, above all having the right ideas in your head is the point of it all. These ideas have hardly anything to do with the compelling ideas of Jesus.

6. Bellah, "Civil Religion in America"; Bellah (1927–2013) was a sociologist whose interests included the influence of individualization in American life and culture, common good vs individualism, and the emergent self-centeredness in American life.

Or I can also work upwards in my food chain of knowledge representation, into my schemata (self- organized clusters of my knowledge, preferred actions, and attitudes regarding some idea) and ultimately worldviews where my ideologies reside. I end up in a different revolving door of circular reasoning, but a revolving door, nonetheless, concluding what is right and wrong in what I have already assumed to be right or wrong. I can take up conversations with others or privately within myself, big issues like death with dignity, sexual orientation, and abortion. But I will likely end up again, simply accommodating a current concept to whatever feels comfortable and preserves my sense of security and significance. I will easily get away with safety in thinking, circular reasoning, and really bad ideas about Christianity when I do not live into the kingdom of God, take up right relationships with the Creator, self, others, and the created and natural order. Is the mind a problem? Yes. Is the mind part of the solution? Yes. The message of this book is that right relationships, developed through being in the world in ways taught to us by Jesus lead us gently into solutions. Read Romans 12:1–2 if you do not believe me.

The evidence is there. There is something happening here, though what it is might not be exactly clear. But maybe, just maybe, the change we need today is more like reclamation project, a regeneration of old ideas into new practices.

One final note. The time periods noted for each paradigm are general and rough approximations. No paradigm shift comes to screeching halt in a day, month or even a year. But nesting each paradigm into a time frame can be informative in our understanding of what was going on politically, economically, and socially. There always has been a progressive, mutual accommodation of Christian practices with the culture in which it finds itself.

Let us take a closer look at what odd ideas might be reclaimable from times past and regenerated into new practices.

Big Idea #1: The Way of Jesus: 0–150 AD

The essence of Jesus's teaching was simple to understand and practice, but apparently, given history's long, terrible story, not easy. The kingdom of God is a way of being in the world that comes about through right relationships with God, each other, ourselves and the created (cities, neighborhoods) and natural order (creation). When we take up and practice his way of being in the world, it produces right relationships.

If this sounds like a tautology you are not reading it right. If this sounds all too easy, then you are not reading it right either. The kingdom of God is ontological. *Being* is more important than thinking and doing. The simplicity of being is at the far end of the complexity of practicing right relationships.

The way to follow Jesus was through right relationships, beginning with following him. The way into right relationships was not through memorizing Jewish scripture (though Jesus memorized scriptures), showing up at meetings, or even doing the right things, The means to the end of being in the world in particular ways did include certain ways of behaving and thinking, practicing life, as well as being intentional about developing healthy mindsets. These were necessary but not sufficient. That is if we are to take up what Jesus taught us

The means to the end of being in the world in particular ways does influence the development of right relationships. We know that today. We can and do learn from models of virtue and character, to inhibit bad behaviors and to disinhibit good behaviors (practicing what was previously an inhibited behavior, perhaps for fear of embarrassment-such as standing up for someone who is being treated unjustly). Models of character are important; they provide a picture of what is right and good. Right relationships can and do lead to new possibilities for us in our journey to true selves. We do the heavy lifting of dealing with deep wounds and imagining new possibilities for ourselves, each other, the world, and our hand in hand walk with God. The right relationship with God through Jesus was both the end and the beginning, the source of ideas for the new practices in education and the hope for new outcomes of new practices.

The initial paradigm of everything rising and falling on right relationships was doomed before it could fully set in and be operationalized. The shift to other paradigms, was inevitable and unavoidable. Here is why. Paradigm shifts are caused by anomalies. An anomaly is an idea that does not fit with the normal, it is a taken-for-granted thinking. The protestant Reformation was an anomaly that changed Christendom. The holocaust was an anomaly that, for many, changed the map of the world. The first nuclear bomb dropped on Hiroshima was another anomaly that changed perspectives about human beings–especially of the American persuasion of being good. Solzhenitsyn was right, it appears, that the dividing line between good and evil runs right through the human heart. American and western persons' hearts too.

Jesus's followers knew a Jewish system of education, an oral tradition in which the learner was to be a cistern that would not lose a drop. However, Jesus's kingdom idea of right relationships trumping right ideas was an anomaly, with enough upsetting qualities to bring his ultimate end. But the leader of this movement of right relationships was murdered. The long hoped for Messiah had not come for sure and was certainly not this Jesus of Nazareth. He offered no military freedom from oppression, nor did he systemize better ways, or a new expression of Jewish education.

The system of education that Jewish people knew and practiced was oral, a tradition with an emphasis that information trumped everything-to know the right stuff was the point of education in the rabbinical schools. The rabbinical schools were themselves an anomaly that would not go away or be accommodated to this outrageous idea that everything important simply rose or fell on right relationships. Jesus was calling just about everything into question.

A small handful of first-and second-generation Jesus followers understandably tried, at all costs, to promote and preserve the way of being. Letters were written to people who were gathering to practice Jesus's teaching, designed to encourage and affirm, and in some cases disaffirm practices of being in the ways described by Jesus. It was a good effort, but by the mid second century sects and strange spiritual practices had sprung up. The first 150 years following Jesus were awash with other messiahs, sects, and religious systems. Underground meetings sprung up, but so did some unusual expressions of the way of being-unusual interpretations and, consequently, expressions of spirituality that were contrary to the way of being that Jesus described and represented.

Maybe Jesus's way was too simple? It was certainly too upside-down, too opposite to what was expected and wanted. Maybe it was too political-take care of the poor first and foremost? And of course, Jesus death sealed the mindset deal. He could not be the Messiah then could he. The seeds were sown, and the first wobbly, not firmly established paradigm initiated by Jesus was about to shift. Our flagship got lost at sea, very early on in the voyage.

Big Idea #2: The Didache, Way That Leads to Life and Way That Leads to Death 150–300 AD

The big idea from the Didache, a document found initially in Constantinople in 1873, was that there were two ways, one leading to life and the other to death. It presented Christianity as a way of life that needed to be practiced, to be understood and nurtured. The Didache proposed these two categories—life or death—and by choosing a particular-way of being in the world, one chooses life; right choices led to life. Christianity is "some kind of life," an intentional, purposeful way of behaving, a lifestyle of actions and behaviors.

The Didache is a manifesto for how the Jesus followers understood their need to practice, or take up, Christianity. There were two ways: one way leading to life and one to death. Life was not found in memorizing anything, getting your facts straight. or practicing some liturgy in a building. Those are all not bad ideas, but just not central to this big idea that being a follower of *the way* was about just that, taking up the way of being that would lead to life.

We do not know the motivation, the reason for writing the Didache. Maybe the document was written in response to the springing up of unusual interpretations and strange expressions of the way of being? Within the first 150 years following Jesus's death, unusual interpretations arose of what Jesus meant and who he was.

Was the Didache onto something about two ways of being in the world? If we take seriously the recent research on brain and behavior, we might conclude that, yes indeed, a deep wisdom was woven into the document. Here is why. We know today that the brain is an adaptive system; it does not lead as much as it follows. Behaviors and actions, even emotions, create neural pathways and shape our thinking. It appears that indeed we do act our way into new ways of thinking.[7] The writers of the Didache may not have known the science of it all, but they chose to align their thinking and writing to a simple notion—Christianity is a way of being in the world. What is produced is right thinking. Right thinking does not lead the way; it follows.

---

7. Palmer, *Courage to Teach*; Palmer (1939–present) is author of "The Courage to Teach and To Know as we Are Known." His writing is often characterized by themes of personal identity, authentic self-hood and development of a true self, particularly for teachers.

Reclaimable today is that Christianity is a way of life more than a system of right beliefs. The initiating event into the way of living was Christ's death. From the initiating event of Christ, we begin our own personal dying and rising with Christ, and from Jesus's teachings on how to live in the meantime.

But once again this early paradigm was going to have a very short shelf life. The irony, however, is that what developed in the next paradigmatic period, often called the Catechumenate, could have preserved this essential idea of the way of being. The catechumenate was an organized system of rites of passages to induce young people into the faith, a way that came to be called Christianity. The system included formal study, preparation for baptism, and scrutiny by persons who had already passed through the system. It appeared to do just that except for one thing. The times were changing; the economic and social conditions were about to change as well. The slippage was well on its way, away from the way of being based on relationships to a way of being based on organized systems, and a complicated one at that. The reasons for the shift and the end of the catechumenate were complex and beyond the scope of this book. However, one thing is clear and is a regenerative idea, that people are social beings. For group dynamics and right relationships to be good group dynamics, maybe teachers and parents do need some catechumenate-like system or patterns of ways of being so that relationships can be nurtured.

However, duty was about to replace intimacy; regime replace friendship; systems and formula replace knowing. The soon to emerge educational practice was one of rigorous, rite of passage and systematic progress through to of how to regenerate the old ideas from the catechumenate into a new practice of authentic friendship and community.

Big Idea #3: The Catechumenate-Community is Essential 300–400 AD

The essential question being addressed by referring to the catechumenate as a unique, standalone paradigm is-how do we grow or develop as Christians? The answer includes the essential role that the community plays. Not the building that we mistakenly call church, but the visible, local, proximity-based community where the liturgies and systems necessary for right relationships are practiced, active, and participated in. The catechumenate was a formal designed system intended to nurture people, often young people, into Christianity as a total life. It was made up of what was called the '*accendente*,' inquirers who had been evangelized and were put through a rigorous review of their life. Acceptance into the catechumenate was followed by up to three years of engagement in the community. When transformation was evident (sometimes earlier than three years), the person underwent scrutiny to see if they had done justice, good deeds, and used Scriptures to form a lifestyle. If judged to be so, they joined the *elect* at the beginning of Lent. They then learned the creed, Our Father, and were baptized and confirmed. They entered then into what was called the *mystagogy*. A teacher, not just a cleric, could bless the student. For us today what might be reclaimable is the need for a framework that identifies and marks progression of development. What we might regenerate is some form of a rites of passage system into our new practices of this old idea. Here is why.

The word faith taken from the Greek word means trust and action, with a cognitive element. The abstractions of the way of being, which were originally intended to be the end, the result of being in the world in a *particular* way, must have been pre-imminent. Beliefs not only became synonymous with faith, but they also were emerging as the very essence of faith. Beliefs assumed the lead role in the story of Christian life. This anomaly continues to haunt Christians today. The abstractions of Christianity, knowing the right concepts, lost their place in the place in the food chain of knowing and being. Belief in the abstractions was no longer the product or the consequence of being in the world in the particular ways described by Jesus, but devolved to being the foundation, the starting place. Faith devolved from trust nurtured through right relationships with God, into a large concept that was more important than anything, including right relationships. This idea of faith as the organizing concept for Christianity required mental ascent and alignment of ones thinking. What was emerging, and vestiges of which remain today, was the importance of knowing the right stuff, a person's cognitive-based alignment with some abstract concept like salvation.

Today, given the long-life span leftover of this paradigm, we hardly know how to best to question many of our taken for granted Christian ideas, and to teach young people how to be critical questioners of ideas and practices. We do not feel good about calling into question the inherent contradictions of such practices as making a decision for Christ as the deciding factor in our eternal destiny or doing whatever we can to avoid falling into the hands of a very angry God. If the inexplicably always angry God is what we know, then our resentment, not relationship with God, just might be justified. C.S. Lewis puts it this way, 'The worst we have ever done to God is to leave Him alone-why can't he return the compliment?' [8] We carry on today, affirming the ascendency many strange, less glorious ideas as our pinnacle religious response, instead of giving in to the evidence that from the very beginning we were destined to a big idea, that we were destined for a relationship with the Creator. Some paradigms are continuous, sadly.

We are not dissuaded by these strange ideas, even when we negotiate our way through mental machinations to accommodate them, to explain for example, what happens after death to aborted babies. I once listened to one of world's leading theologians explain to a young theology student that we all deserve hell anyway and it is only God's election that saves some people and not others. Aborted babies just may end up in hell. Concepts indeed!

The theological machinations get worse. On one hand, who decides given our life and death issues? Young children may die before even being able to either decide or respond, and then it is up to God's whim? What, then, is the point of teaching young people who are fortunate enough not to die before they align their thinking to an abstraction like decision-making theology, or people who have never heard of Jesus?

And, what if I am of the persuasion that instead of it all being up to God, I need to get in to the Christian party and ultimately heaven, only through praying the sinner's prayer and having faith in Jesus. Again, why bother with teaching anything to young people?

Do you see the problem? Outside of an operationalized system or framework through which thinking is socially constructed, and knowledge can become a social construction within the curbs of what right relationships and the teachings of Jesus mean, we can believe any kind of self-serving, proof-texted nonsense. We can easily take a scripture and make it support our ostensibly good idea. That is called proof-texting and it is a bad use of Scripture and a bad idea.

However, our reclamation project includes the role community can have and right relationships to come to understand what is true and right. To be clear, I am not referring to the ubiquitous, everyone has a community interpretation of community, but propinquity based, proximity

---

8. Lewis, *Problem of Pain*. p35 In his arguments throughout he guides the reader to think again about their philosophical presuppositions that are not based on the real universe and grand narrative of scripture.

oriented and neighborhood community, with authentic rites of passages, real liturgies of eating and doing life together, and ways of being that are modeled and taught, acted into and taken up.

Events were about to happen that would further erode the possibilities earlier offered by Jesus for being in the world in particular ways that come about through right relationships. The anomaly of a strange marriage of church and state was one. The imminent onset of what we today call the dark ages was another-feudalism replaced community; monasticism for the few who would preserve much of what was written and considered true replaced the systematic induction of young people into the faith.

Big Idea #4: Augustine[9]: Stories Trump Facts 400–500 AD

What is reclaimable in the time-period, just prior to what has come to be known as the medieval period or dark ages, is that thinking is socially constructed through stories; knowledge is a social construction. Augustine had an intellectual conversion early on. He maintained a conviction of Christianity's truthfulness throughout his life. He was influenced by reading the Neo-Platonists, that knowledge has a pre-existence nature. He was over and against the heresies of his day-Gnosticism (hidden or secret truths), Manicheanism (evil comes from the will) and Pelagianism (if you don't do it, no one will do it for you).

Augustine raised the notion of knowing and not just in some abstract sense but in the sense of physical knowing or being intimate with real issues of original sin, sexuality, and morality. From this paradigm we can reclaim that God indeed might just show up disguised as our life and that God has nothing else to work with other than our small stories of forgiveness and celebration, pain and exodus, relationships and separation, and how language expresses all the above and more.

Augustine not only raised the question of knowing but of how to promote knowing. The student-teacher relationship therefore was important. Teachers were to bring people to know God but in the Hebrew sense of deep, intimate, and experiential knowing. Ordinary people had to be bound by the community so that knowing was also bound, not free

---

9. Augustine (354–430 AD) was a Christian bishop and theologian who helped create modern Christian thought through some of his works like "Confessions" and "The City of God."

to roam into heresies. The teacher-student relationship was important as were the stories told by others in the community.

Augustine was an advocate for the idea that God loves us, a reality that we need not understand, nor is it a puzzle to be solved. It is a mystery to be lived into, to be practiced. He clearly affirmed a person's role and place in the Christian story. One possible and arguably legitimate reclamation idea then is that the narrative in our lives, the story line, can be a recapitulation of the larger narratives we see in the scriptures. The story of the Exodus is therefore best understood by understanding our own exodus, our individual stories of birth, captivity, wilderness, release, and celebration.

To reclaim and regenerate the power of story to express what is true about the facts of our lives, may be a most effective way to come to understand what is true about what we have been told is true, the scriptures.

Big Idea #5: The Medieval Period: The Role of Conservation in Communities of Faith (500–1250) AD

We know little about how faith and the Jesus way of being in the world were nurtured during these dark ages, the time-period often referred to as the holy Roman empire. We know that monasteries in places like Ireland preserved written documents, including the Bible. church-government marriage. By Charlemagne, the church and state were one. We know that Alcuin and Charlemagne were among the few well documented people of the middle ages. The catechumenate was no longer the main educator. But Jesus's message survived, perhaps attributable to written creeds that codified beliefs; perhaps in homes with families teaching young people how to live Christianly. We just do not know enough to be sure.

What we do know and can take away from this era is that whether through the creeds, the liturgies that came to characterize being together, or families who chose to teach young people, something went on that led to the conservation of the practices of the faith. We do know that the monasteries preserved the manuscripts. We know that prayer life became more liturgical, and formalized. We know that the Visigoths destroyed the intellectual life so formal educational practices likely were non-existent. We also know and have preserved the idea that praying in a common way had a unifying effect. The means of conservation surely was holding on firmly to what is essential to the formation of right relationships.

Questionable low-lights of this era included emergence of a state-church marriage. And we know that this era also included many questionable practices within each, such as paid indulgences for sin's forgiveness, land holdings by clergy, and the crusades. I struggled to find anything worth reclaiming from this period. Human history does appear often to be a long, sad story of trying to find anything other than right relationships to be happy. Our understandings and educational practices can come from the lessons learned from great and not so great people and practices. The Hebrew understanding of the future is curious and offers one important perspective here. It is not the future we are to face but the past. The future is firmly behind our backs. The word אתמול (etmol) roughly translated means living into a new future by looking backwards to our past, from where we have come. The word מחר (machar) is connected to the concept of being behind, like sitting in a rowboat focusing on a point where you came from, with glances over our shoulders to where we want to end up. Maybe the best takeaway from this period is an educational one, to guide young people away from endless searches for that elusive thing called the will of God and into what has been and is true about 'what is.' The rowboat metaphor to end this brief section on the medieval time-period but then to look forward to the next.

Our next reclamation project is to conserve, look backwards with wisdom to decide, individually and in community, what is worth holding onto, conserving, and breathing new life into.

Big Idea #6: The Role of the Mind: Necessary but Not Sufficient (1250–1550)

Thomas Aquinas[10] and the scholastic tradition are the iconic representations of this era and point us towards our next reclamation project. The scholastic tradition emphasized dogma and tradition, as well as a system of theology and philosophy that drew heavily on Aristotelian logic. Understanding begins with knowledge or insight that lays compacted, amorphous, waiting to unfold in the presence of right conditions. Insight began internally and, unlike the Platonic idea, that generally proposed a big idea that there existed an external source, a third reality outside of what

---

10. Thomas Aquinas (1225–1274) was a Catholic priest and one of the top thinkers of scholasticism. He came up with the natural law theory, which states that the first principle of human action is based on reason.

we see or can imagine, and therefore what we understand. The platonic idea, for example, was that the pinnacle of existence was something they referred to as the good. The good was the source of all things; that expressions of good would be recognizable as good only if they corresponded to the ideal of good. Scholasticism drew from a different viewpoint, that the good wouldn't exist until it did, that it developed and began within the person. Scholasticism was taught in medieval European universities, and its curriculum was based on, and drew heavily from, the writings of the early church fathers. Aquinas's understanding of Christianity led him to conclude that people are responsible for their own agency. His line of reasoning was that what is true about life is within the person waiting to unfold there, and not in some platonic ideal.[11] The best education was one that drew people to pay attention to the data of their life and to their generally, and to understand this data by using tradition, the ideas of early church fathers, as well as current church teachings. The learners' task was to judge or pour value into the insights that were emerging and then act on it.

The big idea, the take-away is the essential role of reason in the nurture of Christian faith. However, today more than in any paradigm, we remain more than a little suspicious of the mind and the limitations of reason to explain and encompass everything that is Christian. Thomas Aquinas's understanding of people and the shift from a spiritual knowing (wisdom) to a rational knowledge remains a stream of influence to this day. The result? We do not tell the story as much as we take up and deliver a short, pithy, metaphysical explanatory summary of the story. We love to broker in abstractions, particularly if we get paid to do so and need the affirmation of an audience. If we are preachers and teachers, we have found a way to make a living, by delivering information. The result? Going to church or school is primarily about sitting and listening to transmitted information.

However, not all leftovers from the scholastic paradigm are problematic. The lost big idea is faith is a way of knowing, that includes the mind, but cannot be totally dependent on the mind. Faith is more visceral and as the next paradigm claims, is initiated not by us but by God. The result? A new concept of faith, more like a body trustingly falling backwards as it were, into trustworthy hands. The reformation was about to change everything.

---

11. Thomas Aquinas was an influential philosopher in the tradition of scholasticism; God's existence could be proven rationally among the tenets of scholasticism.

Big Idea #7: Ongoing Reformation Required (1550–1650)

The Reformation was a massive paradigm shift of understanding and eventually practices regarding what it meant to be Christian. Martin Luther[12] is often credited with significant influence in the Reformation and forwarding the premise that the just shall live by faith and it is through grace that that people are saved; by grace, and not through any works that they might to try to do be saved.

Aquinas and others up to this period advocated for a notion that you were an individual by virtue of being a member of a village, town or group, and an individual as an individual. This notion seems to have been lost with Luther. The emerging individualism, that the individual trumps the group, would take hold eventually and firmly later in the twentieth century.

Luther's success was both timely and, in many ways, predictable. He was in a paradigm shift himself; economic upheaval that saw barter begin to transition to money; peasants becoming aware and knowledgeable by the emergence of villages and towns that could be containers of the word on the street; rationalism in Europe was arising and portending the enlightenment period that would take hold some decades later. The papacy was arising to a more politically strong entity. Revolt was common. Laxity in clergy was commonplace. And the buying of indulgences for a way out of purgatory was a common practice. Rather than flee in the face of these conditions, this paradigm shift and void in practices of the teachings of Jesus, Luther chose to fight. Accepting salvation as a past tense, already accomplished, was his biggest gift to us.

Luther left us with questions that have a variety of theological answers, problems with a number of possible answers. For instance, what is the role of the church? If we are saved by grace, then what are our requirements for living day to day? What is the role of right relationships in nurturing the Christian life? What language should we use? What does it mean to make a decision for Christ? Or to accept Christ? Receiving? How does grace, with its new reformation-based understandings, influence day to day life? What is the role of human freedom? Does grace cover or redeem human nature? Do we objectify evil and subjectify good? Should

---

12. Martin Luther (1483–1546) was arguably the most significant person during the Reformation. Today, the evangelical and reformed perspectives include the belief that salvation is not earned by good deeds but only received as a free gift of God's grace.

we begin with secular education and be taught how to be over and against the church and Christianity?

We are still today in the questions, problems, and issues. Many have chosen not to conserve what would have produced right relationships, perhaps because the questions, issues and problems seem formidable and perhaps are harbingers of an absurd universe. There is no meaning, no purpose to it all anyway. Learning processes honor the content; the method becomes the content. If you want love, lead within love. If you want clear hard-headed thinking, then teach this way.

The old idea to be reclaimed is that reformation should be inevitable and unavoidable in our understandings and practices in families, churches, schools, and organizations that claim a stake in the education of young people. However, if reformation is to be the new normal, transformation and change the new constant, the guiding question remains, towards what end? To reform is not to deconstruct. To reform is to remain committed to conserve, to keep our eyes focused backwards to the way of being in the world that comes about through right relationships.

Reformation has to do with courage to act based on Scripture. Logic, rationality, and general revelation should contribute to reformation. Luther teaches us about the life of activity, the habitus, the courage to think theologically for ourselves, not merely follow what others have said. It is important for any reformers to recognize the cost.

The reclamation project from this era is conservation, to hold on to understandings and practices that can and do produce right relationships.

Big Idea #8: Different Ways of Knowing (1650–1750)

The transition to the importance of knowing, away from the importance of teaching, is most important. The transition is still ongoing today, educational practices that place the learner in the center and reason for teaching. This transition began with Luther. Like a thread linking a garment, the emphasis on the individual would show up in John Amos Comenius[13] and his notion that learning to have faith is a natural process and learning therefore should be an organic and personalized activity. Catechisms emerged with the onset of the printing press and opportunities to codify what emerging sects saw as central for young people to

---

13. John Comenius (1592–1670) was a Moravian philosopher who is considered the father of modern education.

learn. However, what emerged was what we live with today—the ghettoization and sectarianism of the particular way of being in the world into smaller, much smaller interests-serving practices. The catechisms took the form of sermons and became the center or locus for learning. Both provided security but worked against the relationship idea of Jesus. Any goal of people living into a universal principle that would explain and encompass everything, that of relationship and the kingdom of God trumping everything else, was lost. Faith remained a deposit, a thing, a noun, not a way of life/living.

The good news, however, is that like a stream of water flowing into a larger and good pool, keeping fresh the larger pool of water, a learning centered theme would carry on, in fact right to today. From Johann Herbart[14] and the importance of design in and for learning, with awareness and attention to the teaching-learning act itself, and onto others for whom family had to play a central role in nurturing faith. Catechisms continued to be used to help create an identity and an ethos within a community.

For the now well-established Moravians and, particularly, the Moravian John Hus,[15] religion had to influence life now, not just salvation later. A social concern movement began in earnest. The Salvation Army (1865) was birthed and to this day practices addressing social and economic differences.

The old idea to be recovered is that to know, and perhaps more importantly, how we come to know what we know, is important. Knowing how (procedural knowing) is not the same as knowing what (semantic knowledge). Both and more ways of knowing will be part of the new practices outlined later in this book.

Big idea #9: Women's Ways of Knowing (1750-Still Emerging)

A feminist consciousness began to emerge in Europe, primarily in the new world in the seventeenth and eighteenth centuries. It was a small start but a start, nonetheless (Mary Wollstonecraft's (1759–1797).[16] The

---

14. Johann Herbart (1776–1812) was a German philosopher who founded pedagogy as an academic discipline. His concept stemmed from logic, metaphysics, and the analysis of experience.

15. John Hus (1369–1415) was a Czech theologian and philosopher who outlined his reform of the church in his book "De Ecclesia." He was later burned at the stake as a heretic and his followers launched a civil war against the Holy Roman Empire.

16. Mary Wollenscraft (1759–1797). A controversial person for two reasons,

movement met opposition and remained largely an individualized effort regarding specific social issues like women being part of the leadership in the church and suffragette. The big idea from this emergence of a right way of being in the world is to remember our usable past, our forgotten history. Our current sensitivity today to gender equality and gender issues generally is a start. We need to reclaim and share together the tension that was then, for minorities and disenfranchised to matter and be equal participants in social life, and that some us experience today. It might be worthwhile to take up what some anthropologists refer to as the borders of separation, are thickest when we celebrate differences, and thinnest when we celebrate similarities. The question for us is given the end we desire, the kingdom of God, the particular way of being in the world that comes about through right relationships, what wisdom can we transfer to other differences and similarities, and our thinking about both in today's education of young people?

Big idea #10: Education through Nurturing (1750–1950)

The idea that began to emerge with the writings of Herbert, Comenius, followed by the work of John Dewey, Maria Montessori, and Emilio Reggio was that the education is natural, that is, until we make it unnatural. Young people have inherent capacities to both learn and teach; in fact, this inherent capacity lives in each of us. We should find, tease out, and create conditions in churches, schools, and families for young people to inquire, solve real problems, and take up both roles of learner and teacher.

However, questions have emerged from this paradigm shift to learner and learning away from teacher and teaching. Where will we draw information from? Books? We have preserved a consciousness that arose decades previously that all truth was in books. Knowledge has already been assembled. The disciplines provided their teaching and learning logic. Science and math offered deductive method. The Bible was to be

---

advocating for women's rights to be achieved through education and personal lifestyle decisions.

Horace Bushnell (1802–1876) Bushnell called into question the evangelical emphasis on how one becomes follower of Christ. Being a Christian, is not a one time, decision based and emotional response to a feeling or idea. He proposed that training over a lifetime is the alternative and if properly trained a person can claim to be follower of Jesus, a Christian. Bushnell emphasized to parents that train their children should start right at the onset of their lives.

learned and learning meant memorization. Society was a source of curriculum construction—deductive—know about it; inductive know it, socialization knowing their knowing of it.

Throughout the last one hundred and fifty or so years we have been reminded that experience sets in motion a person's understanding of truth. All truth-knowing begins with experience. Here we need inductive methodologies—people look for interpretations and applications for themselves. The corrective to an over emphasis on experiential learning is, as we have noted in the introduction, that we are not hard wired or soft wired to learn as much from actual experiences as we would like to think. It was John Dewey who corrected us by implying that we do not learn from experience but from reflection on experience.[17]

Big idea #11: The Role of Family (1950-Present)

From the Enlightenment through to the era of the early twentieth century with the emergence of rationalism, logic. and scientific method, the church and families, schools, and organizations with a stake in what and how we teach young people took up minds-on, enlightenment informed ways of teaching. Notions emerged and to this day inform our teaching and learning practices—notions like scaffolding, concrete operational based teaching, identity formation over a person's life span. Friendship was taught and practiced before talking about Jesus as a friend, inner turmoil was understood before teaching for understanding how and why Jesus calmed the waters, sharing needed to happen before talk about the church, exodus before Exodus.

We should not be surprised at the limitations and opportunities of families to be co-creators and leaders, generators of the way of being in the world taught to us by Jesus. The limitations have rarely been discussed with enough analyses for us to recognize and acknowledge the inherent and profound limitations of the nuclear family. After all, this family structure in the western world is designed to disintegrate. Young people leave home, eventually. It has never been a strong enough scaffold to support the unusual pressures and demands imposed on it.

---

17. Dewey, *Experience and Education*; He may have been the first person to cogently tell us that we do not learn from experience, but we learn from reflection on experience. The result has been an important and useful heuristic for teachers, a guide to what a learning experience needs to include for young people.

The family as a nuclear structure is dying a natural, slow death. No point in ignoring the bigger idea of right relationships and putting the family on a life-support system. The point is to take up the old ideas and new practices of the kingdom of God. Into this new territory we now go, of right relationships and how to teach our young people to go there.

SECTION II

The Program of Studies

Introduction

EVERY STRATEGY I DESCRIBE, every tactic, logistic, and relationship builder described in this section and in each chapter has been chosen and included for its tried and true contribution to the development of right relationships. Each chapter offers teaching ideas that are practical and have a track record of success with my fifty years of being a professional educator, university professor, Associate Dean of Education and school administrator. The core theme throughout each chapter is that your prime teaching directive, your educator's assignment, should you choose to accept it, is to guide young people into 'particular' ways of being in the world through right relationships. Your job does not have to be a devolution to a delivery of abstractions, nor a curating of shadows, what we know better as words. Everything described in Section II is all about right relationships and how to teach for their development and nurture.

You will find nothing in this book that sets forth educational activities that are purposeless, including the old, tired Christian ideas and practices of educating young people in Sunday school type education programs characterized by brokering in abstractions. Everything described in this program of studies has a real purpose, and that purpose starts and ends with right relationships. Scripture? For a purpose of knowing what Jesus described as being true about right relationships. Kindness? Prayer? Church participation? All useful but only to serve the interests of young people being in and participants of the kingdom of God. No mere moralizing was allowed into this book either. No prescriptions or have to(s). You will find no emphasis on hands-on learning either, without some form of reflection attached to it. We do not learn very much at all from mere experiences, unless those experiences are somehow connected to experience-expectant or experience-dependent synapses, better known as the brain. Let us put to rest once and for all our well-intentioned but wrong-headed and short-sighted ideas about hands-on learning. We are neither soft wired nor hard wired to learn very much from actual experiences. We do learn a great deal from reflection on experiences. Learning is minds-on.

Chapters Ahead

The four chapters in Section II are the promised handbook of new possibilities regarding tactics, strategies, logistics, and relationship builders. Each chapter refers to a specific developmental phase of young people, an invariant, sequential pattern of ways of being, made up of typical developmental and psychological needs of young people in each phase.

Chapter 4 includes a description of the program of studies for right relationships, a curriculum, the course for teaching young people in what arguably are the most developmentally sensitive years of all, the 4–13 years of age time span. A foundation is laid in these years, one full of good memories, competency development, awareness of personal attributes and their contribution to developing right relationships.

Chapter 5 includes a description of the program of studies for young people in the 14–17 years of age time span. This period is the transition phase, the experience of young people, for most young people, is like being in the borderlands, a liminal space between childhood and adulthood. The safest journey though the borderlands is when the young person feels protected and safe, while taking risks in being in relationships.

Chapter 6 includes a description of the program of studies for young people in the 18–21 age time span. This time-period is almost exclusively experienced as an internal negotiation of identity, who am I, what do I stand for, how would I like to be known and live. Identity issues of intimacy vs isolation, questions and problems about one's role and future place in the world, are best be addressed in this time-period. According to James Marcia (2011)[1] some young people foreclose and settle quickly

---

1. Marcia, *Ego Identity*; Marcia was influenced by Erik Erikson's work, as have been

on an identity. Other young people choose a moratorium approach wait and see and a continuation of investigations of personal and relational ways of being in the world. For others, their identities remain diffused and continue to remain unclear well into later adulthood. The premise in this chapter is that in and through being guided into right relationships identity issues resolve into healthy ones.

Chapter 7 is a description of tried and true tactics used to develop leadership attributes and skills. Learning is experienced, ironically, through teaching. Competencies to lead with integrity, risk-taking, and love are the ultimate outcomes of a relationship-based education program of learning.

---

many social psychologists over the past number of years.

4

Early and Middle Childhood

Ages 4–13

I Am Just Going to Be Nicer

My daughter came home from her grade one class one Friday late in September. She sat quietly at the table, uncharacteristically quiet. After a few minutes of painful silence and no response to that typical parent question, "How was school today?" She burst into tears, ran upstairs, and slammed her bedroom door. I followed her upstairs and listened outside her door to sobs and crying. I went in and sat on the edge of her bed. I waited. She hid under her blanket. I asked her what is going on?

The story came out between sobs. Her school mate was having a birthday party. She had handed out invitations to her party to all the girls in the class, except one. Yes, except one, my daughter. After a few minutes three things happened that I am sure I will remember for the rest of my life. First, she said, "Daddy, will you call her mom and ask her to invite me to the birthday party." After some more sobbing she declared that from now on she was just going to be nicer so kids would invite her to their birthday parties.

I recall thinking then, okay, here she goes, down that long, terrible road of trying to please people so that they will invite you to their birthday parties. The separation of her false self from true.

I did not say anything. I may have missed a teachable moment. I am not sure to be honest what I would have said to a very upset 6-year old girl. I never got the chance because of what happened next. She crawled

Early and Middle Childhood

up out from under the covers, sat on my lap, wrapped her arms around my neck and snuggled into me and fell fast asleep.

At that moment, with my daughter in the arms of a loving father, there were no spiritual scorecards needing to be kept. No past or even future. No worries or anxieties. Not even any forgiveness or bitterness. It just was. The most important truth of all had become flesh and blood. No more abstractions required.

Three life lessons learned from a failed birthday party. Three ideas explain and encompass everything that is important for teaching children. Practicing asking God to fix it; brokering in thankfulness coupled with lots of 'wow's trumping brokering in abstractions; being guides for children on the beginning of their long life-time journey of finding their true selves.

The Foundation

Chapter 4 is titled Foundations, for a reason, for parents and teachers of children 4–13 years of age. Children are not miniature adults; they have their own developmental and psychological needs, and experience unique identity, cognitive and moral questions, and challenges. Erik Erikson (1968)[1] the grandfather of social psychology theory and standard fare for every student of introductory psychology, tells us that the main developmental crisis or turning point for young people, aged 6–12, is development of competency vs inferiority. These young people need to get good at things. Lots of things or just a few, does not matter as much as we might think. Competencies developed in these years are the most desirable intended outcome of educating children. Jean Piaget (1964)[2]

---

1. Erikson, *Identity Youth and Crisis*; The grandfather of social psychology probably best describes Erik Erikson's contribution to our understanding identity and how one's identity is formed.

2. Piaget, *Construction of Reality in the Child*; Piaget (1896–1980) was a biologist who contributed some important early understandings of children's and youth's cognitive development. A stage theorist who proposed that children progress through four stages that are invariant and sequential, but not universally connected to specific ages. Generally, with exceptions, children progress through stages from sensori-motor (0–2 years), psycho-motor (2–6 years), concrete operational (6–11) and onto formal operation thinking. Piaget contributed a language that still is valid today including schema, assimilation, accommodation, and equilibration. However, his theory has been called into question and is less persuasive than more recent cognitive psychologists such as Alberta Bandura and Lev Vygotsky. An old idea, yes, but a new practice

was a biologist who took some of the obvious biological functions found in nature, such as assimilation, accommodation, adaptation, and equilibration and applied them to the cognitive development and phases of a child's development.

Piaget was one of the earliest scientists to tell us that these young people are concrete operational thinkers, that they make sense of new information, assimilate new ideas and accommodate their schemata by connecting what they are learning with what they have concretely experienced in their past. We have mistakenly misapplied concreteness in thinking to mean that children learn best by concrete experiences. That is partly true. However, Piaget knew (as well should we) that mere experiences do not teach us as much as we give them credit for. Reflection on experiences is better. Minds-on learning experiences are best, ones in which children are guided to be divergent thinkers thinking of new and creative expressions of learning, connecting new experiences with leftovers of old experiences they have had. Memories are those leftovers from previous experiences mindfully attended to, brought up into the working memory, the active memory where learning takes place. The best teachers you know are masters at "teaching the unfamiliar from the familiar."

The big idea of Chapter 4 is that an educational foundation for children between the ages of 4 to 13 is best laid in a teaching and learning context loaded with inquiry, mystery, awe, wonder, and magic. The foundation is a Narnia Chronicles[3] foundation, a magical mystery tour that includes, along with mystery, the intended outcome of getting good at things. The end or ultimate goal is competency development through inquiry, not a passive "sitting and getting" learning experience, but a set of active, hands and minds-on learning experiences, designed for young people to ultimately "get good" at doing things, from making friends to answering real questions, solving real problems that live in their world.

Why a foundation?

A foundation is a base. It is an underlying set of something, like simple skills or attitudes, on which something else, like a more complex

---

in his evocative claim that we can teach any subject, to any child, at any age in any intellectually honest fashion.

3. Lewis, *Last Battle*. The last story in the Chronicles. In one scene, Lucy asks Aslan to do something for the traitorous dwarfs as they are huddled together just before the end of time. Aslan lets out a roar that sets the universe shaking. The dwarfs turn to each other believing that 'they' do it with a machine of some kind. They agree to not be fooled. Aslan claims the obvious, that they are prisoners of their own minds, so afraid of being taken in that they will not be taken out.

skill or attitude, can be built. It is the feeling of being loved, on which the ability to receive and give affection is built. It is the trust that comes from a mother's touch that leads to feelings of attachment. It is a child's practice of making personal choices that lead to healthy adult assertiveness. It is a child developing basic skills and competence in school that will lead to later work-place confidence. It is an identity, that idea one has of who one is and what one's gifts are, that will be the basis of being able to be intimate with others in Godly ways.

How successfully a person hits a tennis ball is dependent upon the previous development of an underlying set of skills like being able to anticipate and watch a ball all the way to one's racquet. How successfully a person writes is dependent upon a previously developed underlying set of knowledge and skills that includes word identification, eye-hand coordination, and logical thought. The new skill is really an accommodation of a previously learned skill; the new concept an accommodation of a previously understood concept, even if that skill or concept is vague, inaccurate or in some way only an approximation of the more accurate concept or skill. They are still the connector, the meaning maker for children and their learning.

The best teachers design learning experiences so that children develop a repertoire of executive, control functioning. That term sounds academic but simply means children "using" self-regulatory functions that they have come to understand will help them solve a problem in math, address a relationship issue out on the playground, find an answer to a question. Executive controls function in the mind, when called up and are pulled into the short-term memory, the "workroom" of a child's mind where learning occurs. These executive control functions are like a CEO running a company; they determine the best old concept or skill to deploy in each specific situation they encounter. They can be taught. That is important for teachers to know.

How successfully a person lives into right relationships, finds their true self, hangs out in friendship with the Creator, remains thankful and full of the "wow" response to everything, is dependent upon an underlying base or foundation of "something," too. And, in the same way that other skills and knowledge need a support on which more detailed and sophisticated skills and knowledge can be built, so too "being" a mature adult who lives into right relationships is dependent upon, and builds upon, a certain foundation. This is not to undermine the Creator's role. It is inclusive of it. A foundation produces the predispositions, the mindset to be able to pay attention to the data of one's life that does include a Creator. A foundation is learned. There was much to learn about the upside-down way of being in the world. Learning to be in the world in particular ways is in part sequential, and its skills and knowledge are best learned in iterative ways, cumulative and assimilated over time.

The foundation of being in right relationships is laid down in these sensitive years, when young people are increasingly susceptible to environmental influences. 11 to 13 years of age is probably the second most sensitive time-period in human life, next to the embryonic time in the womb. The brain and nervous system are undergoing massive physiological reorganization. Neurons are rapidly connecting to other neurons; experiences and mindfulness are most influential in these sensitive time periods.

More important than watching *Veggie Tales* is to "train" a child in the direction of his or her predispositions, personality and interests, their bent and innate sense of justice and being fully alive, their "older" concepts and skills. Most critical now is for children to hear "yes" more than no, to talk about real issues that they are now facing and imagining, including sex, death, worries, and fears. The true self needs this freedom for significance and security to be experienced in their relationships. From a good foundation comes the possibility of understanding what is true and not true later regarding one's spiritual journey. Intellectual conversion should begin here, and from a person's foundation of hanging out with the Creator, with a bit of awe and wonder, comes a foundation for the future.

A Right Foundation of Relationships

Like the kingdom of God that Jesus taught us, it just seems upside down to make right relationships not right religion the big idea of teaching young children. If you want better scripture memory techniques, more reverence and right "Christian" ideas to populate the file folders of your children's minds, the schemata that align with what correct theology, then it is now time to put this book away. What you will read in this chapter is uncommon to what has been up to now "common practice" and taken for granted understandings of teaching young people. I predict that the ideas in this chapter are going to be disruptive. You may have to suspend your disbelief and read to the end. Look ahead to the curriculum

Early and Middle Childhood

found in Section III in this book. Consider the ideas in the light of the big idea of this book, the kingdom of God being all about right relationships. Consider the ontological argument I have made in Part I of this book and evaluate this and each subsequent chapter with the kingdom of God being an interpretive key, as well as the beginning and end of our educational practices with young people.

Foundation's Big Ideas

The right foundation for young people's relationship with the Creator, the intended outcome should include a Narnia Chronicles[4] foundation—one that guides young people into a way of being characterized by mystery, awe, and magic. For the young person, life should be experienced as a mystery, and though they will not be able to say it, they experience that ". . . there is something going on here but what it is not exactly clear." Learning activities should not simply be some sort of trivial pursuit type of activities, doing crafts or subjecting young people to a parade of words, largely meaningless abstractions, like "God loves you." Or far worse, leaving young people with the hidden curriculum effect, the sub text of some message that the Creator is some huge "man" who is running some sort of cosmic worthiness contest. The end is not about ought to, should or have to, but a program based on wonder and curiosity, practice and thoughtfulness, inquiry, and training.

The right foundation for young people's relationship with themselves should also include "getting good" at as many activities and skills as time and resources will permit. Competency development should characterize their identity. Competency precedes confidence. Boy Scout and Girl Scout programs are exactly what young people need. Choose programs that award badges or acknowledge in concrete ways the achievements of young people. Like *AWANA*, make sure, however, that the program does not include achievement that is explicitly a result of winning over and against another child. The right foundation is the development of pro-social skills, sport skills, inquiry-based skills through which they can ask questions and be guided to answer those questions. They should desire to see problems and want to solve them, handle issues that are of concern to them and be guided to address those issues.

---

4. Maybe the Narnia Chronicles might just be best way, even for a sceptical adult, to understand the most essential of concepts of being a follower of Jesus

The right foundation for young people's relationship with others should also include a virtues-based curriculum. The desired practices in this curricular focus are opportunities to practice respect, kindness, honesty, and other virtues, and be guided to understand why and how the virtues are mission critical to being. Programs like the Virtues Project or the Circle of Courage are exactly what young people need in the first fourteen years of their life. The Virtues Project is designed to systematically develop daily practices of virtues, one at a time. The program includes five strategies—speak the language of virtues, use teachable moments to teach, set clear boundaries, honor the spirit, and offer companying support.

The Circle of Courage program is designed to develop four developmental needs of children and youth—independence, belonging, mastery, and generosity—usually presented in the form of a native medicine wheel and implemented in real practices of each developmental need. For example, in large meetings of children in an "assembly," children are permitted to present verbal "bouquets" to one another for accomplishments and acts of kindness. The disinhibitory effect on children can be very real; children who may have been inhibited to give and receive kindness now can move outside their inhibitions because they have observed kindness in action and have experienced the effects of kindness on themselves and others.

Finally, the right foundation for the development of a young people's relationship with the created (society) and natural order is service. The desired practices are first to "make my immediate neighborhood" a better place, and then, second, "make the world" a better place. There is a reason for this order, and you will have to read on to see why.

A Normal Christian Birth

David Pawson in his book, A Normal Christian Birth (1997) suggests that often, spiritual disease can be traced back to an inadequate initiation into Christianity.[5] They have begun wrong. They have not been coached, initially and correctly, into the foundations of right relationships. The default teaching approach then is to remedy the poor birth with setting

---

5. Pawson, *Normal Christian Birth*; Pawson (1930 to present) is a British writer and pastor who proposed in his book, "A Normal Christian Birth," that what is most wrong with Christians today is that they have had a poor spiritual birth; they have started wrong and needed a normal Christian birth that included rites of passages, community and more than just praying the sinners prayer.

young people up not to be participants but spectators, to observe that "parade of shadows," to be subjected to listening to the rules that are offered to them as correctives. The result is confusion and anxiety. In far too many cases the results are that young people ". . . are motivated to meet [their] needs for significance and security in ways [they] unconsciously believe will work."[6] The result might help explain the bewildering emphasis on "knowing the right stuff" type of Christianity.

Even when we say we believe one thing about religious matters, we often do (behave, act, decide) something else. We believe that gossip is wrong, but we destroy people's reputations with our tongues. Not a problem in destroying someone's reputation, but we get twisted out of spiritual shape regarding sex. We have college students and professors sign behavioral covenants largely about sexual matters. I recently read about a female professor at a Christian college being dismissed for living with a man. I have never read about anyone getting dismissed for gluttony, gossip, destroying a reputation, or not forgiving someone. How odd!

The Beginning of Self-Worth

Many Christian adults struggle with feelings of poor self-worth. For many of us, a simple yet important foundation of love and physical touch was never laid down in our lives. Many of us will struggle all our lives with poor self-esteem. The irony seems to be only will be through painful experiences, perhaps a parental rejection or an illness, that we will eventually learn to see our own worth. But painful experiences can work their magic only later in life, after the early twenties and after a suitable foundation has been laid. Painful experiences like sexual abuse, rejection, racist attacks, or bullying lay down *ruts and grooves* (C.S. Lewis) [7] in the landscape of the child's subconscious, on which behaviors later in life will travel.

My father was the thirteenth of nineteen children born into a French Canadian, Roman Catholic family. Maybe they did not know what was causing it? My father never experienced any love. His own child-rearing philosophy grew out of such discipline experiences as being locked in a cold, dark cellar for hours, and from an attitude that parents do not respect their children, but children, at all costs, need to respect their parents. My father's love for his own children was, in turn, filled with harshness,

6. Crabb, *Effective Biblical Counselling.*
7. Lewis, *Miracles.*

duty, and responsibility; it was empty of any warmth and richness. There will always be one part of the developmental foundation missing in my life. My view of God has been influenced by my father. Today, I behave toward the Creator much as I did years ago towards my father. Neither my father nor I had a very good foundation. Yet, the story is not all bad. I have never had much of a problem with deciding right from wrong. My conscience has been sensitive from five or six years of age. The foundations of responding to what is right developed early through rigorous, consistent training. We were told as children that there was a right way to behave and a wrong way. We were told what the consequences are of wrong behavior. We were dealt with swiftly and often severely when we chose the wrong. The net result is a "good news, bad news" story. I do not like regrets and for that reason alone I practice choosing what I think is right. I try to keep a short list of sins, as one of my friends used to teach me. On the other hand, to love the Creator seems like a nice idea but for me remains an implausibility. The best I seem able to do is to give in and look for evidence that the Creator loves me. Maybe that is good enough, for now.

The Experience of God

I still wish sometimes that it had been different. At times I long for a different foundation, one that has not needed to be rebuilt as often as mine has had to. In a paper titled Children and Religious Experience[8] Maria Harris gives examples of the religious experience adults remember having as children. In these experiences is the very heart of what I believe is a successful foundation.

As a small child one of my favorite festivals was Trinity Sunday. It seemed to me quiet and beautiful, and happening around midsummer became associated in my mind with green trees and flowers in bloom. It was "mysterious" and right, something far bigger than the words used in church about it which sounded to a small child nonsense. But Trinity was not nonsense, it was holy, holy, holy as we sang in the hymn, and even a very young child could join in a sort of "oneness" with all things bright and beautiful and worship this Something so great and lovely that it didn't matter at all that it was not understood. It just *was*. Neither my mother nor my father attempted to explain or describe God to me. He was indescribable as far as I was concerned, a Creator. But I am sure my

---

8. Harris, "Original Vision," p 56–79.

parents increased my sense of God's omnipotence and mystery by their own awe and reserve in discussing the subject.

My first real apprehension of religion that I can recall came from the housemaid, Alice, who was an enthusiastic follower of the Salvation Army. She would teach us choruses which we sang all together, "Pull for the Shore, Sailor," and it was with her one evening that I first got an idea of the immense and lonely blackness of the night, and the distance of the stars, hence a sense of the power and strangeness of God, for I do not think I ever questioned his existence.

As a child, I was told that grandfather spent an hour every morning and evening listening to God. So, when I came suddenly upon my grandfather one day seated motionless in his armchair with closed eyes, I knew he was not a sleep. He was talking with God. I stopped short where I was and stood very still. Perhaps if I listened intently enough, I might hear God's voice speaking to my grandfather. But the room remained quiet, not even the faintest whisper reached my ears. After a long time, my grandfather opened his eyes, saw me, and smiled at me gently. These moments of intense listening for God's voice in the room with my grandfather are among the most vivid memories of my early childhood.

Foundation Building: What Not to Do

What should make up a relationship producing foundation? What should that underlying basis of education be for children? Let me begin by identifying what should not be included in a foundation for children and explain why the following "taken for granted assumptions " should not be included in teaching children 4 to 13 years of age, if we want them to develop a foundation for a lifetime of experiencing right relationships, beginning with these important developmental years.

Principles

In the foundation in these sensitive years, 4 to 13, there should very little, if any, decontextualized emphasis on direct teaching through transmission of ethical and moral principles, the guiding ideas of being in the world in particular ways. Principles are fundamental facts, guiding ideas, e.g., those who serve will be great. But this and other religious principles are for adults, principles designed to be understood by adults, younger and older. The audience that the scriptures, Jewish and Christian, intend to speak to is an adult one. Scripture's principles are designed to guide adult actions. Principles need a foundation to be understood and applied. Good principles or guiding ideas should eventually be taught, perhaps. But for now, the question for teachers is how to design learning experiences so that principles like honesty, kindness, and the joys inherent in serving others are authentic and are experienced in their actions and not being deposited in some file folder of their minds titled "ought to(s)."

I think of my new granddaughter. While she is a child, there is really very little value educationally in simply transmitting, through words delivered to her, principles that represent what she might one day come to understand. Why? Because she might be able to define them, answer a multiple-choice question and tell you what they mean to her. Not only will she not be able to sustain actions of honesty, for example, by knowing about honesty, she simply will not understand the purpose of honesty. Why bother? She will not be able to transfer them to actions, very well or very often. To know principles, in the sense of being able to identify or recognize these principles, will not serve a young person very well in those sensitive years.

To know principles, like someone might be able to define or memorize the principle, will not bring about changes in a child's attitudes and behavior. But two things will. They are children's actual decisions and a systematic regime of training in making decisions. Boy and Girl Scouts are far more important than catechism class on Sundays. When teaching children, take principles out of the words and put it into rigorous practice. Rather than tell your children about servanthood, condition your children to be servants. Instead of preaching concepts about kindness to children, practice with them being kind to your next-door neighbor; instead of teaching them how to think about the Bible stories, read them together with all the suspense, mystery, and drama that most of the stories can serve up.

To understand why training, not rote memorization, is important when children learn principles, consider this. I am an adult. I may know that I should not eat chocolate bars, or that I should exercise every other day. I may understand and agree with the literature that cogently identifies the reasons for avoiding junk food and for taking care of my fitness. But I am exactly like you. I do not always, in fact rarely do I consistently, choose what is right for me simply because I can remember the facts about what is right. Not only will I rarely choose what is right based on knowledge alone, but I also often feel guilty when I watch someone running or eating properly. Why? Because I am acquainted at a low level of understanding with all the benefits. My knowledge becomes a heavy burden, a legalistic policeman. To relieve the guilt, I will simply try not to think about it. My "knowledge" becomes a stumbling block, not a motivator to behaving properly. If we believe that we are laying a foundation by some soppy, once a week, in Sunday School "deposition" of Christian principles into our children, then I believe that we are shortsighted and wrong-headed. To have a foundation means to have been trained, like an athlete has been trained, to perform appropriately. But more of that later.

Banking Teaching

Another practice to avoid when laying a foundation is "banking" teaching. The "banking" concept of teaching that all parents use to teach, and too many pastors use to preach, is based on one huge myth. That is, "depositing" enough good knowledge into them, (like putting lots of money in a bank) using a big parade of words, is meaningful and effectively leads to a deeper and more right relationships and intimacy with the Creator, each other, self, and the created and natural order. Teaching and preaching based on banking ideas into children's heads works in one way only to bore the life out of them. Some parents seem to believe that if they have kids in enough Sunday school classes, osmosis will occur. Hear enough Scripture and like mud thrown against a wall, some of it is bound to stick. If they accumulate enough Christian information, some magical transformation of their declarative or semantic knowledge to procedural knowledge will occur. A rich friendship life hanging out with God the Creator comes not by learning about prayer but, through hanging out with, being friends with the Creator.

In the beginning, "banking" teaching should be minimized. Again, a solid developmental and spiritual foundation is best laid down when young people are guided to progressively and mutually accommodate themselves to the settings with people in the contexts young people find themselves.[9] Principles are best assimilated and accommodated, not as

---

9. Bronfenbrenner, "Bronfenbrenner's Ecological Systems Theory of Development." Like Piaget, Bronfenbrenner took an "in-nature" phenomenon and translated it into a model for describing human development.

deposits but as sources of equilibration.[10] I would suggest instead of a "banking" way of teaching, we use an "athletic" way of teaching. We are like all the world's religions in that we have our limited selection of key markers, found in the catechisms, the Lord's Prayer, the Creeds, the commandments, the beatitudes, and whatever other forms that right relationship principles have been given to us in the form of stories or Bible. Have a once a month focus for the young person, for example being a peacemaker at school, standing up for the other child who is being bullied. Far more influential in developing the right foundation than preaching the concept at them of being a peacemaker.

Playing on a sport team is far more influential in children's development of a good foundation of "wanting what's best for others" than preaching to them using the words in the Bible. Young people fall under the disinhibitory effect in gradual and graduated ways when coached by a woman or man of character and integrity. Look for a team and coach who models both character and integrity, one who sets up a team manifesto that makes right relationships with teammates, other young people on the other team more important than winning or losing. Add "fun" to the coach's repertoire of coaching attributes and you have an important influencer in your children's life.

Knowing Christian Concepts

A foundation is also not laid down in emphasizing Judeo-Christian, ethical and moral concepts particularly when the purpose is for the child to apply to their lives and obey these notions and concepts. An ethical concept may be giving sustenance to mature people who get it, and practice right relationships. But knowing a concept, like honesty, will not automatically make a child be honest or practice honesty. Similarly, knowing that the Scriptures have a lot to say about sex will not keep a fourteen-year-old from sexual shenanigans, or from losing faith in the truthfulness of biblical notions regarding sexuality.

For example, one intriguing notion we read in Philippians 1:6 is that the good work that God begins in certain people will be faithfully completed. This abstraction remains just that, a concept until it is lived into, reflected on after experiences. You and I, I bet, have had a wealth of experiences, both negative and positive, into which I can assimilate this

---

10. Piaget, *Construction of Reality in the Child*.

concept and some sort of change happens in my own mind and behavior. As the years go on, I find it easier to accommodate my experiences to this concept. Now, I can view my negative experiences as not so negative after all. They had a reason for being, that only reason and time would one day make clear. I have slowly come to know the concept to be true. I have heard lots of people preach to me about it, but it took natural life experiences, both good and bad, for me to understand and trust in a Creator's faithfulness in helping me be kind or quit a lot of self-defeating habits.

The young child can never give the same intellectual and trustful allegiance to the ethical and moral concepts and notions in the Bible that encourage you and me. It is far better for a parent to be relaxed, to let the child be honest with feelings, with their doubts, their pain, and their frustrations than it is to "preach" a concept at them. For example, a death of a friend might include a time of anger or doubt towards God. A rejection by friends must be viewed as simply painful and inexplicable. Yes, forgiveness must be encouraged, but anger needs to be expressed. Sexual pressures need to be discussed honestly. If these occurrences are treated in a "natural" and relaxed way, friendship with the Creator will not devolve into avoidance tactics of someone who, for them, is impotent, far off, or cruel. Preaching to young people about sin, their "sin" in particular, may be just what will keep them far away from wanting to hang out with this Creator.

The insight eventually comes to all of us and to children in ways that they cannot speak about or explain. They do not need to. There is a deep way that something is wrong with everything, as Larry Crabb (1984) put it there is something wrong with everything, and some sort of 'wrongness' has seeped into all creation.[11] People die. We get rejected and bullied.

We experience loneliness. As someone once wrote, we learn early to just try to survive between happiness surges. As adults, we know that pain will show up. We can and do intellectually embrace pain as some strange sort of refiner in our lives. C.S. Lewis put it in an odd way, that we have no right to happiness anyway. It appears that our right to happiness, being one unique expression of a humanity that has gone sideways from the very beginning, was forfeited. Pain means that we can learn more of

---

11. Crabb, *Encouragement: The Key to Success*. Important notions that Crabb seemed to drift away from in his later writings, preferring instead of strong psychological premises to draw from sociology, the church, and notions like the safest place on being community that cares for each other.

God, but only eventually, and only based on how well the foundation has been laid.

To force a young child into aligning their questions, issues, and problems with biblical notions as they are interpreted by mature adults will give a child a tangled, confusing mess to be sorted through later. It is preferable for you and me to let struggles and doubts be experienced naturally in day to day living. Let the mental and spiritual questions and perhaps confusion occur naturally. Then pour meaning into their doubts and struggles by discussing (not telling) over weeks and months how those experiences that resulted in pain and doubt confirm or disconfirm what they believed about the Creator and how what they believe about how the Creator confirms or disconfirms their experience. Thomas Groome, in his first book *Christian Religious Education: Sharing Our Story and Vision,* calls this process "shared reflection on action"[12]

A smart relationship-oriented parent wants a child to eventually align behaviors with the principles of the Creator's design. But the foundation of alignment and obedience will result in part when a parent naturally informs their children of how their experiences and ideas look similar to what Jesus taught us. This teaching approach takes time, patience, and reasonable expectations. Only then will the outcome be what every smart parent wants. Their child will take up the silence and the good, the mystery and the bad as well as good experiences of daily life, as if a Creator (who they cannot see) wants to be friends with them. Jesus slowly becomes someone who they grow to like. Slow and steady guidance of a young person's behaviors and ideas with Jesus's ideas, delivers young people, not into a whole bunch of dos and don'ts, but into an apprehension of being in the arms of a Creator who likes them. Being liked and friendship-based relationships are the best scaffolds for a child to be obedient to the virtues of truth, kindness, and love.

---

12. Groome, *Christian Religious Education*; Groome (1945 to present) currently is a faculty member at Boston College. He is an author, a former priest, and a strong supporter for women included in the Catholic priesthood. His book, "Christian Religious Education," is now considered to be a classic and an important foundational text for use for teaching young people. I studied with Thomas Groome at Boston College and to this day remain strongly influenced by his interpretations of praxis, how people learn, the role and place of scripture, and his clear and evocative style and content of teaching.

Catechisms

The foundations are not laid down by a catechism-based program of definitions, theological ideas codified into words and formal doctrines. Doctrine is that "religious" body of knowledge that gives direction and stability to life. It is like the rudder that keeps the ship heading in the right direction. All religious systems, including Jewish, Muslim and Christian, are full of doctrine. We have doctrines of practically anything you can name. They indicate the direction our lives should be headed. But they should be introduced in adolescence, not in childhood. The reason is because of the abstract nature of these rudders we call doctrine. To understand something abstract, children first need to understand something concrete that they have experienced. Kindness is best understood and practiced on a foundation of giving and receiving kindness.

Children often understand what something is by understanding what that "something" is not. Hope is not giving up. Trust in the Creator is not just an idea in your head; it is like falling backwards knowing that you will be caught. Love is wanting what is best for someone (including you) and not just some sort of feeling good emotion. If young people have heard the expression "no marine left behind," use that expression to make visible the Creator's choice for each of them, that no "child" will ever be left behind by their friend, the Creator of everything.

A counter-intuitive, visible expression of love and friendship is a picture of the "cross," a symbolic reminder for young people that something is indeed going on here on earth but it is okay to not be sure of what it is. To present to children a cross attached to a theological explanation is a waste of time. To present it as something to be apprehended, not comprehended, is right and good. It symbolizes love. That is enough for now, for the young person. Children need the cross, to see it often, wonder about it, worry about it, ask about it. The cross should only begin to interpret them as much as they interpret it. No need for formal answers, slick theology, or complicated interpretations. It just is, and that is enough up to the age of thirteen.

Integration

The foundation is also not laid down by parents or teachers attempting to "integrate" a Scriptural idea into a "natural" idea. Most attempts at integration are either just proof-texting or devotionalizing. In proof-texting, a parent or teacher begins with Scriptures then uses them to "prove" an occurrence or an idea. For example, parents may be generous with charitable giving and feel they are being blessed by a God for doing it. But to take a scripture like "give and it shall be given unto you" and use that scripture as some proof given to their children for the reason for their material blessings, is giving the child an incorrect perspective on the Bible and on its overall meaning and intent.

To talk to a child about a sunset and then add a perfunctory reference to a Bible verse like "the heavens declare the handiwork of God" is fine. Far more influential would be for you to say instead, "incredible." To expect that you are accomplishing a foundational integration of scriptural truth with "natural" truth by devotionalizing is an error. This is an example of devotionalizing, maybe important for your reformed folks reading this book, but to do so is not foundational.

Guide a young person and look out at a million light years of space, what some have called "God's first Bible" and a billion stars on the clearest, darkest night of the year and say, "Oh wow God". That heartfelt, honest response will do more to lay a proper foundation than will memorizing all the verses in the Bible that declare how incredible a Creator God is or devotionalizing everyday life and its events.

Church-Going and Bible Memorization

The foundation is not laid down by a reliance on memorizing scripture or by showing up at church service. Think about the value of the following approach to guiding young people into Jesus's teachings. In his approach to discipling new Christians, Robert Jacks states that he tries to keep new Christians away from formal church. In his book, *Your Home a Lighthouse: Hosting an Evangelistic Bible Study*, Robert Jacks advocates laying down a foundation first of friendship, regular devotional times that are authentic and meaningful, and open, judgement-free conversation before encouraging church participation.[13] For young children to formally and rigorously memorize Scripture has potential to reduce the Creator-human being story to just some more "words on paper" that adults like to read. The Bible becomes one more book in everyone's list of super books. A well-meaning teacher once said to me that she encourages new

---

13. Jacks and Jacks, *Your Home a Lighthouse*; Robert Jacks (1943–2014) was an Australian author of *Rules to Live by* and *Just Say the Word!*

Christians to memorize scripture because it will all come back to them later. I think that memorizing scripture for the new Christian might smell like incense in a church. I think it might taste like sawdust, sound like Russian, and seem heavy as mud. Later, it might be important that they memorize Scripture. But a foundation is best laid in hearing Scriptures as narratives, stories that surprisingly ring true because they are our stories, our narrative lines. When the Scripture is interpreted into meaningful and truthful story-like summaries for the child, then the child can assimilate the truths therein. Children's Bibles, illustrated and summarized, are excellent resources. When the Bible is retold in stories, and retold with excitement, drama, and flair, then the stories keep their innate attraction.

The best teachers begin a Bible-based "learning experience" with an advanced organizer, the children's experience first. Teaching even the most difficult theological concepts can begin with the child's experience. Teach the story of what some traditions call the eucharist or communion through their story of experiencing eating together with people they love best.

The richness of the Scriptures is its story telling, usually with nudges to put the Creator somehow first and foremost in daily life activities. Bring in a pail and using physical objects to represent daily events (apple for food, toys for play, small book for school, etc.) fill up the pail as children tell you what a day in their life looks like. Finally, add a picture or small project representing Jesus. If prepared to do so, the Creator will not fit into the pail. Repack the pail by putting the Creator in first and, lo and behold, everything now fits in the pail. Kids will remember this for a long, long time.

Rather than just insist that Scripture be memorized, either read the Scriptures to children, or tell it in a story. Encourage them to fall in love first with the Scriptures as a big story made up of lots little stories, chapters, and very cool stories of good and bad people. But force-feeding is bad idea. They must learn to love the stories because they are cool stories, right from the beginning of their experience with the Bible.

Now let us move on from what not to do to with a few suggestions for what to do. Let us examine more closely now the "what to dos" and how teachers can design learning experiences for children 4 to 13 years of age that result in the best foundation for the development of future right relationships.

> Train up a child in the way he should go (Proverbs 22:6, KJV)

> The only crown I ask, dear Lord, to wear . . . is this, that I may teach a little child[14]
>
> These commandments that I give you today are to be upon your hearts. Impress them on your children. Talk about them when you sit at home and when you walk along the road, when you lie down and when you get up. Tie them as symbols on your hands and bind them on your foreheads. Write them on the doorframes of your houses and on your gates." (Deut 6:6–9, NIV).

From the Jewish Scriptures and the book of Deuteronomy, we get this blueprint for teaching children the foundation of being in the world in that way called the kingdom of God. Contained in this Scripture are the five practices needed for parents to properly lay a foundation.

1. Build a child's secure inner emotional life.
2. Train children in their day- to-day endeavors, daily occurrences, and relationships.
3. Model a Christianity of relationships.
4. Speak about Christianity as if it were life, not as if it were a "way of life."
5. Work with the natural developmental and psychological needs of a child.

Build a Child's Secure Inner Emotional Life

My daughter and I used to battle over her messy (my opinion) room. When she was five, I began to deploy the heavy hand approach to get her to clean her room. She would come downstairs for a meal and I would ask her if her room was clean. She would honestly reply, "No, it isn't", to which I would reply (angrily), "Get up and clean it now." This scene repeated itself three or four times. By about the fourth time, I expressed more anger, and lots of frustration, when she truthfully told me that her room was not clean.

With tears in her eyes, she dutifully went up to clean her room. Now, my daughter is intelligent. What is associated with telling the truth (a much more important issue than a messy room) is my anger and her subsequent emotional distress. The fifth time (or thereabouts) that I

14. Craig, "My Opportunity."

asked her if her room was clean and she said, "Yes, it is." It was not. The new battle began over what a "clean, neat room" meant. I was beginning that spiral down the black hole of lousy communication patterns between father and daughter. But worse, I had instigated the logical, natural tendency of my daughter to lie to protect herself. I was not building in her a positive, healthy emotional life; instead, I was an architect and a lead builder of a liar. This tendency towards dishonesty may become a hiding place for my daughter, a protective layer keeping her from giving and receiving integrity and honesty.

I see parents do this all the time. We associate negative experiences (our messages, anger, frustration, shock) with our children's lived experiences. Mothers assure daughters that "they can tell them anything." When a daughter tells her mother about her struggle with sexual fantasies, a mother expresses shock. End of story.

I tell my daughter to tell me all of what happens at school. She does. I react angrily at a teacher's impatience. No more communication. At least not honest communication.

Telling the truth, open communication, expression of deep needs, honest statements of struggles are all originally neutral. That is, until they are associated with a stimulus that is not neutral, then they produce a physiological, real response. It is with the association of a neutral stimulus (telling the truth) with a decidedly non-neutral stimulus (my anger) that the problem occurs. My anger naturally produces a negative emotional response in my daughter, e.g., anxiety and anticipation of receiving a negative response. When anger is there continuously and occurs just before or at the same time with telling the truth (originally neutral), telling the truth produces a negative emotional response—anxiety and high-handed participation of receiving a negative response. There no longer needs to be the negative, anger-filled response of the parent. The conditioning effect is in place, and there is almost certainly a generalized effect. In a similar situation, with a teacher for example, all self-respecting children will lie when in these conditions. The conditioning of children's emotional life is firmly set in the direction of fear, self-protection, wariness, anxiety, and dishonesty. In other words, parents and teachers for sure have built part of our children's emotional life, but the result is far from what it should be, or what it could be.

A child's inner emotional predispositions are the screens through which ideas will later be sifted. People with pain-filled experiences tend to learn to understand the suffering side of being in the world. People with happy experiences, the blessing side of being in the world. Being a child should be an enjoyable experience. Going to children's church, playing with friends, and hearing stories about the truly great people of faith should be fun. Early experiences with religion should build positive memories, enjoyable memories, in young people. If going to church (originally neutral) is paired repeatedly with a non-neutral stimulus (exciting activities), participating with the church can produce excitement.

We all want to report what we enjoy doing. The foundation should be laid with enjoyable, potentially repeatable, activities. The association of spiritual things with enjoyable things creates the emotional predisposition that religion, Christianity for example, is an attractive and worthwhile "idea." This foundation of "good memories" will be an important foundation in a person's eventual maturing. Negative experiences, no doubt, will eventually come but the person will handle them more meaningfully and successfully with a positive emotional screen firmly in place.

How is this foundation accomplished? The following strategies are children's gateways into wonder, into nurturing their imaginations, into building good memories and desirable relationships with the Creator, self, others, and the created and natural order. The foundation is not built on what is known but on development of what John O'Donohue calls a divine, wild imagination (p 33), a birthing of ways of being in the world that are tinged with freedom, memories of experiences and good thoughts, feeling sheltered and protected by right relationships, belonging to something big and being enveloped with the mystery of everything.[15]

Exploration

Allow the child to function naturally and freely. Naturally, they are self-serving and will do and say stupid things. But they are also inquisitive and need to learn by exploring, probing, asking, and creating. A curriculum for young people that will lead to right relationships should include lots of minds-on-on, fun-oriented, exploratory activities. They are children; their job description includes being crazy, scattered and not always doing what you ask of them. They are trying to learn the boundaries. Keep that in mind before you give them time outs or worse. Use word pictures instead of preachy "you better not." A word picture is an image created in the mind of a child. "No marine left behind" is a far more effective

---

15. O'Donohue, *Anam Cara: A Book of Celtic Wisdom*, 33.

scaffold for young boys and girls to learn to "love your neighbor" than is a sermon on the golden rule.

Love

Pour unconditional love into their lives. This means communicating to children that they are still lovable even when they are not. Hugs, touch, and kind words build security. Regularly scheduled "love-ins" should be part of every curriculum anywhere. Here is your teacher's "measuring stick" for knowing if your children experience being loved unconditionally. Is your children's "lived experience" with you made up of "if/then" conditions? Is the hidden curriculum laced with conditional love—if you clean your room then you are acceptable and approvable? If you quit stealing, then your father and mother will love you. Seeing you hurt and experiencing your love, deep, emotionally laden love when "bad" will do more to teach them not to steal or to follow your instructions (even if short-sighted and wrong-headed like always keeping a clean room).

Greenhouse

Protect or "green-house" them from what is not yet tolerable, developmentally. Open the wings of a butterfly before it is ready, and you will harm the butterfly. Expose young people too soon to the soft underbelly of life and you will harm the child. Death depicted in newscasts, violence of any sort, including verbal violence, and even the taunting and teasing from peers, should be censored. The time will come soon enough for the "real world" to be experienced. Schools are most problematic because of the dangers that reside there—dangers of rejection and pain that come when children are not protected from abuse and harm.

Avoid Arguments from the Real World

Please consider rejecting, now and for all time, the arguments from the real world, particularly when it comes to teaching children. Most real-world arguments are nonsense arguments infested with adult logic. Kindergarten is preparation for college; competition experienced as winning or losing against another person is good for young people, as is rejection by friends; children need to experience the "real world." I have experienced the short-sightedness of these kind of "arguments from the real world." Here is your measuring stick. Does your argument for an activity and program of learning align with the child's deepest needs now, where they are in their developmental and psychological timetable? Their deep needs are for security and significance. Does it develop competencies? Or does it set young people up into a pattern of learning to fail, be layered up and perform to keep safe? Competition is a good thing, just to be clear. Beat a previous best, perform against a standard, modify the learning conditions like distance, time, and materials, and within these conditions encourage competition. But forget the "I beat you" concept of competition.

Communication

Communicate with them, not to them. This is accomplished by asking them, "How does what you are experiencing or feeling confirm or disconfirm what I have taught you or what Jesus seems to be teaching you?" Thomas Groome says that this type of sharing can begin even before children are school age[16] It provides security that questioning is okay, and sharing is a good way of life. The best communicators with children pay attention to tone or "how" they communicate with children; children hear far more than the words you use, they hear your emotion, your feelings for or against them.

Motivation

Keep all tasks within the range of fifty percent chance of success. Motivation remains optimum as a result. Failure teaches children how to fail, success how to succeed. Too many lines in the Christmas play, or too much confusing theology in a Sunday school class will quickly undermine a secure emotional foundation.

The results will be evident in your child's relationships. They will be free from the fear of failure and will be careful risk takers. They will have been conditioned classically to associate the best emotions with a Creator, and a loving Creator at that. As soon as positive emotions are

---

16. Groome, *Christian Religious Education*; His work has remained seminal despite criticisms of his notion of shared praxis, which aligns well with how children and adults learn but not so well with fundamentalist type thinking about the Bible and where knowledge resides.

experienced, they will associate them with the Creator; the emotions will be "God coming to them in disguise." They will maintain their natural empathy for others, important inner response that was always there, hidden but evident in them when they were infants.

And they will have an inner emotional foundation laid of security and significance built through their practices of relating positively to the natural and created order around them, in their families, schools and neighborhoods.

Training in Life's Day to Day Things

There is one very good and true reason why we all need to be trained. We are self-serving and prone to protect ourselves first and foremost. We have well developed ruts and grooves laid down in our minds[17] on which our behaviors travel when threatened, anxious, angry, or frustrated. As a result, we are prone to self-protective conscious actions, the source of which is the sub-conscious. These attributes produce, in turn, disaster in our lives. To be trained early on to respond in correct ways will help screen us from wrong decisions that will hurt us in this world. I may not feel like being a non-gossiping employee, nor think that I should be one. Habits trump good intentions, however. Only training in speaking positively about others, even others in authority, has promise in it that I will speak positively and bring about good, ultimately.

We need to train children in day-to-day habits like keeping promises to parents, kind actions to friends, taking responsibility for a room, a pet, or a job. Through learning how to respond rightly in the world and its ways, comes the ability to respond rightly in relationships. It is useful, though perhaps theologically questionable, to view the spiritual and day-to-day worlds as distinct, not separate. In fact, some argue that there is no distinction between the spiritual and the day to day life in this world. They are one and the same so development in one area is automatically development in the other. The secular and sacred may be distinct in the abstract, but they are not separate with the time-space world we live in. The book of Proverbs is full of advice on exactly for what to train, providing practical tips for day to day living. The Bible has much to say on how we should

---

17. Lewis, *Miracles*. p272. The context of Lewis's metaphor-ruts and grooves-is his description of belief feelings that he claims, do not follow reason except by ruts and grooves that already exist in the mind. Feelings are not very good proofs that miracles exist, or anything else unseen for that matter.

"behave" in the day to day world. Jesus clearly saw a separation when he told his followers that to feed the hungry and clothe the naked was to do likewise to him. (Matthew 25:35–40). He also said that if his kingdom is not of this world, he would have told us (John 18:36; John 14:2).

Training is not mysterious, but it does take hard work. Rewards, punishments, and the threat of the removal of rewards help condition a person into correct behavior. Also, keeping those windows into the soul, the eyes, and ears, clear of harmful messages that come particularly from images that arouse, helps keep sinful drives at low arousal states. In addition, recognizing that aroused states come when some drive has been left unchecked helps in the conditioning process. If boredom or tiredness result in the aroused state of frustration or anger, parents can respond to the drive, and therefore to the aroused state by giving alternative, positive actions. Training includes goal setting, physical activities, and attention to regular habits.

Goal Setting

Set clear goals for your child. Better yet, teach young people to set goals. Keeping the child within a program of goal setting helps keep the forward momentum going. Goals that are too high, too vague, not meaningful, or which can be easily blocked will give rise to negative emotions. Goals are not the same as desires. My desire might be to have a good night's sleep. My goals are what I do to ensure that happens—exercise earlier in the day, avoid eating late at night, and so on. Children need to know the difference between what they want and what they can do to get what they want. Desires are legitimate, but desires are only realized when goals are set and reached. Goals can be written out weekly and a log or diary can be kept of how the goals are achieved. Shared goal setting creates a sense of ownership and partnership.

Physical Activities: Modified to Fit the Child

Physical activities are mission critical, particularly a program of pursuits that lend themselves to young people's practices to keep goals, record progress and invest something cognitively into the activity they enjoy doing. Individual activities like swimming, tennis, or judo, will help implicitly to socialize them into such habits of deferred gratification and overcoming obstacles to reach goals.

Modify skills to fit the child; do not modify the child to fit the skill, particularly in the early phases of developing a skill. Let the ball bounce when learning to play volleyball. Let children catch the ball, throw it over a net (lowered of course). A six-year old's reaction time is twice that of an adult. A bounce slows the ball down for a child. This is not how volleyball is played," you might be tempted to say. Forget it. If your daughter tries out for the national Olympic volleyball team, and lets the ball bounce, we have a problem. If you are interested at all in your daughter developing a base of skills that underly volleyball, and all sports and physical activities, then modify skills progressively. Take pedals off a bike when a child is learning to ride. Catch with larger than normal balls; throw with smaller than usual ones. Play t-ball; avoid formal fastball and baseball to start with. Not all modifications are good ones. Water wings when learning to swim is a bad modification; arms are the prime movers in swimming. Use your common sense and basic knowledge of the approximation of the final skill.

Habits

Young people thrive on routine, on work and learning habits that create a sense of predictability for them. Skim a reading first before reading for detail is a habit. Asking yourself if you can be successful in the task or learning to come; and if the answer is yes, what do you need to do? We call this meta cognition. It is a good habit for kids to develop. Routines should include meaningful work habits like caring for a garden or a pet, cleaning dishes, or tidying a room. Too much screen time and not enough routine time characterizes the lives of most children today. Later in this book, I will suggest how to incorporate gamification and use screen time to your teaching benefit.

Modeling Authentic Right Relationships

In the Jewish Scriptures, we have lots of advice that implies that modelling works. An axiom we often use affirms the advice and goes something like this: "Values are caught, not taught." This axiom is true. Models are people who get our attention, and who break through into our minds and hearts. Madonna was once a model, as was Mother Theresa. You decide who to showcase and offer up as models? We respond to models. We tend to remember and imitate certain models for certain reasons. They often exhibit unusual, challenging, or exciting behavior. They repeat their unique behaviors regularly. That gets our attention.

We become like the people we model, not overnight but in iterative and gradual ways. There is a universe of truth in that. Harold Morris in his autobiography, *Twice Pardoned*[18] (1987) say that who you become friends with will determine your future. He should know. He spent ten years in jail because he became friends with the "scum of the earth," a term he uses. One very good reason for people to participate in some form of active, propinquity-based community is so that our children will be exposed to good role models. The church, as a community, unfortunately has come to mean the gathering of people into a building, usually on Sunday. The church should have a deeper and more inclusive meaning. We should be together as often as possible, practicing right relationships. It means continuing the conversations about the way of being in the world, what we are learning about the opportunities and challenges to be in the world in particular ways.

In relationships we should be enjoying people of all ages. Our young people should be hearing the stories of the older people. Different types of people with a range of experiences should be invited to speak to children, young and old. One seventeen-year old struggling young boy once told me that if he hears another "preacher in a suit and white shoes" tell him about Jesus Christ, he will get sick. But to hear, as he put it, someone with "scars and knife wounds" tell about Christ, that would make a difference to him. Modelling works because young people do imitate and do so anticipating some of the same consequences the model gets. They should see religion "work" in our lives. Modelling includes storytelling, fellowship, and having people around us to look up to.

Storytelling

Important for young people to listen to stories, watch videos, and hear athletes and other successful people in the world tell their story. I have

---

18. Morris, "Twice Pardoned, Part I"; Morris is the author of "Twice Pardoned," "Beyond the Barriers," "Overcoming Hard times," and many other faith-based books. He began writing in 1984 after being diagnosed with terminal cancer.

forgotten most sermons that I have heard and virtually all the "good advice." But I will never forget David Wilkerson's stories about his work with street kids. I heard those stories on a hot June 21 evening in 1972 in a fieldhouse in Edmonton, Alberta, Canada. I gave up and gave in to Jesus's big idea that night. I did not understand it at all but wanted to. It seemed exciting and big, to be invited into a big story that I could somehow play a part, even write a chapter or two to the story. I am like you. I remember stories. I can enter someone's story better than I can enter someone's "doctrine" or advice. The young child should have a foundation of hearing stories that are not preachy, but which are invitations into the mystery of everything.

Heroes

Young boys and young girls both look up to the young, strong men and women with a story. Cross any gender lines you might have set up here; boys guided to make female heroes, girls to have male heroes. I have played a variety of sports, some at a quite high level. When I tell young boys about having attended a professional football advancement camp, most boys begin to listen. Girls need to look up to women who have served and accomplished much. Girls will admire women; however, more so for who they think these women are, for their character and personality. An equitable right relationship-based education must include experiences talking to and activities with same-gender models. Encourage your child in the direction of those models worthy of emulation, regardless of gender.

Thinking of Christianity as Life: A New Mindset

Children need to have one big idea in place in their thinking before they will ever mature and grow into right relationships. That notion is that a religion is a system of thinking about life and in a sense, the essence of the spiritual side of religion is that truth existed before Jesus shows up on the scene, the place we call earth.

    The particularness of the way of being in the world, the kingdom of God, is actually the very reason for being alive in the first place. It is a way of being in the world, and that way comes about by being in right relationship with the Creator, each other, ourselves, and the created and natural order. You personally may or may not be persuaded that something dreadful yet magical happened two thousand years ago, with a person's death that restored us to that relationship with the Creator first. However, that idea alone is like a shelter, a protection for young children that gives them freedom to take risks, make it possible for them to be in the world in the particular ways. Someone "big" and mysterious loves them.

Thinking of being in the world in this expansive way means to teach with relationships in mind, the means, and the end of our teaching. Our control center is right relationships developed over time, with the Creator, self, others, and the created and natural order. The particular way of being in the world that Jesus taught us is our "Houston" overseeing and monitoring our programs of education, the reason why we bother at all to teach and live in the hints and guesses of life and engage in prayer, thought and action, observation and discipline.[19]

Remind them to view all truth as the Creator's truth and all phenomenon, and all life for that matter, as a rhythm and very sacred. How to do this is not easy at all. Various books have been written around the theme of integrating or synthesizing Scriptural truth with natural truth. The problem often is that the net effect is not always what we think. Instead of coming to an insight into the truth that a relationship with the Creator is life, young people move further to viewing life in a reductionist way.

The best way to truly synthesize or integrate is first through the child's emotional life. It is important to lay down first a screen of positive, joyful experiences. Children can and should come to associate religion with you and their relationship with you. Later, when the young person is trying to synthesize, this screen will serve to filter out myths and errors regarding the world, and to sift through truths regarding the Creator and the Scriptures. Following cultural myths, like money is the key to happiness, will not produce the same joy and peace that the early experiences following after the way of Jesus in fact do. Giving can and does make us feel better than getting. Children need to experience this truth, not just hear about.

---

19. T. S. Eliot (1993). *In the Dry Salvages, April (Vol. VI, No. 4)* His conversion was to a Catholic expression of Christianity and incarnation was a persistent theme in his writing from then on.

Work with Developmental Stages

Most things in life, some argue, are unpredictable like the weather, the economy, illness, and the timing of death. The unpredictability of events can create insecurity. The deep existential insecurity we all feel at times is partially because of the unpredictability of other people and events in our lives. I believe that is why the Creator taught us that faith is so important. Since unpredictability is a constant thing, the only antidote, the best way to land down on peace and psychological security just might be trust in a Creator's care for you. Maybe it is a good idea to use the word Creator in place of God. God has become a largely meaningless word. The cognitive concreteness of young people renders this image of a Creator meaningful. They create; if something they create "exists," there first had to be a "thought," if a thought, then a creator. The principle here is to teach the unfamiliar through the familiar. Their creation patterns are the best scaffold for teaching at least in small part the Creator's pattern. If something exists on earth, the solar system, a universe, there first had to be a thought of a thought, then a thinker.

Nothing Self Exists

Not everything is unpredictable, however. Children's development is predictable to a degree. Most children, most of the time, predictably pass through the same developmental stages. Most children develop sequentially, being able to walk, crawl, talk, respond to touch, and so on. What is unpredictable, however, is the time in which the child begins a certain developmental stage. Some talk earlier, some later. Some think abstractly earlier, some later. There is great solace to parents here. A child who is not using some language at all at eighteen months is not unusual if he eventually speaks. He is simply going to enter that developmental stage later. He is wired to march to the beat of a different drummer.

There is a great deal that is predictable about learning and children. While some development is normally autogenous, or automatic, learning is not. It needs a set of circumstances for it to occur. You and I needed to learn to write and needed a certain set of circumstances to be present to do so. We were not soft wired or hard wired then to do a lot of what we adults do today.

Learning and Its Conditions

What is important to realize is that it is possible to predict that certain types of learning will occur if certain sets of circumstances are present. Children will learn to feel secure if they have an early and consistent experience of touch and love. Children will learn to read if they are exposed to language, and when they "decide" that mystery of the interrelationship among letters, words, and meaning. Children will learn to memorize if they are taught some fundamental skills of associating, chunking information into smaller pieces of information, and rehearsing. Children will learn that learning is fun and important if they are free from the tyranny of failure, and from the expectations of others.

Learning can be predicted to occur if certain conditions are logical and ordered in our thinking and approaches to task. Math-like problems are fun. Once we figure out a pattern and how that pattern can logically be used to solve problems, we are always ready, it seems, to learn how to solve new math problems. Everything is easy once you know how. Even calculus. Even understanding why men cannot see the mustard container in the fridge when it is right there on the top shelf.

Others of us are more conceptual and abstract. We think "philosophically" and in generalities. We love to tackle ideas and enjoy discussions. Our readiness to learn is enhanced when we are in a "comfortable" learning situation, one that attends to our learning predispositions. Observers prefer to learn differently than those who act first, think second learners, talkers who prefer to talk their way into learning.

Readiness is very much affected by "subjective" conditions. Worry about one's personal appearance or worry about acceptance by peers affects readiness.

Expectations and Feedback

The influence of the expectations of others affects readiness. Children are tyrannized in school, not by the challenge of learning, but by the challenge of meeting some external standards which have little or a negative relationship to their developmental and learning stage.

People observing us when learning a new skill, or practicing a complex skill not yet fully acquired, can negatively affect readiness, as can fatigue, low blood sugar and perceptual problems. However, accurate feedback about the details of a performance can positively affect readiness. Feedback is specific information given specifically to a specific task. You might say something like your writing has improved because your predicates and subjects agree in tense. Or your tennis stroke is improving because you are following through cleanly and smoothly. This kind of detailed feedback both encourages and gives information on which the person can build.

That gushing, general encouraging feedback of "good boy" or "well done" is fine at times, but it is often used unwisely. And when it is used unwisely, it impedes readiness and creates a shaky foundation for a boy's or girl's self-esteem. I used to tell my grade four students all the time that they were "good boys" or "good girls" whenever they did any academic or physical skill correctly. What I began to do was to condition them to view themselves as "good" only when they performed successfully. This created a greater "fear of failure" in them because of displeasing me, someone they loved and respected. And, surprisingly, I have noticed in some of my students a tendency to lower performance to bring my feedback more in line with what they are more comfortable in receiving. Praise can be an odd and misused thing.

If she is "good" only when she indeed does "good, a young person with an emerging identity as a competent individual, can become totally incapacitated." Be judicious in feedback, and keep feedback as specific as possible, and you can enhance readiness. The young person needs to know that she is good because of the Creator's declaration of her goodness and because of your unconditional declaration of her goodness. She can fail and still be "good."

Readiness

Readiness to learn is a complex phenomenon. I have only touched the surface of this important idea. In summary, readiness is enhanced under certain circumstances and undermined by others. For example, physical pre-occupations are strong interferers with learning; thinking about that pimple on a left ear will be hard to ignore if you are 12 years old. If a new shirt or operation to remove the pimple will minimize self-preoccupations, make them happen. Your instincts here might be to pull up that old, tired argument from the real world. The real world is a tough place, get used to it. I hope that you do not go there; get the operation to remove the pimple or buy the new shirt.

Purposeful Learning

The child needs to sense in a concrete way that the new learning is important. They deserve a "real" reason for learning. A four-year old friend of my daughter found a garter snake. He loved this snake. He fed it, took it for walks (true), and played with it. But more importantly regarding learning, he wanted to learn what snakes eat and how they live. He was "ready" to learn because he had a purpose for doing so.

What makes new learning important? There are some right conditions. One is a sense of ownership and participation in the planning of the learning. Also, simply letting your child naturally show you what is important to them then using that natural interest to "teach." I learned to read by reading Superman comics and Hardy Boys mystery novels. I learned to do "science" and to love science by taking a pail and a net to a pond and exploring. I learned to play baseball not by playing baseball but by playing tin can cricket.

Prerequisite Skill

The child needs the prerequisite skills in to be ready to learn other skills. Most learning is continuous. It builds on other learning. Most learning is also dependent upon the developmental stage of the child. An eight-year old will likely not do well in extrapolating from one story in literature or in the Scriptures to another, or in synthesizing a lot of related details into a new story. At twelve or thirteen years old he might be able to do so but rarely will an eight-year old be able to. They are not yet developmentally ready.

What should a teacher or parent do in preparing children to have the best possible prerequisite skills? First, take an experimental approach to exposing children to ideas, skills, and activities. Expose children to as wide set of ideas, skills, and activities that underlie other skills, ideas, and activities. For example, being able to move in and out of balance when setting a volleyball, setting a pick in basketball, moving efficiently on a badminton court, and more requires good balance. Use games that require balance to develop this base skill. Reading comprehension requires predicting skills. Practices predicting in directed reading activities. Developing friendships requires listening skills; practice and develop these skills. Also, use a variety of methodologies from hands-on to visual to auditory to teach any skill in addition, watch your child, look carefully to see where the gap that impedes readiness might be in their learning. Math skills are virtually all continuous. If a child has difficulty with some conception skill, back up to a previous concept. Make sure the child has the "concept" before he has the "mechanics". I could divide and multiply mechanically from grade three on. But I never understood until high school what division and multiplication really were. The result was poor math marks throughout school.

Range of Challenge

The range of children's tolerance to task difficulty is of course idiosyncratic, unique to each individual child. Children's perceptions of the difficulty of a task is one deciding factor causing them to act or not. For example, learning to do a front dive off a springboard or making a new friend will most likely be tried once by just about every child. They cannot help their first try. However, they have no compelling reason to stay with a new and perceived "to be impossible" task, for hours, days, or months. They will not do the second try. If it is too difficult, they do not try; if it is too easy, they become bored. The optimum range of challenge is when there is a fifty percent chance of success, and a fifty percent chance of failure. Add that important second factor, again a perception but this time of the importance of trying the task, and couple that along with a perception of a 50/50 chance of success, a teacher has the optimum conditions for causing a child to act.

Freedom from Fear of Failure

Unless failure is minimized, children will be prevented from learning very little else except how to fail. Failing might cause them to acclimate to failure but does little else. Success teaches children to be successful. Now this sounds all nice and true but so what? Do children not succeed and fail many times in little ways day in and day out? Yes, they do. But children learn how to quietly fail and succeed, on their own terms. Success and failure, these "impostors"[20] as Rudyard Kipling called them, then

---

20. Rudyard Kipling, "If," in *Rewards and Fairies* (Independently published, 1910). The story goes that he wrote this beautiful and profound poem in just twenty minutes, while sitting alone by a river.

have their normal effect when they, and children, are left alone to have their way with each other.

When adults impose some adult expectations and standards on kids, fear of failure, and the fear of success, enters the picture. Why do most adults, and I am included here, choose rather to move away from a person, task, or challenge if failure is possible then move towards it if success is possible? They learned it. Think about it for a moment. You often choose what would keep you safe than what would bring you fulfilment and success. Why? Largely because of the influence of others in your life. You are worried about what others could say if you fail. You are fearful of the reaction of others. What a lousy foundation that is and what an impediment to one's readiness to live life fully. Too close observations, particularly in the early stages of learning, maximizes the fear of failure potential. Let young people keep secrets, particularly when early on in new experiences. Children learn early on that in threatening situations, not risking, and avoiding the possibility of failure, is almost as good as succeeding.

Realistic Expectations

Children need to be kept somewhat safe and free from the tyranny of the unrealistic expectations of others. Authoritarian relationships and parents (no explanations just do as I say) should be the last relationships young people should go into. Joyfulness must be correlated with feeling existentially free, and a million miles away from some mindset characterized by what we think others think of us.

All we should expect from children is what we have trained into them. If they have been trained to be obedient, honest, inquisitive, and orderly, then we can expect that. If they have not been trained to be consistent, deferring of gratification, and kind in speech, then we cannot expect that.

Educate comes from the Latin word *educare*, which loosely means to train by guiding or leading out. Guiding children into right relationships in the first months and years is a good practice, if it is not forced or tinged with ought to(s). Avoid, if you can, watching them too closely and too much. Give them room. Be sparse with both flattery and criticism. Honest praise for a job well done is what will encourage. Let children tell you what they need and desire, then, in the beginning respond to them.

The purpose of laying the foundation is for the child to fall in love with the idea of one day hanging out with the Creator, serving and being kind to others, be a means of grace to neighbors. I believe the best foundation is one where "childlikeness" is encouraged, where it is fun and enjoyable to be a child of the Creator. The painful experiences of life will come; the maturing process will come. If a solid foundation is laid, a person has the goods to be resilient, to persevere through good and bad times.

I believe the foundation should be continuously laid up to the age of adolescence, usually thirteen or fourteen years for boys, perhaps a year or two earlier for girls. Finally, I believe the foundation is laid for a particular purpose and when that purpose is accomplished, then it is time to move on into principles, ideas, concepts, and propositions.

The Strategies and Tactics of Laying a Foundation

The following ideas[21] are useful as they are written for all teachers, and are modifiable for parents who are homeschooling, or who are simply trying to lay down a solid foundation in the lives of their children. They can be modified to be useful to children as young as three or four years of age. Remember to keep the end in mind; a right relationship with the Creator, i.e., young people living into a created world of magic and wonder, giving into and apprehending (not necessarily comprehending) that a reality we name God exists. With themselves, getting good at things, lots of day to day skills. With others, practices of the virtues, kindness leading the way. With the created and natural order, recognizing the landscape around them as God's *first* Bible and treating all life and creation as sacred, are the curriculum of a right foundation.

Brainstorming

Brainstorming is a technique for older children which is valuable for the stimulation and generation of ideas and the facilitation of their expression. The purpose of the procedure is to promote lots of ideas or a specific subject by identifying all possible aspects, ideas, and concepts, related to it. Brainstorming involves the cooperative thinking and acceptance of all ideas of children and parents or teachers toward the solution to a specific problem. It is the time-honored supper talk activity. Topics can

---

21. Means, *Methodology in Education*, 101–18; The methodologies that follow here and in the remaining three chapters have been adapted from a series of methodologies found in Methodology in Education.

range from the abstract (why people are unkind) to the practical (how can we be more kind to each other in school and in the home). The key to successful brainstorming is to not critique or praise a young person's response. You can dignify and honor a response best by taking it up without criticizing it, in an ongoing brainstorming of additional ideas.

Committees

Committee work involves the active participation of older children in small group activity. The committee consists of three or more family or class members and frequently explores phases of a personally pressing problem, issue, or question that lives in their world. Committees with real responsibilities, ownership, and voice given to everyone, sharing in the topic through a problem-solving approach. Committee work is usually an ongoing type of experience which may culminate in a project after a designated period. Committee work trains children to prepare, to be organized, to set goals, and to finish tasks. Examples include raising money for a family or mission project or learning how to involve a new family in the church. Up to eight or nine years of age children's preference is for associative rather than cooperative activities. That is, they are psychologically prone to be more comfortable in adding a piece of a committee's output to another person's output, much like building a jigsaw puzzle. Later, after the age of 13 or 14, young people are more comfortable in co-creating an output, cooperating together on delivering a product.

Problem-Based Learning

Problem-solving is a complex integration of many kinds of responses that vary from one situation to another and take many different forms. It is not an isolated process, but rather one that seeks new ways, modifications, and patterns of behavior in attaining a goal. It involves the presentation and analysis of a problem to arouse curiosity, interest, and student activity which culminates in a prayerful and carefully thought out conclusion or solution. Examples include solving the problems found in being in relationship with others like rejection or unkindness, or solving problems of "life" and theology, like why do you think things die? The end-product or deliverable of problem-based learning can be a prototype, a visible expression of a possible solution. A simple water purification system for use by people in water challenged areas of the world, a strategic plan for bully-proofing against what most of us inevitably come up against, a bully.

Buzz Sessions

A buzz session is an informal group activity designed for smaller groups, for ongoing discussion purposes. The buzz session can be effectively used to deal with difficult questions, problems, or controversial issues. If children are listened to, they will develop a positive emotional life. Parents or teachers will offer the synthesis of the groups' ideas and the best conclusions. Leadership is required here. The how is more important here than the what, or topic of a buzz session. Your number one role as the teacher is to create an appreciative inquiry atmosphere, a dignity-preserving way for everybody involved to respond to ideas, even very unusual ones. The hidden curriculum will be at work here. What is it you want your children to really learn from the buzz session? What they will really learn is how they were responded to, not what you taught them.

Role Playing

Role playing is the spontaneous acting out of a situation. It is a form of improvisation in which any age of participant can assume the identity of other persons and then react as they perceive their behavior in a particular set of circumstances. Spontaneity and invention characterize role playing with an emphasis upon individual performance and the role itself, rather than a coordinated group experience centered on the problem. Role playing renders the heroes young people look up to, more identifiable and relevant to children. Bible stories, men and women of God and even local well-known people and events can be played out. I remember being one of the three wise men, each year in the Christmas pageant in my Catholic school. Me and the two black kids. I never knew the significance of all that until much later in life. Your children will remember their role and attributes of their character for a long, long time.

Storytelling

Storytelling is the narration to children of incidents or events which may be true or fictitious, and read, told, or presented through various forms of expression. Its general aim is to present a message, interpret the literature, or inspire reading and expression. The procedure can be used to initiate new units of study, foster imagination, build new vocabulary, create a sense of reality, stimulate creativeness, and provide a common background experience for the development of ideas. Children love stories and storytelling, and it is stories that have perhaps the largest and richest educating history of all the methodologies listed here. Invite young people to tell each other who they identified with? Who did they like best? Not like? When were the most engaged? Least engaged? Reading is in one sense a psycholinguistic guessing game-read, summarize, predict, confirm prediction, repeat all within less than a second eventually for a proficient reader. Reading practices for children should include asking them to practice predicting, from illustrations, headings, and their summaries.

Gamification

If you have not noticed, young people are playing games on electronic devices. The challenges here are immense for teachers and parents who want to somehow limit or use this phenomenon in positive ways. I propose that we use games, and electronic games as well, to teach. A game is an educational play situation possessing some structure by virtue of a set of rules or procedures to be followed. Board games, modified games of Pictionary or charades, and active games of exploration and creativity on playgrounds or in water can lay a foundation of success experiences. My grandkids love Mind Craft. I kind of like it, too. I sit next to them while they are playing, and I pose prediction questions. What might happen next? What would happen if . . . ? The cognitive ability to predict turns out to be a key characteristic of both fluid and crystallized intelligence. Why not nurture this ability along their developmental highway.

Pageant-Maker Faire

A pageant is a type of drama usually produced out-of-doors. It commonly is based on history and frequently associated with a kind of special occasion. Various musical devices, humor, commentators, and other variations of theatrical art sometimes are used. Pageants make clear the behaviors and successes of the models we wish our children to imitate. Easter, Christmas, Passover, Advent, and other times and events of history can be used for pageants.

Drama

Drama, theater, and pantomime are variations of role playing and other dramatic expressions. They differ in that gestures, facial expressions, and overt movements take the place of spoken words in the portrayal of character roles and situations. Sometimes an unobserved announcer is used to briefly describe the action as it occurs. Pantomime is a valuable way to demonstrate the "right and wrong" or "do and don't" of a situation which involves feeling and action. Children pantomime creation, the passion and death of Christ, and any Bible story. A picture is worth a thousand words. We humans know more than we can say, or, for young people, a lot more is known than what can be said. Art in all its forms is the teachers' and parents' gift in helping young people develop a foundation.

Play

A play ordinarily is defined as a carefully rehearsed dramatization that involves a pre-determined script, costumed performers, and rather elaborate scenery. It can be extremely useful in portraying important concepts particularly of a social nature. Play scripts are available in printed form from online sources or may be developed as a class or family project. A family can work together to produce a play to present to another family or class at school.

Projection

The projective procedure involves the use of a stimulus to encourage spontaneous and uninhibited discussion or reaction to social, spiritual, personal, or real-life problems or situations. It is used to reveal attitudes, beliefs, ideas, and adjustments related to specific problem situations. Open-ended or association techniques usually are utilized as stimuli such as completing a sentence or story, responding to a word or phrase, or describing a picture of symbol. Projections can be done around a meal or before special events at church or school. For example, ask children to project what Christmas will be like for the single parent family across the street. Or what was the hero of the story thinking when she saved the dog from the fire. Bigger ticket items are fine too; what was someone thinking when they did not stop to give money to a homeless person. What was the homeless person thinking?

Rhymes and Songs

Rhymes and jingles represent a creative writing experience involving the manipulation of words to produce a form of rhythmic meaning. When used sparingly and with discretion, the approach provides personal satisfaction, serves to emphasize important points, and motivates the development of certain basic writing skills. Performances by young people are always fun and a means to gather the family and perhaps neighbors into a party. Use percussion instruments to accompany singing and the fun starts.

Open-Ended Inquiry

Allow children to turn rocks over, poke around a pond, ask questions about why animals die, and how did you get those wrinkles around your eyes. Guide them to select and repeat what they enjoy doing when inquiring. Take time to do this with them. Leave the learning ends, the intended outcomes open and unstated. Forget the teaching 101 lessons about always having to have goals and outcomes.

Tableau

The tableau is a picture from a French word meaning picture. The tableau is a picture-like scene composed of individuals arranged against a kind of background. It is a motionless as well as a silent portrayal of an event, circumstance, or situation.

Circle of Courage

The Circle of Courage presents four developmental needs of children and youth (belonging, mastery, independence, and generosity) usually in the form of an indigenous medicine wheel. You would find the principles and practices of the Circle of Courage in well over 100 books, articles, curricular programs for schools and agencies that work with young people. Two of my children attended a high school with many of its practices drawn directly from the Circle of Courage. Their lives were changed in this school and its practice.

Virtues Project

A Canadian originated program designed to systematically develop daily practices of virtues, one at a time. An award-winning program that has been deployed in schools, families, schools, churches, and workplaces. The program includes five strategies: speak the language of virtues, use teachable moments to teach, set clear boundaries, honor the spirit, and offer companying.

5

Middle Years

13 to 17 Years of Age

Prisoners of Our Minds

"Their prison is only in their own minds, yet they are in that prison; and so afraid of being taken in that they cannot be taken out."[1]

The Fascinating Years

THE MIDDLE YEARS CAN be the most fascinating for parents and teachers of young people, roughly aged 13 to 17, that is, if the realization is that these young people are far from the finished product. They can be self-preoccupied, often hormone driven and as someone once wrote, just trying to survive between happiness surges. They know more than they can and do say, and they are quick to take up a cause and defend that cause. Their emerging abilities to think in a new key, to imagine possibilities not connected to their past concrete lived experiences, and unique identity and moral challenges, makes them even more fascinating. As one of my mentors once told me, preserve the relationship during these challenging years because when they come out of them, and they will, if you have lost the relationship you have lost everything. If you have preserved the relationship, when they come out of the challenging years, and they will, you have kept everything.

---

1. Lewis, *Last Battle*. The last book in the series, the Chronicles of Narnia

These years call for a curriculum of new practices. What I propose as a new curriculum will be one that you may not recognize. Old practices like some form of Christian boot camp, Christian school, or forced participation in youth group are not the answer. What is the answer is for teachers to align tactics and teaching strategies to the deep developmental and psychological needs that are alive and well in these young people during these years. My doctoral studies focused on the lived experience of middle school aged young people and what I found continues to influence me and in large measure is the reason I chose to write this book. Simply put, what is often claimed as effective teaching for middle school-aged young people is not. What I found to be true was that young people want to experience belongness; they desire real community but settle for what will immediately meet that need. They will look for shelters, psychological ones, while they try to survive between times spent playing computer games. Those shelters are almost always their friends, good or bad. They want to grow into an identity of their true self and above all want life to be meaningful, to have a purpose. They are not always very good at telling you any of this, however. They know more than they can say.

At this period, too often young people experience religious teaching and learning that is tinged with a sub text, some sort of insistence that they need to find that elusive thing called God's will, then beat their thinking and actions into some alignment with this 'God's will.' John O'Donohue puts it this way, a curriculum that emphasizes "an awful lot of theology and spirituality (that) goes badly to ground in an excessive concentration on the will of God."[2] The result? The lovely opportunities to work with the lively and imagination-producing minds of these young people, the result is an image of the Creator that is crippling and negative. God becomes that giant chess master moving pieces along the chess board of life, or worse, some mean old man who needs to be pleased. Hopefully, if you align your life to some of this grumpy man's should(s), you may just be alright. Unless, of course, you are of the elect, the predestined lucky few that have won the lottery and are getting in, regardless of any alignment. Both outcomes are simply not aligned with the Creator Jesus taught us about.

The emphasis in these years should be on the declarative or semantic principles of living in right relationships. But the teaching pathway is a form of misdirection Do not lead your teaching event with the

2. O'Donohue, *Walking in Wonder.* p 17. His wisdom is earthy, and yet just feels eternal and important; I recommend his book

abstraction, instead, start with an activity into which you pour meaning. Learning needs to be active and minds-on; again, designed for young adolescents to address real problems, solve issues, and answer real questions that not only live in their world, but also in the world out there, their immediate context first-family, neighborhood and city, then in the wider world. Erik Erikson tells us that these young people are struggling with identity vs role confusion. Who I am really is a big question? This question trumps learning abstractions, principles that are paraded by them in schools, homes, and churches. In the list of priorities for young people, principles do not rank very high. Principles, guiding ideas for living into right relationships will be used instead of the word doctrine, and for a reason you will read in this chapter.

The big idea of this section is the importance of young people developing executive control functioning, the ability to know how to self-regulate behaviors and mindsets. This is the ultimate—goal—a set of personally developed self-regulatory strategies that have real world promise and appeal to the young person.

Principles

Principles are guiding ideas. They are the markers, the signposts that point to the particular way of being in the world. Not every idea is a good signpost. As inclusive as Jesus was, he left us with a closed set of principles to be used to direct us into right relationships. Saying the right words does not do much good at all. Saying "Lord, Lord," apparently leaves the Creator underwhelmed. Doing right things like feeding the hungry and being a peacemaker does not. A principle that is true somewhere, is true everywhere.[3] When Jesus teaches us to feed the hungry, give to the rulers of a country what is theirs, do not worry or be anxious about anything, he meant exactly what he said. It was always supposed to be the case, the taken for granted practice of people. However, as we know, and I am sure Jesus knew, people would need to take up many good and useful interpretations, and lots of applications, of what he meant, including spiritual, personal, psychological and quite practical ones. This is how the Creator made us. This is the fun part of the program of studies for

---

3. Rohr, *Immortal Diamond*, 135–36. Father Richard has influenced many and while he remains controversial, he remains even more so an influence for people to find their true self and get on with living for others.

middle years' young people, guiding them to proceduralize, take up possibilities in interpretations and applications. And, because their thinking is being socially constructed, their knowledge a social construction, they need lots of different kinds of conversations and social engagements to develop right relationships.

The World of the Mind

The world of the mind, the young adolescent mind, is the world we now enter. The program of studies now shifts from nurturing a psychological and developmental foundation in young people, one full of practicing virtues, training and modeling, all tinged with messages that they live in a world that is magic, to a program of studies designed develop healthy and relationship-producing mindsets.

The big idea of teaching young people, 13 to 17, includes guiding them to unpack the meaning of principles. To pour personal meaning into principles and experience learning for some young people might best be described as re-socialization, a re-patterning of concepts and schema, but hopefully for most young people with a good foundation already in place, a socialization into the mysteries and wonder of the mind.

Jesus's descriptions of the particular way of being in the world becomes "religious" when people proceduralize a principle and make decisions based on that principle. The principle in Luke 6:38, "Give and it will be given to you" is one idea intended to help guide people's use of money. Principles are just abstractions. They are declarative or semantic pieces of knowledge that serve as guides, that by following the dictates of a principles we save ourselves from bad decisions. Principles are means to know how to practice right relationships, forgive others, and use money. Knowledge of principles is necessary but not sufficient, if a teacher is interested in young people developing right relationships and taking up Jesus's teachings, practicing both. Knowing semantically a principle does not and cannot automatically transfer into practicing principles, like the golden rule. What does? That is the question I address in this section. You need to read on.

Jesus's way has a religious element. The Scriptures generally, including the Jewish Scriptures, and Jesus's teaching specifically, include lots of principles for living, sometimes hidden in parables, other times quite clear and forthright. There is nothing wrong with "religion," if life is not perceived solely as, or lived only as, a religious walk on some moral tightrope. Life is not primarily a set of ostensible fun-destroying religious ideas. The life we want for our young people is a way of being in the world that comes about through, or by, right relationships. Being in the world in these ways in turn bring about the right relationships. So, what does religion have to do with our relationship with the Creator? What do principles have to do with our relationship with ourselves, others and the natural and created order? And how should we teach young men and women, adolescents who are emerging into early adulthood?

Well, I am glad you asked.

Executive Controls

The desired end, the intended outcome of teaching principles to young people aged 13 to 17 is first to guide them into developing more complex, personalized executive control functions. Simply, our job as teachers and parents now shifts to guiding them to develop their own set of domain specific procedural strategies and tactics, logistics and relationship builders that will serve as self-regulators of their behavior. Because their imaginations are now able to consider possibilities that they have not concretely experienced, young people need to experience genuine freedom to draw into the workrooms of their mind, their active or working memory, executive control functions that will direct them ahead to recognize and choose new possibilities, new futures. Our teaching assignment is to teach them a "so what, now what" approach to living, to imagine new possibilities, what it could mean for them to have a relationship with the Creator, self, others and the natural and created order.

Our teaching program of studies includes coming alongside young people, a coach to help them put words to what is emerging in their imaginations, their identity, their sweet spot mission in life, their relationships. The desired end in their relationship with the Creator, the learning output in a young life is a "giving in" and recognizing the evidence that love is the answer for the world today. It is far more important for them to know and practice that the Creator cares for them then some abstraction that they are supposed to love God, or else.

The desired end in their relationship with the created and natural order is for them to imagine and then practice how to solve real problems, address real issues and answer real questions that live in the world.

For the young person to experience coming to know and recognize what a right relationship can bring to life, to ways of being in the world.

The desired end in their relationship with themselves is negotiating the identity crises that they are fully engaged in at this age, intimacy vs isolation. A teacher's best gift now is to coach them to imagine new futures for themselves, the possibilities of living in freedom to be their true self.

The desired end in their relationships with others is one characterized by virtues. During these years the adolescent brain can be adapted through lived experiences to understand that virtues can be a nuanced, that respect, kindness, and peacemaking and all virtues include speaking out against injustice, calling into question dishonesty, and deciding which cultural values to accept and which to reject. Heavy intellectual lifting but for a teacher maybe teaching discernment is the most important intended outcome possible.

Our Mindsets Affect Relationships

We are immersed in a culture of doubt and disbelief, it seems to me. It feels easier sometimes to accept everything rather than believe in anything. Our culture is sometimes described as post truth, where what is most important is a pragmatic and individualistic way of being in the world. A pursuit of meaning, critical thinking, and pursuit of the truth, even in universities that should know better, seems to start and end with basing the curriculum on carefully selected principles that serve only individualized interests. Young people will progressively, mutually accommodate themselves to all this unless mentored to think differently. These years are opportunities, chances to challenge assumptions that the world is meaningless. My experience has been that simple logic helps. I ask them if the world had no meaning, would we have ever discovered that? To be taught to fairly test the world is now the essential program of learning.

These years are sensitive ones, benefiting from learning to hear from each other; to listen to each other's stories and experiences. Middle years aged young people have a limited habituation range. Without discrepancies and unusual stimuli, they will not exert that energy we know as 'paying attention.' They will listen to and learn from others telling their stories of experiences with the Creator, others, and self, but the style and form of the stories become the message. They need to hear others be candid and transparent about the consequences, good and bad, of life decisions.

Attention is not something they possess; it is not a noun. It is a verb, something like energy that we do not have but can make. My point is to not waste the power of the story by boring the life out of these young people.

Here is one reason why an expansive, imagination rich principle that truth is to be pursued is important. The Scriptures, both Jewish and Christian, did not produce any new truths, add any new truths, or in any way introduce a Plan B. Life was always meant to be lived in relationships; Jesus was always divine and the Creator, and the way of Jesus was always the plan. "Blessed are the peacemakers for they shall be called children of God" (Matthew 5:9) did not become true because it is in a section in the Bible. However, what is true about what is true is still worth the conversations among us, and with middle years' young people.

Let us start with some assumptions worth considering for your program of studies with young people. It is in the Bible because it is true. The poetry is true, the history is true, the metaphors are true, the cool ideas Jesus taught us are all true. All factual? No, some not literally, anyway. A 7-day creation story is a true story, probably not a factual story. The guiding ideas, the principles in Jesus's sermon on the mount did not pop anything new into truth, and certainly nothing new is introduced because we get to read it all today in the Bible. Principles are transcendent, past tense, descriptive not prescriptive and have always been true. Until Jesus told us so, we were not aware of just how important pre-existing principles are within the kingdom of God. Our teaching mission now is to guide the re-imagining of new futures of young people with the self-regulatory principle of what trust can we place in the truthfulness of our friendship with the Creator, others, self, and the created and natural order.

There is a Creator. That is a second assumption worth considering for your program of studies. Jesus taught us a great deal about this Creator, his Dad? He also taught us that self-serving behavior may make for a lived experience of wilderness, an ongoing, longer than necessary, and awkward time wandering around in some psychological borderlands. Hard to experience love here, despite all the noise in the bible about love. More assumptions follow in the ages to come in this chapter.

Paradigms-Directors of Behavior

It is important for young people to develop concepts as accurate as possible (not complete or thorough) images and beliefs about the purpose and nature of life. Our concepts are ordered rules that determine what something is and what it means. You recognize something that barks, wags a tail, and chases cars as a dog only because you have the concept of dog in your mind. Otherwise, you would have no idea of what you were seeing, and what it means. In the past, I taught high school in a rural area of Zambia. I would sneak across the Luangwa River with farmers who delivered maize to markets in Mozambique. The last time I did this we encountered hippos who decided to pay attention to us. I recall the event very clearly; first, telling the farmer that I thought that I could spit on the closest hippo. I then noticed his panic and cranking his small outboard motor up to full blast. His concept of hippo was far more accurate than mine. Dangerous animals, very territorial and, rumor had it then, that they were the most dangerous animals in Africa, and I was going to spit on it?

Concepts direct and regulate our behavior and the ripple effect of our images touch all aspects of lives. My image of my father influences how I view God, men in authority, and even how I view myself. Principles that are interpreted accurately are important precisely because they can give us correct images of a right relationship-based life. Correct knowledge of a principle has potential to correctly direct and regulate our lives; and more importantly, to direct us over time into an ongoing intellectual conversion to understanding more about the essence of right relationships.

Let me try one more illustration regarding the principle of forgiveness. I grew up being told that I was to forgive those who hurt me. Being conditioned to respond without question, I would say that I forgave someone because I was told that it was in the saying that was the forgiveness. Unfortunately, I never really forgave very many people. In fact, I often plotted and schemed to get back at people. I had heard all the religious arguments in favor of forgiveness. God forgave me, so I should forgive others. Forgiveness can mend and make right broken relationships, or simply do it, forgive, because you are supposed to.

All the arguments amounted to absolutely nothing in my life until the deepest truth of forgiveness leapt out at me from the page of a book, the name of which I have long forgotten. But I have never forgotten the deep truth. Forgiving others heals me when it includes a certain kind of forgetting those others. It releases the anger and revenge from me. It restores me to psychological health. It needed practice and a new concept made a big life change.

That insight has opened something about the nature of truths generally, and concepts specifically. It is simply this. The Creator and Jesus's concepts about what are true, are for me. I may be for the Creator but I am not for the concepts of the particular way of being in the world. I do not serve them, they serve me. The Scriptures, and all holy texts, are for me. I am not for them. There will not be a short answer quiz needing passing at our meeting face-to-face with Jesus, needing 100% to get into heaven.

The Creator is for me even when I am not for the Creator. Knowing that Jesus's concepts are for me has been liberating. Forgiveness is not an abstraction but a another of that set of particular ways of being in the world, that preserve relationships and gently move me into the deep settled joy described in the Beatitudes, the blessedness that results from right relationships. This, and all Jesus's upside-down kingdom principles, are gold for a young person, a treasure to be found and enjoyed. Teach your young people that all truth is God's truth, even if it is not in the Bible. To do so gives them permission to see sacredly and begin to imagine new possibilities, new futures for all their relationships.

One final comment here. Principles that do not make sense, or have meaning for you and me, will not influence me. Meaningful concepts will. Meaning is a social construction. Thinking is socially constructed. This may be the most important reason to teach principles of the kingdom of God to young adolescents in relationships, with their emerging concepts of what right relationships mean as their interpretive key to unlocking the meaning of everything.

Teaching Principles

Knowing a principle like the golden rule might lead to a sensitivity in the conscience. However, it will rarely if ever alone motivate someone to correct action. What a principle can do cause conscious disequilibrium when a certain principle-directed action is not followed. That is not a bad outcome. Principles also give us a language, words, which in turn give us meaning. The language of principles precedes the meaning of the principle. Words are very important. Calling something "abortion" is different from calling it "freedom to choose." Not the same thing. Loads of different meaning are inherent in both concepts. Language precedes meaning here.

The point is that the words used to teach principles must be chosen carefully if an individual's meaning is to conform to the truthfulness in the principle. I spent a couple of years in a religious organization, a system organized and run around one man. Historical landscape is littered with the problems that come about when authority is given to one man. The principle of leadership espoused by this organization was best summed up in this statement from one of the church elders when he said, "The truth we follow around here is the truth as preached by Pastor Smith." For someone like me who had been conditioned and failed to learn to live freely in an authoritarian home, the results were devastating. I would literally lose a night's sleep over not attending a particular church function that the pastor said we should be at. I am a recovering fundamentalist, like many of you reading this book.

Knowing a principle holds some people more accountable than others to responding to that principle simply by virtue of personality or predisposition. Principles when proceduralized (i.e. practiced) can influence people's lives, and profoundly.

How Principles Can Be Taught

The reason I suggest waiting until adolescence to begin to teach principles, is that it is at this age young people begin to think about new possibilities that exist in the world, but do so without the anchorage of concrete past experiences. They can and do think in new kinds of abstractions, in ways that are consistent with their emerging independence, and with this newly developed skill, can be creative as well as imaginative. David Elkind in his book entitled *All Grown Up and No Place to Go* says that they think in a new key.[4] They can now make correct inferences, can successfully extrapolate from one story or situation to another, and can synthesize unrelated ideas into a new or original plan. They have potential to move from fantasy-based thinking and writing to imagination-based thinking and writing. They can be creative, based on logic and what truly exists. They can evaluate based on objective criteria, that is, they have potential to be analytical, not simply critical. They can also imagine alternatives

---

4. Elkind, *All Grown Up*; Elkind (1931 to present) is an author whose books for years were required reading in university and teacher colleges of education. He writes along a line of reasoning shared by others such as Goodman (Growing up Absurd), that young people's developmental psychological realities need to be taken into consideration when designing teaching and learning experiences. Pushing children too fast to soon interrupts their normal development. Good reads of Elkind's include "The Hurried Child," "Miseducation and All Grown Up," and "No Place to Go."

to what their parents and teachers do and alternatives to what their life might be like.

This precondition, or antecedent, of thinking in a new key is necessary, if principles are to be understood and practiced. Why? A principle that is true externally to knowing it, is still true somewhere. And young people are still accessing meaningfulness of principles, second hand, through an interpretation by someone else, of what is right and important. For the adolescent, principles need to be discussed with them, not delivered to them. Why? Because thinking is socially constructed; knowledge is a social construction. Young people will construct meaning one way or another, with one source of information or another. Why not that source be you.

Finally, principles need to be nested within executive control functions, those cognitive based self-regulatory ways of thinking that serve as guides, or directions to what to do with a principle when and how. The young person in these years is primed to think how to think and be an independent problem solver, issue addresser, question answerer.

Obstacles

Presenting too many principles overwhelms. Presenting too few may result in a truncated, improper perception of what is unique in the particular way of being in the world. Presenting principles in a dry and uninteresting way may dissuade someone from being attracted into the way of Jesus. Sex is a big issue for middle years' young people. I am told that it is a popular activity for them. It is uninteresting and not very effective to nest the topics of sexuality and their personal questions, issues, and problems related to sexuality into a set of thou shall nots. The result? A doorway opens to additional concepts regarding sexuality that are unhealthy and wrong-headed. Given the current evangelical over and against stance to gender, homosexuality, sexual expressions outside of marriage, one might be tempted to conclude that the unforgivable sin must have something to do with sex.

Teaching Principles: Strategies

There are four strategies I recommend for teaching principles to middle years' young people. They are direct instruction approaches, reflective action and ethical decision-making, the insight-generating approach, and problem-based learning.

Strategy 1: Direct Instruction

By far the most common approach to teach principles is direct instruction or transmission of information. Often, too often, this approach is a *one and done* experience characterized by a teacher's stand and delivery activity. Often, direct instruction is used in responses to a young person's actions, behaviors, and decisions. It is reactive and not proactive. Its teaching presuppositions are traditional. Ostensibly, all the meaning young people need is right there, in the fact being transmitted. Another presupposition is that we have a cultural and educational mandate to conserve, to preserve the best of culture, of religion. We need and expect young people to take away and conserve something meaningful and necessary to living. Lecturing, talking at, using words delivered to teach has always been a preferred method of teaching principles. This method is easy, neat, and tidy. Teachers and parents deliver words, a parade of abstractions, and then hope, and sometimes even expect that young people will understand and proceduralize the abstraction.

Then what is the problem? This direct instruction approach without designing attending conditions for learning being active, rarely works. It is largely a waste of teaching and learning time. If you doubt me, tell me what you learned, really learned and no apply to your life from the last sermon you heard, tape you listened to, class you sat in passively and listened to. What are the conditions necessary for direct instruction to be effective? I am glad you asked.

Learning happens when someone first becomes attentive, then recognizes and interprets certain words, hopefully in as close a way as possible to the way they were presented, categorizes in their minds their interpretation, and then remembers those words. The purposes and aims of instruction or the "why" and "what" of teaching, is usually said to be for a young person's development. The objectives are usually behavioral and are determined and prescribed by the teacher or parent to specify exactly what the young person should know or believe. The methods are usually lecture and question/answer.

Direct instruction might work but under a set of learning conditions, when certain teaching strategies are used that help the hearer engage with the message, cognitively as well as emotionally. The next section describes instructional strategies that can be used by a parent or teacher to help someone understand accurately the message taught in a lecture.

Titles

Read the following paragraph. Your task then is to immediately tell someone else what the paragraph is about.

They set off into the blackness towards what many feared was the abyss. The three with one intention, moved on together, with dreams of riches they moved into the unchartered blackness where stars beckon their twinkle welcome. The unknown was no less ominous by the twinkle, the fear no less pressing by the strong presence of one who demanded allegiance if their task were to be successful. (Author unknown)

Star Wars? Some science fiction story? If you guessed that the paragraph is about Christopher Columbus discovering America, you are right. Now, using the title *Christopher Columbus Discovers America*, reread the paragraph. The title organizes your perception so that recognition and interpretation of the meaning of the paragraph is made easier when a title is used. The first step in using the lecture or catechetical approach is to use a title. The Bible could be retitled *Restoration: The Story of God's Connecting to Everything*. That title makes every story and every idea in the Bible mean something quite specific.

Prerequisite Information—Teaching the Unfamiliar from the Familiar

When my daughter was much younger, I began asking her to wash her hands after going "potty". She asked why (typical of a four-year-old). I replied, "Because after going potty and wiping yourself, there are germs on your hands." One night, after the practice of handwashing was firmly in place, I asked her if she had washed her hands. She replied, "Yes," and proceeded to put her hands into my face and said, "See, I have a whole bunch of clean germs."

Her recognition and interpretation of the "facts" was skewed because I did not give her sufficient information in advance around which she could organize her perception, that is, her ability to recognize and interpret the new information. The result would have been different had I said to her in advance, "Gabrielle, washing removes bad things from our hands, like that sticky honey yesterday." She understands sticky honey. Washing germs is like removing your boots after walking in the mud (she can understand removing boots). Poop has germs in it; they can get on your hands when you touch it. You should remove the poop-germs by washing them down the sink. Middle years' young people are no different.

Information presented to children of all ages in advance of a presentation can help them recognize and interpret more accurately the information that is to come, provided the information is understandable, it relates directly to the key points found in this information that is to come, and it is a summary.

Analogies are excellent advanced organizers, as are stories and illustrations from the world of science. Before teaching about Jesus's parable of the seeds and the sower, a parent can put seeds in a cup of water, watch them germinate over days, plant them in different places in the garden, and watch the results. Some grow; some do not. The basis for understanding the meaning in Jesus's parable is in place because of the advanced organizer's effect.

Set Induction

What I am about to tell you next could save you from intense pain, perhaps even death. It will certainly save you from embarrassment. Please read this very carefully. Do not put your face on a hot stove.

There, I had your interest for a few seconds. An emotional bridge was built between the two of us; we were connected. You anticipated what I was going to tell you. You were aroused, attentive, and eager to read on. (I think I gave you good advice, don't you?)

A set induction is that activity or idea, usually offered up early in a teaching and learning event, that builds an emotional and cognitive scaffold between a teacher's intention regarding learning and a learner's prior learning experience, the leftovers of that experience we call memory. A set induction could be a story that the learner can relate to or has experienced personally, a real-life example or a visual.

You can build that emotional bridge between you and your child in teaching by stating something that heightens anticipation. Before teaching my daughter a lesson about how important she is to the Creator of the universe, I told her that I thought Jesus might of liked kids, more than he liked grownups (I'm sorry if that upsets your theology, but I think I am right). I told her that Jesus loved children, they hung around him. He got a bit angry at some men who wanted to chase children away.

My daughter's interest was immediately aroused so much so that for the next two years she said she did not want to grow up. Good for her. She wanted assurance that if she can be a child in heaven she can run into Jesus's arms. Wrong theology perhaps but loved the outcome.

Purpose

How often have you sat in a meeting listening to a talk asking yourself throughout, "Why is this being said to us?" "Why do I have to hear this?" "What is the purpose here?" The same is true in classrooms everywhere. The battle cry of a teenager in school is either, "This is boring", "It is unfair," or "Why do I have to learn this math (or any other subject) anyway?" They may have a point. When we have a purpose for learning something, learning is more likely to occur.

Everyone has a different "receptive point" and potential for learning. A young five-year-old friend of my daughter had a garter snake. He took it for walks (true), called it Joe, and was devastated when it escaped. But before it got away, he wanted to learn everything about snakes. He had a reason to learn, a purpose in reading about or hearing someone talk about what snakes eat and how they live. A teacher or parent can begin to lecture by stating there is a very good reason to hear this story (or do this activity).

Learning Outcomes

If I would have known more of what was expected of me as a husband, my first year of marriage would have been less troublesome. My wife, thankfully, was patient. She made it clear what her expectations were and encouraged me to do the same. The result—the best marriage in the solar system. Beginning with the end in mind and planned for, working backwards towards the desired end is the key to effective direct instruction.

Middle years' young people need to know what is expected of them in a learning experience. What are the learning outcomes? They should contribute to or at least hear what they will be expected to do, know, or feel by the end of the lesson. Not only is that good pedagogy, but it is also a polite and respectful thing to do.

Capturing Attention

Any parent or teacher who has tried to teach anything to a child will tell you that a main problem is trying to keep that child's attention. We are all psychologically predisposed to respond to discrepant or unusual stimuli (a police siren would capture our attention during too long a parade of words) or wordy writing in books.

Young people's ability to pay attention is poorer than that of an adult. They are still learning to select relevant from irrelevant information and from blocking out discrepant stimuli. Therefore, teachers and parents need to keep distractions to a minimum and help them by providing graphic organizers and outlines that direct them to what is relevant and what is not in a text or learning experience.

Young people's understanding of your intended transmitted information might occur best through your use of non-exemplars. Young people respond well to axioms that clarify concepts and principles, through non-exemplars. Kindness is strength under control, it is not niceness. Non-exemplars can be psychological—worry in order as opposed to do not worry. In the physical, jogging is not running on your legs; it is running with them, taking them along for the ride.

Young people are still quickly habituated to repetitive stimuli. Their attention needs to be recaptured more often than we might think, even in a twenty-minute instructional session. Attention is a verb not a noun. It is not a thing young people have and then use, it is an activity of the mind that like physical energy, needs to be activated. Parents and teachers need to vary the style of presentation within a single lesson. A twenty-minute lecture-based lesson should contain stories, energetic descriptions, and so on. Fortnight and other computer and video games are produced with enough stimuli to keep a 13-year old engaged for hours. Watch one of these games with your young people, (hold your nose if you have to) and watch for the genius designed in the games for keeping attention.

Directed Reading/Listening/Viewing Activity

I recently picked up a book written by John Fischer. It was entitled *Real Christians Don't Dance*.[5] "Don't" was crossed out. I was intrigued with

---

5. Fischer, *Real Christians Don't Dance*; Fischer (1947 to present) is a musician, public speaker and writer, author of "Real Christians Don't Dance" and other books that have helped people recognize what is important and what is not in Christianity.

the title. More so, I began that psycholinguistic (a big word that simply refers to the language/meaning relationship) "guessing game" we call reading. I implicitly started to predict what I might read, primarily but not solely at the level below the consciousness. In other words, I was predicting quickly and without qualifying or evaluating my predictions. I then began to read, in a sense, by testing my predictions out, seeing if my predictions were true. I read the preface. It said, to summarize, that Jesus, the Creator, did not enter into our world and go through hell on earth for us, and the martyrs go to the stake to be burned alive or to be sawn in two—so our pinnacle "Christian" response today is to not dance or drink. That is an important lesson, I think.

By predicting, based on a title or illustration, then reading to test that prediction, I began the activity of reading. By making summaries of what I just read (largely my interpretations influenced by my prediction of what I thought I might read, and certainly influenced by my paradigms, I am reading. I continue reading, predicting, then summarizing. Reading, of course, is more than that. But a parent or teacher can explicate what reading a young person does implicitly. In other words, a parent or teacher can improve a reading comprehension by directing the reading or activity. They can stop after the reading of the first paragraph and invite summaries. Then, they can ask the young person to predict what they might read in the next section (this means that the parent must know what is coming) and continue this directed reading activity through to the end of the chapter or book.

Questions

Consider the difference between these two questions. "What is the definition of the word teaching?" and "What does "teaching" mean?" The difference, of course, is that each question triggers a different thinking activity. One is quite straightforward in its requirement—remember a definition. The other is more complex in its requirement to demonstrate or give evidence of comprehension. To answer that question requires more thought of a more detailed nature. I trust you know which question requires the more complex thinking to answer.

There are numerous ways to classify questions. The most used classification system is the one devised by Benjamin Bloom. It is referred to as Bloom's Taxonomy[6]. Here is a summary of this taxonomy.

Remembering. A person recalls or recognizes information, ideas, and principles in the form in which they were learned. The key concept that a parent should keep in mind in asking a remembered question is memory. Some sample phrases and questions might be: "What did the book say?" "List the three steps to design an experiment?" "Who is the Prime Minister of Canada?"

Understanding. A person translates or interprets information. They explain what they understand about an idea. Sample phrases include "Explain the . . ." "What can you conclude?" "State in your own words . . ." A teacher might ask, "Why did Jesus say what he did to the rich young ruler?"

Solving or Application. A person uses information to complete a task or solve a problem. The key concept in asking application questions is "solution." Sample phrases include "If you know A and B, how can you determine C?" "What would happen if . . . ?" A teacher might ask, "What should the rich young ruler do to fulfil the requirements Jesus placed before him?"

Analyzing. A person relates hypotheses or assumptions or evidence to the tasks of deduction. This is the same as using logic. Sample phrases include "What was the author's purpose?" "Which are facts, which are opinions?" "What caused this to happen?" A teacher might ask, "What is there about the riches that Jesus seemed concerned about?"

Synthesizing. A person originates a new plan. They integrate and combine ideas into a plan that is new. The key concept is creative or productive thinking. Sample phrases include "Make up . . ." "What would you do if you were being bullied? A teacher might ask, "What might you do to avoid being someone who only wants to make money?"

Evaluating. A person appraises, assesses, or criticizes based on specific standards and criteria. The key concept is judgment. Sample phrases include "For what reasons do you favor giving money for social causes? A teacher might ask, "For what reasons could a person have money and still be totally devoted to social justice?"

Asking different kinds of questions before, during, and after a lesson is an important teaching strategy. An evaluation question (considered by

---

6. Bloom et al., *Taxonomy of Educational Objectives*. First presented in 1955 and still referred to by educators, in some form or another to this day.

Bloom and others to be the most complex) can be used to start a direct instruction session, to arouse interest or to be an advanced organizer. Asking a comprehension question at the beginning of a direct instruction session serves an important prediction function, alerting to what information might need to be brought up into the working memory. Asking a synthesis question contributes to the development of creativity.

Cultivating Memory

A typical evening scene in our home used to go something like this. I would ask my son to go upstairs, get his pajamas on, find his blanket, and brush his teeth. He would put his toothbrush on the counter, get his favorite book off the shelf, climb into bed, turn on the light, and wait for me. I would be there in just a minute. Off he went to complete the grand total of two, or if I was fortunate enough, three of his requirements. Was he disobedient and over and against? Of course not. He was limited by his short- term memory capability of holding at best $7+/-2$ (5 to 9) isolated, pieces of information. He simply, and honestly, forgot. To get angry at him for not listening was ridiculous and inappropriate. Middle-aged young people with well-developed self-regulatory strategies may be able to compensate for this inherent limitation and have learn ed to handle more discrete pieces of information in their working memory.

Proceduralizing Semantic Knowledge: Practicing What You Know

I will be more likely to more deeply understand something if I use it shortly after I learn it. If I speak in front of a group of strangers, then I am very receptive psychologically to an idea or procedure that will reduce my anxiety and make my presentation more effective. The urgency of some application enhances learning. We do learn from experiences upon which we reflect. When teaching, look for ways for young people to apply what they are learning as soon after learning it as possible.

Concepts and Misconceptions

Everything can potentially be meaningful within a conceptual framework; nothing we see, hear, or touch is meaningful without a concept that pours meaning into it. To directly teach important concepts to young people requires attention to what a concept means, what it does not mean, and to present illustrations and examples of that concept. The intended outcome is a guiding principle that serves well the imagination of new futures, working to self-regulate the decision of the emerging adult. Misconceptions can be used as the nexus, the place to start a direct teaching activity.

Strategy 2: Reflective Action

The reflective action method is far less commonly used. Its teaching presuppositions are of a very different nature than in the direct instruction approach. The main presupposition is that education for learning and applying principles is not achieved by directly teaching principles but by leading people out into new possibilities through pedagogic movements. Its main presupposition about the learner is that they are capable of independently and consciously appropriating new ideas into existing mental structures or his experiences. They can assimilate what they see and hear in ways that are meaningful, best accomplished if the teacher has shuffled the information and learning sequence regarding the principle into constellations that can make meaning happen.

This approach is not as Whitehead said "packing articles in a trunk"[7] but is much closer to what Piaget says is encouraging "reflection" or coming to see the truth in something[8]. The approach starts, not with the subject matter, as in the direct instruction approach, but with the lived experience of the learner.

Identifying Current Experience:
Patterns of Decision Making and Behaviors

Now I need to explain this clearly because of the questionable history for Christians' "experientially" based education. The approach of beginning with the experience of the learner, suggests Thomas Groome, is to deliberately and intentionally start with (the learner) by attending to activity of God now, in the present, and only after to the story of the Christian

---

7. Whitehead, *Aims of Education and Other Essays*.

8. Jean Piaget. His theory reminds us of the interplay between nature and nurture, that nature (genetic predispositions) are like an elastic band, able to be stretched or not in the direction nurture takes it.

faith community, and to the vision of God's kingdom.[9] In other words, this approach begins by a movement, a pedagogic movement that opens up the conversation by students gathering around the "what" question. What have you experienced regarding such and such a topic?

The first step, or movement, is what Thomas Groome calls naming one's present action. There is a particular doctrinal focus and the "what" question begins the movement towards gaining true knowledge about the kingdom and to building a faith-full relationship with God. If the focus is the doctrine of prayer, the teacher might start by asking, "What prayers do you say?" or "What do you do with prayer in your life?"

Naming Possibilities for Reasons for Current Patterns of Decision-Making and Behavior

The next step, or movement, in the approach focuses on inviting the learner to reflect on why they do what they do and what the likely or intended consequences of their actions (or beliefs, assumptions, and ideas) are. Regarding prayer, I might ask, "Why do you pray as you do?" "How or why have you come to believe the way you do about prayer?" or "Why is prayer important to you?" What to you assume about the outcomes of your prayer?

The Christian Story and Its Vision

The third step or movement in the approach focuses on presenting that part of the Christian story and its vision regarding the topic at hand and the faith response it invites. In other words, once the learner has grappled with the what and the why, now it is time, not before, to place relevant Scriptures into the learning constellation. The purpose here is not for the learner to deduce some truth but to encounter the truth with the intention of using the truth to critique the what and the why of the learner's beliefs and actions. In other words, the "story," as Groome calls it, is used to confront and call into question what is believed and what is acted upon.

---

9. Thomas Groome. Took a course with him at Boston College in my PhD program. Disarmingly charming and intelligent.

The Dialectic: Moving beyond Our Limits in Knowing

There are limitations in what we will ever be able to know. The purpose in this step or movement is to reduce those limits and move beyond the limits as far as it possible. By appropriating the truth of the Christian story in a way that seeks to synthesize the truth into the learner's story, there will be a moving beyond the limits. Regarding prayer, I may give the accounts of how or why Jesus prayed. I may use stories or anecdotes to identify prayer in action. My intention is to design questions and conversations probes that inquire, "How does the story and its vision affirm or disaffirm, conform or disconfirm, call into question or call forward what you do and why?" "How does what you do, and its assumptions, inform what the story and its vision mean to you?"

Time for Action

The final movement or step is what Groome suggests is a personal faith response for the future. The question asked of the learner is, "How will you now think, act, believe, etc.?" Regarding prayer, after the appropriation of some part of the truth regarding prayer from step three has occurred I would ask, "What do you believe about prayer now?" "How will you now pray?" Now, I believe Jesus taught this way many times. Read the accounts again of Jesus's discussions with the rich young ruler, the woman at the well, Mary and Martha, and more than once with the apostle Peter.

Strategy 3: Insight-Generating Approach

The third approach, using the methodology described below, is by far least commonly depended on for the teaching of doctrine. Its presuppositions are that insight is a God-given potential that resides in us. It is what Bernard Lonergan suggests is an invariant structure,[10] waiting compacted and whole within us, waiting for the necessary conditions that will begin the process of the "unfolding" or releasing of this insight. The unfolding of insight would be "conversion."

Now this may read like some post-truth philosophy. I do not think so. What this approach does is to cooperate with one of the design ways

---

10. Lonergan, *Method in Theology*.

the Creator made us to learn. Lonergan suggests that this is necessary for leaners movement in coming to insight.[11] I call it a new possibility for a new practice based on an old idea.

There are invariant and necessary conditions required for coming to insight.

From Tension to Attention

To gain insight requires certain conditions to be present. First, we need to be attentive to the data of our lives, or to deliberate over something we see, hear, experience. This step may require that the young adolescent be guided to pay attention to some data in their lives. For example, deep emotions attached to rejection by a friend or feeling upset at some tragedy in the world. We see young people in the U.S. speaking up regarding guns and gun control. Young people's insight begins with an encounter with something, to be presented with something, to investigate it, and be curious about it. The intention of the teacher is to create a little "disequilibrium," a little healthy tension in the person's mind.

There are "tension producing" circumstances and people all around us today that can grab the attention of a young adolescent, to start within them the process of gaining insight. Birth and death are two. Poverty in the face of an often-stated premise that God is love is another. A creator God who would die for his creation is one more, maybe the most disturbing one of them all and, therefore, the biggest tension producing premise of them all. Why is there something as opposed to nothing?

Even the physical universe of infinity we live in, or how prayer works, really or good life and happiness some people appear to get while other's do not can get attention and be the scaffold for right conversations and eventual insight.

The teacher's role in this first step is to bring the person into contact with that which will create tension, and disequilibrium. It can be a film, a speaker, a trip, a visit to some place, or just a quiet talk. It is all about guiding young people to pay attention to the data of their lives.

---

11. Lonergan, *Insight*.

From Attending to Understanding

Bernard Lonergan suggests that the next step or movement to bring insight comes when the person understands exactly what is going on with what he has encountered. He needs to be "intelligent" about what he has encountered.[12]

Now the intelligence here does not come from the analytical way we naturally think. It is more to do with wisdom. It is an intelligence that is probing and wondering, imagination-led and not quick to a resolution. Good teachers keep the conversation going. Young people no doubt have heard people say God has blessed them when things have gone well, and often in some material monetary way. Really? Does that mean that the poor family struggling to keep their family alive in Afghanistan, or Tunisia, or Tanzania is not blessed? Sucks be to them? Ongoing encounters with tension producing ideas are central to coming to insight. The dignity preserving conversations accompanied with good questions are all that are desired. Understandings need to be held lightly, like water in cupped hands, and eventually let go. No need to eat again of the tree of the knowledge of good and evil. Understanding with certainty is not the goal; inquiry and more inquiry is.

Regarding birth and death, poverty and ostensible injustice, and the appearance of unfairness with human beings lives, or anything else we have used to get our learner's attention, this "intelligence" can come and almost always over time, naturally, sometimes spontaneously and often in and through art, music and drama.

The disequilibrium produced by tension needs to become equilibrium, however. The tension needs to be eased sometime. It is natural to want to get some mental balance, if you like, on a tension-producing topic. The teacher's job is to help the learner go back to understand, or better, to remember the "bigger idea." It is important for the teacher to review the foundational ideas and most compelling arguments for or against an issue, like death with dignity or abortion. It will take honest dialogue and patience.

---

12. Lonergan, *Insight*; Lonergan institutes continue to operate in Canada. Lonergan, when it comes to understanding 'how we know what we know,' may be the most important thinker in the 20th century.

From Understanding to Judging

The next learning phase emerges when the learner becomes interested in what someone else is saying about the issue or topic at hand. That someone else can either be the creator, teacher, friend, judgment naturally needs to occur. The young person needs to begin to make judgments on what he is encountering and understanding. The meanings he has arrived at in his thinking need to be responded to. The judgment step or movement is where the young person says that something is right or wrong, better, or worse, true, or not true, worthy, or not worthy, important, or not important. Middle years' young people are quick to be critical but often criticism without evidence or thoughtfulness invested into the critique.

Tactics include completing a cost-benefit analysis of a project, SWOT analysis of a school initiative, debate in which they take up both sides of an issue, pro and con, regarding assisted suicide for example. Many teachers default to a simplistic, "Why do you think about that?" question. The subtext of the why question is often read by the young person as one of suspicion of motives or intelligence, challenge to prove and not support a premise and worse, preparation for an attack. Instead, use a tactic that guides the young person to make a judgement. Religion and religious ways of being in the world are now free to be owned by the young person, at least in their minds. They can and do imagine new possibilities for the sacred that can have little or nothing to do with mom's and dad's religion. This disintegration is unavoidable and inevitable and all in all a good and important developmental transition from immaturity to a personal and owned religious way of being in the world. The nesting of religion into right relationships and issues of justice is exactly what middle years' young people need.

From Judgment to Action

The final learning phase or movement to insight is where the young person acts in love on what insight she now has judged regarding the issue. The action may be some practical service or may be prayer, acceptance of mom and dad, and maintenance of love and respect for them or not. It may simply be acceptance of the new reality that they are in transition and in the borderlands, though likely would not even begin to know how to describe it as such. It may be letter writing, discussing, storytelling, or telling others about their transition. The teacher's role throughout, right to this step is "hands off" in the sense of attempting to direct or regulate. The teacher's role is to engage the young person with the issue initially, share intimately and responsibly with the person anything that will help them understand, respond to their judgments by affirming or, if necessary, disaffirming, then providing the means for the young person to act out in love the insight they've come to.

This process of gaining insight happens over years, primarily achieved through mentorship, a learning of a far different nature than what most of us have experienced. I believe it is precisely how Jesus taught his twelve apostles, and particularly Peter. A person's conversion is on course intellectually when insights have come about in this way.

Strategy 4: Problem Based Learning

Problem-based learning is a young person led investigation into a topic that leads them to a designed answer to a question, solution to a problem, or way to address and issue. The young person is responsible for the procedures used in the investigation and design. The end? A project developed to solve the problem, address the issue, answer the question that is first and foremost from the interest and life of the young person.

The purpose of projects is for students to experientially understand and apply solutions to problems, answers to questions, and better than worse ways to address issues. The outcome of projects is an authentic, visible product, an output, a visible expression of the student's deeper understanding and a broader knowledge base regarding a topic.

Projects encourage students to use a coordinated set of skills (including inquiry, problem solving and presentation), to build a base of knowledge about an issue, question, or problem. The best projects include research into living cases, real situations, or an actual problem. For example, students can do projects in supporting an internationally based foster child through an organization like World Vision.

Teachers design the template, or model for students to follow, as they (students) initiate and implement the project (e.g., how to write a formal proposal to a funding agency). In design thinking type approaches to problem-based learning, teachers and parents guide the young person in a series of movements that begin with discussing together what the problem is in the problem, who owns the problem, and how the problem is creating other problems. The next steps include defining the problem empathizing with the problem designing and then testing a prototype, the end-product of the design thinking project.

Projects are similar to case-study research, following a design where the question, problem, or issue is stated, the project's question(s) clearly stated, information is carefully gathered, relevant literature and other information read and summarized, data gathered, themes constructed from the data and conclusions, recommendations, and responses to the original question proposed.

From Strategies to Tactics: Now What? So What?

The tactics described in the following section have a long and good track record in my own teaching and parenting. The theme or connecting thread in each is the focus on the mind of the young person, the potential to develop executive control functioning and a set of self-regulatory strategies that young people can deploy in their emerging relationships, to the Creator, self, others and the natural and created order.

The intended outcome of your teaching program with young adolescents is that they are guided to move beyond the limits of their understandings, to learn and then practice set of useful strategies coming to know what they know, self-regulatory strategies and a trust set of executive control functions for knowing when to use a strategy. The best teachers create the conditions for middle years' young people for doing so freely, safely, riskily, and always with new possibilities worth finding out. They know how to know more about God, self, others and the natural and created order.

Another outcome is a psychological one, that they are developing the confidence and competencies that they can come to know what they know. We call this self-efficacy; and self-efficacy is one big idea, the intended outcome of our teaching program for young adolescents. With your guidance, they can come to know what it is about the Creator that they can live with, for now. Their knowing is not a concept or abstract idea more about coming to know by practicing right relationships in minds on ways.

The outcome of self-efficacy extends to their core self, to their identity crisis of identity vs role diffusion. They can come to know their true self, who they are, what they stand for, and how they want to be known. They can come to know the natural and created order and actually enjoy coming to insights about the nature or essence of things, from sex to creation, space to time. They can come to know and understand others, and that includes knowledge that extends into gender, race, and history.

One final reminder here: the importance of executive control functioning cannot be overstated. The challenge is for teachers of young people in this demographic to include learning a set of self- regulatory strategies. The workrooms of their minds can be guides into best possible application or transference of principles.

Tactics

Case Study

Case studies possess many of the essentials of problem solving. They entail the use of research of individual situations as a basis for instruction and the development of principles of action. They are based upon a thorough investigation of a "case" to shed light upon, pour meaning into the background, circumstances, and relationships. Factual experiences of the instructor, student, another person, or a fictitious character may be used. The stories of the Bible can be useful if taught as a case study, a real story about real people. Unfortunately, these rich and textured stories are devolved into some sort of moralizing lessons. Devotionalizing replaces fascination or getting down deep into the psychology and sociology of the case. The case studies in the Jewish scriptures, particularly of rascals like King David, Saul, and Jacob, are rich and textured enough to ring true if taught as a case study.

Case studies of the great non-biblical men and women therefore might be better, at least until teachers learn how to make the stories from the Bible come alive. People love stories. They can enter a story, dwell in it, move around in it, and learn from it. Asking essential questions helps young people unpack meaning from a case. For example, where in the case were you the most engaged? After reading the case, what would you like to know more about? Which person in the case do you identify with?

Debate

Debates offer a unique opportunity for young people to experience both sides of an argument, particularly if you were to structure the debate so both sides of an issue are presented by the same debater. The result can be a better developed sensitivity to another person's point of view, skill in arguing using another person's point of view and refining one's perspective on an issue. Death with dignity, abortion, guns and violence and many other current issues can be debated in this format.

Scenario Building

Scenarios are descriptions of ideal situations. Young people enjoy this activity and if a sequence of steps is followed, can experience thinking at some sophisticated levels, including analysis and synthesis. First, have the young person describe an ideal scenario, what they would aspire to or want others to aspire to you. Topics can include ones that are relevant to them, like what would be the ideal family, school, sport team, friendship, but could include world issue topics such as poverty, racism, refugees, and countries opening up borders to (or not) to refugees. In the initial description, avoid identifying the problems with the scenario. Problem-identification comes second. Guide young people to first recognize the problem in problem, the scenario, why the scenario as they described it might not work, curate a discussion with them to identify the problem in the problem, or the core problem, the essence of the problem. Next, propose some solutions with them for what they have identified as the core problem. In addition, ask them to identify their keepers in their original scenario, the hills to die on for them. Guide them to consider how best to keep these keepers in the scenario. The intended outcome is for the young person to propose a revised scenario.

Colloquium

The colloquium technique involves the use of two panels—one consisting of authoritative resource persons and the other of selected class or family members. It permits direct participation on an equal status with the invited experts. A moderator ordinarily is used to guide the discussion, direct pertinent questions, and encourage panel and audience participation as desired. One parent can be the expert, another the moderator. Topics can be benign and informal, supper table conversations that range from family decisions regarding the age when young men and women should be intimate, one-on-one relationships, to more controversial ones like how money should be allocated in an age of hunger.

The important question in any colloquium is "why?" A "why" question is easy to ask but difficult to answer. Gently edge into the conversation the possibility that a principle might be drawn from to come to an answer and identify the principle, regarding responding to bullying or to some personal injustice, drop into the conversation Mohandas Gandhi's famous statement that "an eye for an eye would make the whole world blind." The better principle just might be forgiveness that may not solve the problem but could release one from the effects of the injustice.

Discussion with a Purpose

A discussion involves the verbal interaction of individuals who perceive one another as participants in a common activity. It is a socializing procedure designed to utilize cooperative oral participation techniques leading toward the resolution of a problem or question. A discussion may proceed with or without active leader direction, although it usually requires some degree of moderation to guide group thinking effectively. When families fail to "discuss," young people lose a great means of learning to think, summarize, be patient, and convince. Also, we all need to "speak ourselves into clarity" sometimes. We do not always know what we believe, and whether what we believe is true, until we "speak it." Discussions allow us to do so. Think of discussions as brainstorming sessions in which you, the parent or teacher, refrain from making a value laden response to the young person's ideas. Remember CS. Lewis's notion that the universe rings true whenever you fairly test it.[13] Simply point the young person towards new possibilities for testing an idea.

Forum

A forum consists of two or more presentations to a group on the same subject or topic with audience participation. It basically is used to present opposing sides of a controversial question or issue and is followed by a question and answer period directed to the speakers. It differs from debate in that no attempt is made to call into question a particular viewpoint but merely to consider the various aspects of the issue in the beginning.

13. Lewis, *Surprised by Joy*.

For example, a forum is a safe but effective means to accommodate young person's schemata regarding difficult social issues like pregnancy and provision of dignity preserving services for single moms and provision of social and health services for homeless people.

Panel Discussion

The panel discussion is a conversational exchange of ideas by selected participants on a topic, problem, question, or issue. It is a relatively informal oral process which brings together individuals who possess differing points of view concerning a subject of mutual interest providing ample latitude for exploration and discussion. Opposing panels sometimes are used with question and answer exchanges. Christian principles that are in the "grey" or debatable area, for example, gender dysphoria or the reasons for church denominations could be a source for panels.

Workshops

A workshop is a group gathering in which individuals study problems, address issues or attempt to answer difficult questions. The intended output is a product, perhaps a prototype. In a classroom setting, workshop activities often are specifically planned and organized by students and conducted under teacher or parent guidance. Issues related to clean water and the health of children around the world might generate a workshop led by a knowledgeable international worker and may lead to the development of a prototype for sand filtering of water. A new practice to consider is flipping the workshop. Rather than deploying the usual 'one and done' workshop delivery of information, give room and time, with limited instruction, for the young person to develop a prototype. The instruction regarding tactics, strategies, logistics and relationship builders typically delivered in the face to face one and done part of the workshop is instead presented in shorter, more frequent, dispersed, individualized teaching events scheduled over a period time with a learner

Survey

A survey involves the investigation and study of specific problems or circumstances by means of a scientific process. It consists of measurement of personal or social attitudes, ideas, or practices from which a scientific analysis and evaluation can be made. The survey frequently is used to study individual or group practices, current program status, or the interrelationships of social process. Young people can survey friends and neighbors about their ideas and values. Techniques of questioning, recording, and analyzing are developed. Analyzing is often new cognitive territory for young people, and opportunities to identify themes based on language gathered in the survey. The sweet spot for the young learner here is that the survey is authentic, about a real problem, issue or question that lives in their world.

Collection/Portfolios

Collections or portfolios may be defined as materials which are gathered individually or by a group that relate to a topic or subject. The materials may consist of pictures, maps, clippings, letters, charts, books, stamps, leaves, or other similar specimens or objects. The collected materials usually are arranged in some sequence or order to tell a story. Helpful here to guide young people to study photojournalism, to view and discuss the value to them of stories told through visuals. Humans of New York is just a compilation of pictures of the many and varied people who live in New York, together the pictures tell a story. *Touched Down in Flight* is another story, but this one in a video of images only that tell a compelling story of everyday life in Afghanistan. Young people would have models here to follow in their own collection/portfolio activity.

Archetypes

The scaffold into understanding the deep pattern in historical events, the archetype or original pattern or model of which all things of the same type are representations or copies. An archetype is identified through laying bare and identifying the pattern in our lives. Middle years' young people are intrigued with and enjoy relating their life events to some larger pattern or archetypical unfolding of events, e.g., something new comes into being, a period of peace and enjoyment follows, then a turn downwards ensues, a captivity, a wilderness experience followed eventually by a deliverance and celebration. The story of the exodus is best understood and appreciated through the smaller story of the young person's own exodus.

Inventory

An inventory is a form or research used to ascertain the status of an aspect of someone's behavior, or of a community activity, or instructional program. It frequently involves the gathering of information by means of some sort of data gathering then appraisal procedure. The inventory provides a practical base from which to develop programs and activities in a family, school, or church. An inventory can be used by a young person to identify what others believe about issues, questions, and problems, such as dignity-preserving and access to food banks for families. Inventories provide for a sober second thought about some taken for granted as good programs like Operation Christmas Child or food banks.

Online Resources

Online or library work involves planned investigation into additional sources of information on a given topic or problem. It is obvious that all the answers to all questions that might arise will not be found in a single reference. Classroom, school, and community libraries provide ready resources for research. Such reference sources might include encyclopedias, dictionaries, newspapers, books, pamphlets, atlases, magazines, almanacs, and other materials.

Oral Report to a Community Agency

The term "oral report" defines itself. Oral reports are assigned easily and can be presented simply in relation to a presentation of a project. Other instructional materials such as charts, pictures, slides, photographs, and graphs frequently lend value and sophistication to the report and should be encouraged. A "family home evening" can be scheduled where the main event is the presentation of someone's report regarding some insight or discovery, creation or interpretation of a phenomenon experienced by someone, e.g., an accident, meeting a famous person, near death experience. The goal? To give the report in a library talk, a Toastmaster's course, a Rotary Club, or a school staff meeting.

Project

A project may be either an individual or class planned undertaking designed to compile information, collect objects, construct materials, or create something, a prototype. Projects can be a group enterprise. A project might consist of such real-life experiences as purchasing and preparing food for the poor in your city or creating a family newspaper. As an individual learning opportunity, projects might involve painting a mural, writing a story, making clothing and selling online in a shop, or collecting and mounting online of visuals different plant or animal specimens. Projects can be used to make other people's lives better. Statements regarding the doctrines of service and giving can be introduced to bring clarity to the worth and purpose of the project. You may find a location like a library or community center, that would showcase the project. One year I had my grade six class write their own book, I promised and delivered that I would have their book published, showcased in our library, and promoted and marketed to parents and family members. Not a single Pulitzer winner in the lot but a deep well of learning resulted and that was good enough.

Questionnaire

The questionnaire is a well-known and frequently used type of survey form. It commonly is utilized to facilitate student opinion studies or self-appraisal procedures. Questionnaire results often are used in planning individualized programs to meet specific individual and group needs. Doing questionnaires can help young people get a more fulsome picture regarding some cultural practice like special ethnic days and why bother with drawing attention to ethnic food, practices, and peoples. Does doing so create more separation among people? Less? Discernment needs to be introduced by the adult to select out the myths from the truths. You might consider searching for a publication that would receive and publish the findings from of the questionnaire.

Reading Assignment

Well, this sounds about as exciting as watching a haircut. However, reading assignments can be quite compelling if young people have a real purpose for reading something. Start with a big question, issue or problem that lives in their world, move into establishing your genuine interest in their discovery of a real answer to their question, way to address their issue or solution to their problem. Reading assignments enable the learner to journey beyond the confines of the classroom. They merely may involve perusal of a single book or go beyond into the vast world of supplementary printed materials. The use of multiple books, typical reference volumes, current media, and created materials have value as resources for basic or supportive reading. Sometimes I've simply given a friend or student a book to read when a particular relationship principle is being called into question. The Screwtape Letters,[14] by CS Lewis for the sceptic of the Satanic, or Passion and Purity[15] by Elisabeth Elliot for those who might like support for personal decisions regarding sexual activity.

Self-Appraisal

A self-test is a series of questions, exercises, or other means of measuring personal skill, knowledge, attitudes, or other aspects of behavior. The self-testing instrument or device may be student or teacher constructed or in some instances standardized, but in each case administered by and to the individual personally. The Enneagram is good, as is the MBTI inventory.

The fascinating years are about to transition to the identity stabilizing years.

---

14. Lewis, *Screwtape Letters*.

15. Elliot, *Passion and Purity*); Elliot (1926–2015) was a popular writer and speaker, the author of "Passion and Purity," in which she made a strong argument for sexual expression to be within the marriage relationship. Today, this view is considered quaint and hardly relevant to the times we live in, but a sober second thought might not be a bad idea.

6

Later Adolescence

19 to 22 Years of Age

When given an abundance it is not time to build higher walls, it is time to build longer tables.

IRISH PROVERB

Not everyone who says to me "Lord, Lord," will enter the kingdom of heaven; but he who does the will of my Father who is in heaven.

MATTHEW 7:21

Educating for the Moral Order

CHAPTER 6 IS TITLED Systems and the Later Adolescence. Your work as a teacher (and parent who teaches) is far from done. Young people in this age period are still susceptible to acting their way into new ways of thinking. Their brain continues to be an adaptive system and develops as it experiences actions and behaviors more than it guides or leads them. This section is for the later adolescent, the young man and woman falling somewhere in the 17 to 21-year age range. The identity crisis of intimacy vs isolation remains forefront and immediate; lingering identity crises issues related to identity. Who am I, what do I stand for, how do I want to be known may still be negotiated during these ages. The program is shared praxis, action research, and problem solving based. Whatever program of learning that forms and develops the brain systems will be highlighted in this chapter. It is still important for young adults to participate on sports teams, to be in the gym doing disciplined, goal-setting type training, and participating in confidence building martial arts. Group solving of problems over a beer at the local pub might have to trump showing up at church (still not a bad idea to show up at the building from time to time but not mission critical for their development). Real conversations happen over a pint, not sitting for 60 minutes in a building on a Sunday of listening to a talk.

Out of the inner world of a person comes a relationship-based way of being. However, the question for us teaching adolescents in their later teen years is how best to inform and transform their inner world so predispositions and concepts align with choosing good and healthy actions and making life-giving decisions. The big idea of teaching is engaging with them in behaviors that align with what is beginning to emerge for them, that there does exist a moral order. That moral order is not found in some platonic abstractions. The moral order reveals itself in relationships, right relationships practiced that remove disguises and camouflages of the moral order.

My best friend and wife Ann concluded wisely that one intended outcome of our teaching is teach for right relationships in the first twenty or so years of life. Then, later one, like a bank account that grows in interest over time, what we put into young people will pays off eventually and we can take out interest payments later. Interest includes respect, kindness, forgiveness, planning to have each other's backs and much more. What is described in this section is really all about that interest.

These years are about reducing those self-serving behaviors that the person is beginning to realize has kept them from experiencing the promised freedom and peace, and ultimately right relationships and learning more about the nature of this unseen world of ethics and morals, cousins in the universe of systems. In many ways, this is a re-socializing period, a smoothing over of lousy ruts and grooves that, when pulled down into, cause the young adult lots of grief, feelings of being trapped and bad consequences.

For a parent and teacher, the focus and intended outcome of teaching should be on mentoring, walking alongside young people to focus conversations and activities on the inner world of ethics and morals. Forget the low hanging fruit we traditionally pick at such as sex, drinking, dancing, and smoking. What difference does it make, really, if your adolescent prefers computer games laden with violence? Obscenity-laden music? Drinking and smoking? These are just the leaves on the tree of a problem. Henry David Thoreau put it best: for every thousand people hacking away at the leaves of what is wrong, there is one person hacking away at its roots.[1] And then there is sex. I am told it continues to be a popular activity at this age as well. Do you encourage thou shall nots or let us talk about sex, or this music you like and how music and lyrics can and do influence us at sub-conscious levels; maybe listening to obscenity-laden music needs to be called into question or maybe not. Maybe lyrics in the songs that we sing in a building on Sunday also need to be called into question. God seems at times in much music to be more of an errand boy than the Creator of everything.

If a habit or lifestyle is undermining relationships, then we have a problem. A spiritually converted person, one with an intellect well on the way to conversion and one with an inner world being ordered using the principles of the systems of the Bible that I am about to explain, will hear and respond to the Creator, to others, to their inner voice of conscience, and to their emerging sense of the beauty of the created and natural order.

Jesus uses language from time to time that gives away something of the nature of activity requirements of his way of being. He does not say worship me; he says follow me. The goal? "Give it a try." Exploration might be the most accurate description of the nature of your education program with these young people. Their identity turning points shifts into intimacy vs alienation. Their relationship with others assumes new risks and challenges, including moral and ethical ones. The intended outcome is making a difference for good in other's life. The created and natural order should now begin to offer up a career, a vocation choice, a calling. To quote Frederick Buechner, "The place God calls you to is the place where your deep gladness and the world's deep hunger meet."[2]

---

1. Thoreau, *Walden*; Thoreau (1817–1862) wrote on a variety of topics from philosophy to natural history. He had an ability to pay close attention to the messages that nature offered and the meaning that nature offered for how people ought to live.

2. Buechner, *Wishful Thinking*.

The Five Habits of a Morally Converted Person

Every major moral or ethical battle that you have ever fought and won was won a long time before the battle took place. The same is true for lost battles. Where were the battles won against anger, attraction to pornography, gossip, hate or lust for material things? They were won in the ordering of an inner world. A set of five habits won for you the victory. They were firmly in place, practiced regularly, and valued highly. These five habits are: making inner vows; replacing old pictures in the galleries of your mind; practicing habits of right relationships; meditating on the concept of truth; and coming under mentorship.

If we can have these habits working in our lives, and if we know how to teach our adolescents these habits, their moral conversion is on its way.

Making Inner Vows

Very little works so powerfully in shaping not only behavior but also attitudes, as does an inner vow.[3] An inner vow is a promise made to oneself, often in the heat of some trying moment, to do or not to do something. I have experienced the power of vow. My inner vow, not to forgive my father's treatment of me when I needed conversations not violence old did not help me much with my hate for my father for years. The biggest issue for me was not my relationship with my father. I had other friends. It was the commandment to honor your father and mother so it will go well for you. My mom? No problem. My father? Big problem.

But it was during sensitive developmental years my "little vow" grew into a huge lifestyle. I wanted to hurt him, so I nurtured practices and habits of which I am now quite ashamed. Drugs and alcohol were best friends, gambling, too. I can laugh at this now but in 1971, I lost my beautiful 1957 Chevy station wagon in a memorable pool game. That was probably as bad as I have ever felt.

The vow of not forgiving is our most common one. Other common vows that are powerful influencers of attitudes and behaviors include the vow of never taking a risk-from someone who fears failure, ridicule, or

---

3. Sandford and Sandford, *Transformation of the Inner Man*; John (1930–2018) and his wife Paula (1931–2012) together founded and ran Elijah House for twenty years offering people the opportunity to think deeply into the conscious and subconscious causes of why they were experiencing discontent and lack of freedom. Their flagship book is "Healing the Wounded Spirit." Paula Sandford died in 2012.

embarrassment, the vow of never admitting a weakness (from someone who experienced rejection), the vow of never embracing a certain race or creed of people (from someone conditioned against a certain type of person), the vow of proceeding on a course of action in spite of someone, the vow to do something only if circumstances change (I'll love him only if he quits watching hockey games). There are many other vows we make. All are powerful, hidden influencers deeply bedded in all aspects of our lives.

Most vows are negative. They imprison one part of our lives. It is impossible to be totally free, at peace with one's self and one's world if what is at work within a person is a vow to have nothing to do with those three troublesome coworkers of yours. But vows do not have to be negative. I can make a vow to see all people as God's masterpiece. I will think the best of each person, even a person who I have not yet met. In others, I can make a vow to have the same attitude in me that was in Jesus Christ—the attitude to love despite circumstances.

I can make a vow to love my child regardless of what he or she does to me. I can make a vow of honesty, regardless of the cost; to commitment in marriage, regardless of circumstance; to faithfulness to my wife in sexual matters, regardless of pressure.

There are two approaches required of parents when vows are an issue. One is for a parent to search back into his or her life to uncover those too long hidden negative vows. Encourage your child to make good vows and help them disaffirm any negative vows they might be in the process of making.

The second approach is to encourage and confirm the positive vows your child makes. Reinforce these vows; give feedback relevant to the effectiveness of a vow your child has made.

Replacing the Picture in the Galleries of the Mind

A morally converted person has a particular image hung in the gallery of her mind. One would find there, for example, images of self, standing tall with lots of talent and gifts, someone who is effective, listened to, respected. There would be other pictures there—pictures of what is true, pure, honest and of good reputation. There is a picture there of a Creator on our sidelines who loves, and not hate and of people we love, and not hate. The voices we listen to, maybe from our moms or dads from years gone by, may need to be bracketed and replaced with new voices.

Many of us have hung pictures that are not so pretty. Small deities and uninspiring dreams. Dark pictures painted with little hope. These pictures need to be replaced. One way is to consider whose voices you are listening to, who is continuing to paint these pictures of you that you are ugly, stupid, worthless. Often it is a parent or a bully. Why bother listening then anymore? Another is to develop habits of the mind that you dwell in, on what is pure, beautiful, and holy. We need to carefully guard the way into the gallery of the mind—the eyes and ears. There is much we all have seen or heard that we wish we never had. The picture of a person sullied with someone's gossip hangs less brightly in our minds; guard the windows and doors into the mind. Those good pictures are the promises of what life can and should be–holy and pure.

Practicing Relationship; Building Habits

A habit is like a magnet. The closer you get to it, the stronger is its attraction. Every would-be lean, trim exerciser knows that. Once the habit of a noon hour workout is established, the easier it is to keep the routine of meeting your friend for that midday run or fitness class. I tell myself, prior to starting a new routine like a morning run, not to think about it, or feel about it–just do it. By the fifth or sixth session of a morning run, it is decidedly easier to put on the sweats and go out and pound the pavement. A habit is established.

What often short circuits the establishment of a good habit, like working out, is an idea that goes something like this: "I am not seeing much improvement and besides, I'll never be able to do this all year anyway, it's too much." Quitting the habit follows quickly on the heels of this idea. I forget two important ideas when I think like this. One is that my desire (to look like Arnold Schwarzenegger) and my goal (finish one workout every second day). These are vastly different and should not be confused. I cannot have my desire without reaching my goal. Forget the desire and concentrate on the goal.

Second, the intended result (looking like Arnold) and the process (working out) are connected emotionally. What do I mean by this? If I thought that in this year coming up that I would be hand washing over four thousand plates, cups, knives, and forks I might downshift and quit while I was ahead. I used to live in a household of many people, a small community of students and friends. I might get discouraged, perhaps even a bit anxious. No one can wash that many things. But the truth is, I can wash one plate (or fork) at a time. By the year's end, I have washed four thousand spoons, one at a time.

Emotionally, I can handle that. If you set a goal to read a good book through this year, you might become a wee bit worried, if the book is War and Peace, 300 pages of dense Russian literature. Reading the whole Bible? My Bible has about 1,200 pages. Three pages a day, that I can handle; 1,200 pages? I cannot handle that. I tell young basketball players not to try for 10 out of 10 foul shots. I tell them to try for one out of one foul shots. That they can handle.

A relationship-enhancing habit is built this way. One step at a time, gradually the habit's attraction becomes strong enough to hold you to it. When unhealthy habits have been established and need to be broken, the same "one step at a time" principle applies. A battle with pornography is won today and cannot be won tomorrow. When tomorrow becomes today, then it is time to battle.

When a bad habit has been established, one often finds an associated stimulus. Pornography's influence is my daily trip past the drug store. Overeating, with television. Masturbation, with boredom. Rather than fighting the habit head on, it is sometimes more effective to deal with the associated stimulus. When boredom begins to creep in, get up and go for a walk. Change the route home, avoid the drugstore. Read a book instead of watching television. By eliminating those trigger stimuli, the habit slowly recedes.

Meditating

Friends I know have taken up the timeless habit of meditating. It calms their minds but heightens their sense of awe and wonder of just being alive. To meditate is to use a different part of the brain and the result can be a release of tension. Most importantly, meditation draws us into the quietness, the stillness of simply knowing "what is" and this turns out to be the most important knowledge. Meditation might be that new possibility for you and your young person, a new practice of learning to become comfortable with being with yourself.

Mentorship

Mentorship is discipleship renamed. It is useful to rename practices, old ideas with new practices attached to them. In this case, mentorship and discipleship mean essentially the same thing and that is to observe and carefully model someone who is someone worthwhile and from whom much can be learned. My mentors are both far off and close by. Those who are far off include Mother Teresa and Winston Churchill. From Mother Teresa, I learned that to serve other people is a choice, but that vocation comes from hanging around with Christ. From Churchill[4], I learned never to quit. Close-up models include university professors who show character traits that I know to be effective. I have also wanted to be a clearer and more precise communicator. I observe clear communicators and model their technique.

Mentors come in many shapes and sizes. Once a mentor is found, access to the mentor is necessary. We need to see and think about the mentor's work. We need to make a mental representation of the mentor's behavior, then practice that behavior, sometimes over and over.

Mentors are those guides who take us into right relationship-based ethical and lifestyle actions. Most often they are not even aware that they are being observed. That is probably the best way.

The Enemies of Moral Conversion

There are two enemies that have consistently subverted young people in their late adolescent years, young people who have at least wanted to want to live fully in right relationships with the Creator, self, others, and the created and natural order. While both enemies are not obvious, one is much less obvious, and much more insidious than the other. The first is media generated axioms whose subtext is "it's all about me." Similar to the tired old religious systems of ought to, should and have to, our culture offers another Bible of abstractions, but these ones are not inclusive or

---

4. The story goes that shortly after the end of the second world war Winston Churchill, the Prime Minister of The United Kingdom, was asked to speak at Harvard. The expectant audience filled the auditorium to hear the man who inspired and motivated a country and its allies during a very dark and troubled time in history. He stood up, waited a few seconds, then said, "Never, ever, ever, ever quit." Then he sat down. That was it, the entire speech. After a few seconds, the audience stood as if one person and gave him a standing ovation.

have any real potential to bring good into neighborhoods, other lives, society and culture, or above all, individual lives.

It is hard to be different when you are 18 years old. When a young person decides, for example, to avoid the tyranny of the dating game that reduces sexuality to conquests, and chooses to save sexual contact until in a committed partnership, a marriage, that person is flying into the face of what is culturally acceptable. When a wife and husband respect each other, cherish and act in love to each other, the paradigmatic culture says that any submission that results is a wrong outcome. What remains is okay. The woman is being oppressed and the husband is perpetuating oppression. They, too, are flying into the face of our culture when equality and mutual respect become an honoring of both male and female similarities as well as their differences. Accentuating just differences creates denser separation, thicker borders as someone once out, between and among people.

Part of conversion is being "conscientized" to what is cultural and what is good and right, what is self-serving but could be made into something sacred. Some young people I have taught over the years appear to have remained unconvinced and unconverted, still entangled in relationship-disaffirming ways. They promote building higher walls to keep 'them' out, taking care of 'our' children and not the refugee child, and that capitalism is deeply Christian. They choose lifestyles that can harm in many ways, including building lousy memories.

An Enemy?

The second enemy is for many today much more disguised, and more subversive, and likely more influential to more Christians than is culture. The bad guy is the church. The church has been kicked around by non-Christians and Christians alike. So, this might sound like I am putting one more lick on the "sorry old church." But I am not just kicking someone when she is down (and the church is most certainly down and maybe almost out). I am doing what others have been trying to do, to wake up the church from sleep. I like the idea of church. The idea has all the wisdom in it of a loving and just Creator. Imagine a situation where tens and hundreds of people come together to worship their Creator. Imagine a place, a "lighthouse" where people can search together for what is and is not true. Imagine a situation where we can show practical love and receive practical love. Imagine a place where deep hurts are healed, gifts and talents can be used to change lives, children can be nurtured into the things of God, and lifelong, loving relationships can be formed. Imagine a situation where, like soldiers before war, people are equipped and strengthened to do relationship-building battles, to take back enemy territory by sharing Jesus's ideas of peace, justice, and love, inclusive of everyone. Imagine the safest and best place on earth? The church? Maybe not yet.

When You Wish, What You Get Is a Wish.

What is true about the church is something less than what I do imagine. A years-ago interview of Chuck Colson[5] said a lot about how the church is perceived by the culture. In Virginia (I believe) when that state experienced a statewide blackout, the legislative decision was to cut out all non-essential services to preserve power. The first non-essential services to go were the churches. Samuel Clemens (alias Mark Twain) once said to someone, "Don't let your schooling interfere with your education."[6] He also was the one who said "I've personally known many people who have concluded that they don't want church to interfere with their Christianity."[7] This is sad, but I get it. I think you do, too.

From a recent research project by Dr. Bibby at the University of Lethbridge in Alberta, Canada, came a finding that is common to virtually every research project that's ever been done on the topic of church and Christianity. He found that there are many more professing Christians out there who claim to buy into Jesus's teaching than who go to church.[8] In other words, people are opting out from church, preferring to go it alone. It is tough going out there along with people in community let alone "alone."

---

5. Chuck Colson (1931–2012) was a Watergate co-conspirator, writer, and converted to Christianity later in his life. He worked with prisoners in a ministry that has persisted and continues to offer mercy and hope to prisoners.

6. Know.u, "Don't Let Your Schooling Interfere with Your Education."

7. Samuel Clemens; Clemens (1835–1910), alias Mark Twain, was the author of "Huckleberry Finn" and "Tom Sawyer, and was a humorist and speaker. Famous quotes of Clemens include "Don't let your schooling interfere with your education," and "I have had a lot of bad experiences in my life, and some of them have actually happened."

8. Bibby, *Emerging Generation*.

Go into most churches and you will find the major age portion of our culture (16 to 35 years of age) underrepresented. The one exception is the more charismatic, up-beat churches which seem to attract younger people with their music and drama-oriented worship services. What is most troublesome, however, is not the emptying of the pews, or even what appears the eventual demise of the local corner church. What is most troublesome, and what is perhaps the real cause of the church looking moribund, is what it offers up as solutions, "fifth rate poetry set to sixth rate music."[9] Almost total reliance on abstractions delivered in different ways, some quite slick, but most however, largely boring.

Like you perhaps, I remain hopeful about churches and their courageous choices regarding right relationships, in gender, inclusion, homosexuality, or the beauty of the stories of the Scriptures. I wonder about the investment of billions of dollars for the building of churches (that are just buildings where the church meets) while most of the world starves. Pursuit of justice and right relationships seems to be secondary or presented as a by-product only, the results of believing the right things. We need more hints and guesses regarding the particular way of the kingdom, of right relationships first and foremost practiced among people, than we need ideas.

The Church and Systems

Regarding the role of the church and the systems of a right relationship way of being in the world. the trouble has been in the mistaking of what is secular and what is sacred, and the accommodation of what is secular into what is sacred in the teaching and preaching found in churches. The fact is it is all sacred. The way of right relationships is life; it is not a way of life. If it is life, we should be identifying for people the true and holy life–systems as identified in Jesus's teachings. It is all holy in right relationships.

Teachers should be mentioning to young people how to see sacredly, that their lives are already ordered, that their breath, their heartbeat, their lives are sacred. Fathers should be mentioning (through modeling) how to live right relationship-based lives so to be able to come to recognize what they are seeing and experiencing is sacred. We should be mentioning to men how to assume leadership. We should be mentioning to couples that to work for love, peace, and harmony in a marriage is sacred. Forget the

---

9. Lewis, "Answers to Questions on Christianity," 22–30.

submission teaching. We should be mentioning to young singles what to do and not to do before marriage. We should be teaching more about money management principles, practical techniques for loving others and for using the sacred gift of one's time wisely. As Malcolm Muggeridge once said, every happening, great and small, is a parable whereby God speaks to us, and the art of life is to get the message."[10]

There are explicit and implicit systems in ways of being that come about through right relationships. These are the "what to dos and how to do them" practices of the way that arise from an inner world made true. When Christian men and women, friends, and spouses mentor each other when they truly do fellowship together, they are motivating one another to follow the true systems of Christianity.

There are too many relationship building systems which are not being encouraged enough in homes, schools, and churches. Here are some of them.

The Later Years' Adolescent and Christian Systems

For the late adolescent, the teaching of how to be in the world in particular ways, and how to practice right relationships becomes particularly critical. The ruts and grooves are still being laid down in the age ten brain, in the mind of a young person. The systems which need to be taught include chastity, prayer, and selective holy dating practices in preparation for marriage, deferring gratification through goal setting, managing money and time with the principle of stewardship as a guide, systematic and planned approaches to eating, exercise and sleep, regular quiet times, planned periods of active prayer and Bible reading, and the developing and nurturing of gifts and talents. Here the shotgun approach of trying everything needs to be put aside in favor of a more rigorous, focused development of a gifting. Excellence is to be sought after here. It is time to put away childish things in these teen years, and to develop maturity.

In these later adolescent years, there are great stresses in our young people. However, I believe we have created many of the stresses by creating a "cultural adolescence." We have little indication cross-culturally that adolescence must be a time of upheaval, turmoil, and rebellion. I believe we have created a no-man's land between the ages of 14 to 21 when we expect turmoil and therefore get it, and when we give young people little

10. Muggeridge, "Malcolm Muggeridge Quotes."

of the solid, meaningful practices needed to regulate their inner moral/ethical lives. I think sometimes we expect too much and demand too little from the adolescent regarding how they should live.

I believe the chief cause of anxiety and despair in our culture is the absence of systems designed into the structures of organizations, including church, school, and business, that build right relationships. Systems include how to act (golden rule) and think (want what is best for the other), evident and even taught in homes, schools, and churches upon which a young person can regulate their life. Without a system, an adolescent does "grow up absurd"[11] as Paul Goodman said in his book.

The Later Years Adolescent and Right Ways of Being in the World

There are late adolescent systems which have been neglected and the cost has been great. Our future as a healthy society is threatened today because of a huge debt, one part of which you and I carry. The teaching of a system towards a stewardship-orientation and a debt-free approach to money management is needed. Also, we need to hear how to be husbands, wives, and parents. There are systems regarding being a healthy family which every father and mother need to practice. A correct, true system has the father loving the mother, the mother loving the father; together they manage the house, the children. Gender is a schema and not a given. They grow together in relationship-building.

The purpose of teaching systems, re-socializing if necessary, is to order a young person's immediate "inner" world into understanding right relationships, and the new futures that just might be possible. The objectives of teaching any system are generally the same. They are to encourage someone to be responsible to God and to others, to develop discernment regarding what is right, true, holy, etc., and what is not, to promote love, joy, and peace in relationships, and to facilitate success in every aspect of one's life: material, physical, emotional, and spiritual.

The Tactics in Teaching Systems

The following tactics are helpful in promoting the systems of the kingdom of God in schools, homes, or churches.

11. Goodman, *Growing Up Absurd*.

Anecdotal Record

The anecdotal record is a descriptive account of events, episodes, or circumstances in the daily life of the student that preserves significant incidents and information concerning actual student behavior for subsequent review. Like a journal or diary, and as such, it is an aid to help the teacher or parent to determine the most effective instructional and encouragement procedures. The young person is identifying what he is doing (or not doing) regarding, let us say, relationships. The major purpose of the anecdotal record is to provide a clear perspective and reference to certain kinds of behavior through systematic observation and reflection. This is somewhat like a journal. It is not meant to be used against the young person, but to give a reference point for teacher-initiated discussion and ongoing conversations. In an anecdotal record, the tactic is to point out the notion of subtexts, that what is not explicit is far more interesting than what is. To create a new scenario starts with conversations that go to the core or essence of any issue, question, or problem.

Conference: Formal and Planned

A conference is a meeting of individuals for the purpose of presenting information, finding answers to questions, discovering solutions to problems, or of adjusting differences of opinion. It is the pooling of the knowledge and experience of individuals through consultation and discussion of common problems or interests. Then, the mature individual can bring the creators ideas found in the Scriptures to bear on the problem to inform it. The conference may be composed of only a couple of persons, or a large number. All conferences, however, are organized with the definite purpose or objective of confirming or disconfirming systems of living. Conferences also involve discussion through which decisions can be made. The tactic is to permit the meaning of the experience of listening or participating in the conference, reveal itself later. Conversations later with the young person become the gateway to meaning.

Counseling

Counseling consists of individualized and personalized assistance, advice, or deliberation designed to help the young person make necessary adjustments or achieve that which she could be accomplishing. In use by the teacher, or parent, counseling usually is conducted through personal interview in which the student is aided to make certain choices or decisions. Relational principles are used as the basis for decision making. For example, counseling from a personal perspective would encourage a young person to forgive, rather than forget, or to know how to say sorry, I was wrong, how can I make it right, rather than to just feel sorry.

Drill

Drill consists of the systematic and repetitive practice of certain fundamental skills to help bring about automatic response, accuracy, perfection, or speed of performance. It can be used for the corrective purpose of eliminating errors, or for overcoming hesitancy or uncertainty. I wonder, if we were drilled in how to demonstrate respect for individual differences, this wouldn't help but develop the habit of being more respectful in our relationships. Training, the athletic metaphor, is a dying idea in teaching the systems necessary to live fully as we all would desire.

Coaching

Guidance is a form of systematic assistance to help young people assess their abilities, capabilities, and limitations in order that they might learn and live more effectively. The approach involves a dynamic interpersonal relationship designed to influence the ultimate behavior of the individual. It can be carried out individually or in groups. Modeling is a powerful, "implicit" socializer. A young person will only allow guidance in her life from someone she esteems and trusts. Ruts and grooves need to be smoothed over in re-socializing educational programs; new ruts and grooves need to be laid down in socializing programs. Here you need to resist the urge to be a sage on their stage; rather, you need to be the guide on their side. You do not just send them along their merry way to a six-day hike through the Rocky Mountains, you go with them.

Interview

An interview is a face-to-face procedure designed to elicit information outside the classroom or home, which is related to a current personal problem, issue, question, or topic of study the young person is intrigued with. Interviews of appropriate individuals are best conducted in groups of not more than three. Opportunities to report back to a family, group, or peer, in summary form, is fun. Teachers also use the interview technique with students and parents. Interviewing can be very enlightening, used as an informal tactic by young people. The relationship big idea is to practice interviewing skills that keep conversations going. Appreciative inquiry tactics open up responses that any critical response simply will not.

Lectures

The lecture method is a formal presentation of information, usually an oral exposition. A TED talk is a form of lecture. It generally uses certain essential facts or basic information to impart knowledge, create interest, influence opinion, stimulate activity, or promote critical thinking. There is a knowledge base in the systems of Christianity. Parents and teachers can clarify and interpret for young people regarding what this knowledge means for them by formally presenting it to them, or better, going along with them to a formal lecture given by an expert.

Lecture-Discussion

The lecture-discussion incorporates the desirable qualities of both the lecture and discussion into a formal technique. It consists of a verbal form of presentation with provision for clarification and further enlightenment through class and children participation and intergroup exchange. Young people could design and present TEDx talks themselves for example, become the lecturer and discussion leader. I would have TEDx talks be an assignment in my university classes and the results were amazing. I would commit to showcasing these to see if we could have one or more actually live as official TEDx talks in our city.

Outside Speaker

The outside speaker, sometimes referred to as a resource person or guest speaker, is an individual who is invited to talk to a group on a given topic or subject. The person usually is selected because of some special knowledge, talent, or experience which classifies him as an expert or an authority in the field. The most memorable times in my university courses were when I had a Syrian refugee speak about being welcomed home by a customs officer at the airport, a student with dyslexia explain how she compensated and became an A student, and a Kenyan man and father to the largest family in the world (over 12,000 children adopted) speak about what motivated him and his wife to give their lives to addressing the great injustices of poverty and abandonment of children.

Question and Answer

The question and answer technique ordinarily is developed in a discussion-type setting. It is best used with resource persons. The question and answer approach could be silent and non-threatening. The tactic for the teacher is to dignify the wrong responses (Maxine Greene)[12] to permit the important process for some young person to think their way out loud to some clarity.

Review

Review entails the re-examination or re-evaluation of material or discussions previously presented or studied. It involves an overview to attempt to identify the most important ideas and concepts. The review represents a guided effort which facilitates clarity of understanding and the formulation of final generalizations. A variety of related techniques is commonly used in the review session. We forget episodes of deliverance in our own lives. Review helps us remember. We forget the systems; review helps us remember. Simply ask young people the question of "Remember when_____?" Young people are not over and against testing; in fact, they respond to it with energy and intelligence. Standardized tests, trivial pursuit type of questions (e.g. name that river), and 'guess what is in our heads' type of questions are largely useless. Create a new prototype, prove a concept, write a story and more are the best ways to test. More below.

---

12. Maxine Greene (1917–2014). An educator and philosopher, her seminal work was *Releasing the Imagination: Essays on Education, the Arts, and Social Change*. In addition to reminders to teach for social change, she tells us to remember to include those who have previously not had a voice in our education.

Assessment and Evaluation

A test, examination, or quiz is a device or procedure used to measure ability, achievement, attitude, interest, understanding, or some other aspect of behavior. It may be objective or subjective in its measurement. There are numerous types of tests, such as those designed to indicate aptitude, appreciation, comprehension, character, cooperation, deduction, intelligence, knowledge, and personality. The teacher ordinarily is concerned with oral or written tests incorporating questions of an essay, multiple-choice, matching, association, true-false, identification, missing parts, completion, short answer, or problem-solving. The problem is that testing, like training, has fallen on hard times. If you have used any kind of testing with young people, you will see just exactly how engaged they become. The issue is not with testing per se, it is with what is done with the results. The practice of explicitly comparing results with other young people's results is thankfully a dying practice Young people are perfectly capable of comparing results and will do so, but to legitimize it by explicitly doing comparisons induces low achievement needs in some young people, ones who have a history of low achievement as determined by comparisons.

Maker Space

Maker spaces are set spaces set aside and designated to develop projects. Maker exhibits exhibit are displays of projects and other visible expressions of learning. The aims can include informing observers about a subject of educational significance and affirming the work of the presenter. It usually provides a realistic impression using three-dimensional objects rather than flat materials, and frequently makes use of sound, color, and motion. An exhibit may include posters, pictures, charts, graphs, specimens, and other similar materials. It also may incorporate recordings, films, slides, and other audio or visual materials.

Cartoon

The cartoon is a form of comic art which can be used in education to depict important events, personalities, or circumstances. It presents a simulated but usually easily recognized and popular illustration of selected activity or behavior. The technology advantage is for young people now, for producing video, you tube and other forms of technology-based cartoons that showcase something true about right relationships, but in light, non-turgid ways.

Research Project/Chart

The chart consists of visual symbols which may be used to summarize, contrast, compare, or explain subject matter. Charts reflect a wide range of interests and are commonly referred to by type, such as narrative, skill development, creative expression, reference, experience, teacher composed, informational, or guidance charts. They represent one of the oldest forms of teaching.

Graphing

Graphs involve various levels of visual expression ranging from a simple presentation of information to the most abstract statistical analysis. Graphic presentation serves the major functions of providing a concise summary, indicating a comparison, showing a relationship, or otherwise explaining a concept or idea. Young people enjoy graphing their progress in all kinds of areas in their life such as soccer goals and assists, number of accomplishments in school and results of observations in the natural and created order like changes in landscape.

Mapping

A map typically is a representation, usually on a flat surface, of the face of the earth or some part of it. It shows relative size and position according to a scale, projection, or represented position. Maps can be metaphorical, including concept maps, mapping out circumstances, people and events that have led the young person to where they are today in their relationships. I ask my students to map their life story and place stepping-stones on the map of people, circumstances, and events that have taken them to where they are today.

Model

The model is a recognizable three-dimensional imitation or replica of a real object. It usually is identical to the original in most respects except size and incorporates the essential features of the object or procedure. With 3D printing and design thinking as an educational program, model making is exciting. I have an Ugandan friend who has conceived and is currently making prototypes of models of wheelchairs made out of bamboo, an incredibly strong and eco-friendly source of material, at a fraction of the cost of a regular wheelchair. Who would have thought it?

Mock-Up

The mock-up is an instructional device that approximates a scale model of a real object or part of the object. It alters the elements of the original object, often simplifying or exaggerating details, to concentrate only on certain aspects to make them more teachable. Mock-ups commonly are used to help understand complex processes, whether an engine, a certain function of the human body, or the way right relationships can and do work.

Pamphlets

A pamphlet is a paper bound or website loaded document, usually consisting of a limited number of pages, which is ordinarily devoted to a subject. The content often is quite restricted in scope and covers a given subject in a somewhat general manner. Many free and inexpensive pamphlets are available for instructional use. My university class made a set of pamphlets titled, "Welcome Home," to be used by agencies in Calgary to provide newcomers with information regarding recreational possibilities, agencies that help newcomers with language training and access to free resources in libraries.

Poster

A poster is a pictorial or symbolic visual representation designed to catch and hold the observer's attention long enough to implant a significant message or idea. It is intended to convey a single easily grasped idea in an emphatic fashion, either in hard copy or digital format. The use of the poster is many centuries old having been utilized by early traders and merchants to advertise their wares. In the early years of my teaching, my students would create posters titled, "*Classroom Manifesto*," developed together and highlighting the ways we were to be respectful to each other, the classroom and to themselves. Personalized co-creation of these manifestos meant long lasting effects. Websites are today's best locations for posters, particularly if the student is promoting a personally designed social enterprise or business.

Current Events

Current events are concerned with immediate or recent happenings which may be expressed through various means of communication. They include important circumstances reported through newspapers, periodicals, popular magazines, radio, television, interviews, or other informative sources. Current events serve as a medium for relating local, state, national, or global occurrences to an understanding of everyday life. More so, current events can be opportunities for young people to clarify and sharpen perspectives on hot button items like global warming, immigration, and nationalistic movements in some countries. One opportunity provided with attention to critical events is to think critically-analyze information sources, learn to compare to other sources of information regarding the current event, deduce motivation and assess the track record of person's involved in the current event.

Demonstration

The demonstration is a process of graphic explanation of a selected idea, relationship, or phenomenon. It involves the use of materials and provides a visual experience which is usually increased in value by verbal explanation. The demonstration generally is utilized with a group of observer/participants by someone who is an expert on the given subject. It often is used to set a goal of activity or to define standards of performance. Performances can be recorded and if permitted, posted in social media or on a young person's blog or website.

Travel

Travel to some location other than the normal classroom for educational purposes. Most cities have ethnic communities full of interesting places. Confirmatory field trips serve as a reinforcement for previously acquired learning while the exploratory excursion fulfills the basic function of discovery. Each approach is a structured attempt to provide an on-the-spot observation of some specific process, undertaking, or activity.

The next age phase is best described as the journey from learner to teacher. The transition is from learning through minds-on doing of activities that build relationships, to leading and teaching relationship building activities.

7

Young Adults

21 to 24 Years of Age

Whereby are given unto us exceeding great and precious promises: that by these ye might be partakers of the divine nature, having escaped the corruption that is in the world through lust. And beside this, giving all diligence, add to your faith virtue; and to virtue knowledge; And to knowledge temperance; and to temperance patience; and to patience godliness; And to godliness brotherly kindness; and to brotherly kindness charity. For if these things be in you, and abound, they make you that ye shall neither be barren nor unfruitful in the knowledge of our Lord Jesus Christ.

—2 PETER 1:4–8, KJV

Putting on Big Girl and Boy Underpants

THE TEACHING STAGE IS set now for some of the most effective possibilities in new teaching practices based on old ideas. This stage covers the period of early adulthood when people are doing more than just inquiring into intimate relationships; they are taking exploratory trips into intimate relationships, learning to love with promise and commitment, in all its fire and fury, inclusive of all its perturbations. Hopefully for the young adult, being in right relationships is now understood as the way to live. Obviously, given the epidemic of loneliness and depression, alienation and angst, right relationships may or may not be understood as the way of being in the world that alone brings life, but it is not always practiced. Perhaps it all seems too risky, to love and live fully alive, and the back door of lots of young adult lives is slippage back into isolation, into alienation.

It is in the early years of adulthood when the idea of friendship with the Creator is either fully embraced as being good enough now for the long haul, or too simple to be true and there is more comfort into slipping back to some image of a scary, hard to please God except with embracing some religious markers like making a decision for Jesus, believing that if the Bible says so, then it is true, and keep a short list of sins. It is early adulthood when the desire to seek justice for a world is longing for a real place to be, a lever to stand on, a scaffold to live on and out from. Young adults are warm to the practice of seeking justice for the neighborhood rather than choosing the way of building higher walls and loving your neighbor as yourself.

I appear to be _____ but really I am _____.

Do this writing activity in a workshop with young adults. Ask them to complete the stems, fill in the blanks. Promise that you will protect their anonymity and set a stage of trust. Collect the completed stems and read them back to the group. The responses will be sobering, and many questions raised that will take time, opportunity, and mentorship to address. But let us start here with a look into the level of personal reality we call the subconscious.

Who do you appear to be? Who are you, really?

A Psycho-Social Perspective

Erik Erikson tells us that for the young adult man or woman, with an already well-developed personal identity, the possibilities are good for the development of intimate, long-lasting and secure relationships, perhaps even one special relationship.[1] Love, the ability to give and receive

---

1. Erik Erikson; Erikson (1902–1994) was the grandfather of the theory of identity and its formation over time, in stages and throughout a lifespan. A life-crisis is characteristic of each stage of a person's identity development. For example, young children aged 6 to 12 are resolving the life crisis of competency vs inferiority. The resolution of this crisis is along a continuum and rarely to one end of the spectrum or the other. In other words, young children develop an identify towards competency provided they get good at activities like friendship making, sports, school, and other activities. However, if they do not have success experiences, they develop their identity towards inferiority. Erikson proposed eight life crises, each with a resolution and

affection, nurturing, and appreciation, is the virtue that is the result of the successful resolution of the young adult's core life crises of intimacy vs isolation. A sense of isolation and loneliness is a lousy resolution, and more likely for people who do not have a well-developed sense of self, an identity developed through successful resolution of previous life crises at previous stages.

A Cognitive Perspective

From the cognitive development world, Jean Piaget[2] has told us much about the stages of young people's cognitive development. His groundbreaking theories of cognitive development have influenced teachers up to, but not necessarily inclusive of, early adulthood. Piaget describes the new cognitive abilities of young adolescence as "formal operational thinking." Later, developmental psychologists have conjectured about an early adulthood fifth stage of cognitive development called *post formal operational thinking*. For the young adult, relativistic thinking begins to slip into the crevices of thinking that up to this stage, while imaginative and full of new possibilities, has been often characterized by absolutes. Thinking in a new key for the adolescent now takes on acceptance of ambiguities, new possibilities that may have different entry points, different expressions, and consequences. We see evidence of post formal operational thinking in young adult's acceptance of LGBTQ.

For the young adult, life is now being experienced as full of complexities. Up to young adulthood, complexities were just not that important or relevant. Absolutes, particularly religious ones, answered most questions, or they did not. But life happens to even the most absolute of thinkers. The causes for the shift to relativism from absolutism are largely experientially driven. Young adults inevitably experience broken relationships, consequences of wrong-headed decisions and many other major and minor setbacks and disappointments. The disintegration of their birth family perhaps has been resolved; maybe a new integration has resulted, maybe not. Life now feels like they are moving from the minor leagues to the major leagues. Money, once necessary only for personal

---

identity development outcome along a continuum.

2. Jean Piaget's work reminds us who teach that while development can follow an invariant pattern, the timing of the onset of a next phase of development is not invariant but unique to each person.

luxuries, is now a non-option if rent or mortgages need to be paid, and relationships like marriage and jobs, careers and religious organisations, perturbations, ambiguities and differing opinions are acceptable. Like a silent informer, however, absolutes still lurk in some file folder of the mind and when considered do provide the most psychological security.

Young adults can be firmly over and against climate change while being able to consider the sources of evidence, the rationality of arguments for and against and logic. For the young adult with religious inclinations, the Bible is now a suspect document. They know that a 7-day creation story is just that, a story. But who can they trust to talk about their beliefs? The Bible now takes on significance for what it really is, a bit of history, lots of poetry, narrative-rich with stories about nations being captive and making lots of bad and sometimes good decisions.

The issues of intelligence turn from "How intelligent are you?" to "How are you intelligent?" Young adults have developed recognizable intelligences in some recognizable area[3] (Howard Gardener). You have met young adults with high interpersonal intelligence, are simply good with people; or musical intelligence and are expressing this intelligence with music. These are the lucky young adults; they have a scaffold for effective relationships, a talent, an intelligence that can serve them well in making and keeping intimate friendships.

A Moral Perspective

Lawrence Kohlberg tells us that young adulthood's moral thinking may be characterized by a morality of contract, of individual rights, and of democratically accepted law.[4] Similar to other stage theories, some individuals never reach this stage of social contract, or, something is right and decisions should follow based on the law and what is best for society and everyone else. Because Kohlberg was influenced by Piaget and the

3. Gardner, *Frames of Mind*; strongly influence by Jean Piaget, his ground-breaking theory began with an observation that most theories of intelligence are too narrow and therefore limiting for understanding how people learn.

4. Lawrence Kohlberg (1927–1987). Stage theorist, influenced by Jean Piaget, whose research was about judgments people make in hypothetical moral situations. Initial stages of moral judgements aligned closely with Piaget's concrete stage of operational thinking; therefore, moral judgements were based on what is concrete, e.g. fear of punishment or seeking rewards. Upper stages of moral judgements were more aligned with Piaget's formal operations and could be as high as based on some universal moral principles.

concepts drawn from stage theories and cognitive psychology, progress to higher stages of thinking may or not be characteristic of the young adult.

However, young adults typically land down in post conventional morality (aligned with post formal operational thinking) is the stage individuals will value the desires of the majority and the well-being of society; their thinking is centred on these concepts. Some adults do move into the rarified atmosphere of universal rights and wrongs influencing thinking.

One critique among many of Kohlberg's work is that he is largely cognitive based, male-oriented and his stages do not necessarily predict how people will behave and what they will do. For example, when there is conflict in a controversial issue like right to die with dignity, post conventional young adults may believe that it is better if people simply follow the law. However, in the higher stage of post conventional moral thinking (Stage 6), individuals thinking may be characterized by "universal ethical principles." In this stage, individuals do what they think is right, even if it conflicts with the law. At this stage, people act according to their internalized standards of morality.[5]

Because so few people attain stages 5 or 6, Kohlberg questioned the validity of these stages at his Level 3, though he later proposed an additional seventh stage, which he described as the "cosmic" stage in which individuals are able to consider the effect of their actions on the universe as a whole.[6] Carol Gilligan[7] tells us that Kohlberg's work was male-oriented (it was) and male orientations to justice are quite different than that of females who are more relationship-based and considerate of people more than abstractions; prefer to think through the framework of relationships over some absolute concept of justice.

A Faith Development Perspective

James Fowler says that young adults may be at the Individuative-Reflective Stage when they start seeing and thinking in new possibilities, and that, in fact, believe that there just may be new possibilities of being a human being in a difficult and confusing world.[8] Their own beliefs are now up for questions; disappointment with previous ways of being "in faith"

5. Papalia et al., "Physical and Cognitive Development in Adolescence," 376.
6. Papalia et al., "Physical and Cognitive Development in Adolescence," 377.
7. Gilligan, *In a Different Voice*.
8. Fowler, *Stages of Faith*.

can slip into disillusionment. It is not uncommon for young adults to be viewed as fallen Christians, Jews, or Muslims. They are moving towards a stage characterized by skepticism and for some adults this becomes a permanent home. Constructive faith is also lurking ahead; however, where older adults are ready to accept ambiguity and not just logic only as trustworthy a foundation for faith.

A Psychoanalytic Perspective

Young adults are actively interested in, intrigued by and open to personal understandings of their subconscious. Early adulthood is often a time of awakening to issues of false self/true self. The psychoanalytic perspectives of Freud, Adler, Erikson, Fowler, Kohlberg, Gilligan, and ultimately Jung, may provide some important insights, leads into understandings for young men and women about who they really are, what they stand for, and how they want to be known. Most importantly, the psychoanalytic perspective can help the young adult begin the hard work that for many is a lifelong endeavor, understanding and resolving the causes and effects of early childhood experiences. For that reason and others, doing the Enneagram is an important activity sometime during early adulthood years.

Here is why? The main theme of all psychoanalytic theories is that personality is a dynamic (verb) activity, an interplay among forces in the subconscious. Personality is not static (noun). The subconscious (below the level of what you and I are conscious or aware of) forces developed through experiences, often in childhood, lead to the emergence of a personality.

Revisiting Freud

For example, in Sigmund Freud's theory of the personality[9] a strong ego (or weak one) emerged in the young adult over the previous two decades of their life. The ego serves the interests of the id, the passionate, self-serving part of the personality. It protects the personality as well by developing mechanisms that turn out to work well, so the young adult has learned. Projecting blame on another for one's mistakes, for example,

---

9. Sigmund Freud (2007). His influence continues to be evident in counseling and therapy, despite criticism that he generated his theory based on limited research with a small sample of women.

are there and active to manage the agenda of the passions we experience, rationalization; the hunter's explanation for killing animals, it is a necessary part of good conservation (instead of I get a kick out of killing an animal). Sublimation-writing the naughty novel (instead of watching pornography or visiting sex trade workers). Rejection-she hates me (but I really hate her). Repression-pushing it down deeply into the subconscious. Displacement-satisfying an urge with something else-kick the dog not your professor. And denial-it simply did not happen.

Freud proposed as well that a father's protection and the experience of feeling protected is more important for healthy psychological development than is a mother's love.[10]

Carl Jung

With Carl Jung, we have an emphasis on archetypes that live in the subconscious of all people.[11] Archetypes are universal, mythical, and character-based human motifs that drive us forward to fulfill ego-defined agendas. One may be more influential in our personality, but more likely that more than one influences our behaviors. For example, I have come to recognize that in my life the archetype of ruler or lord may be the archetype of a lord or ruler, whose behavior above this subconscious reality is lord-like, ruler, and boss. My behaviors in early adulthood, particularly in raising my children, were ruler-like. They served my ego-based interests in, and deep need for, security and significance. However, in my later adult years, I came to see that who I was, that really, my true self was an archetype that had been largely unexplored, under nourished, underdeveloped. My true self was that of a nurturer.

For Jung, the cast of archetypical characters found deep in people's sub conscious, developed through early and middle childhood experiences, good and bad, include ruler, sage, jester, rule breaker, and hero. Jung named these ego types. Each ego type has a set of observable characteristics that are dead give-aways of their ego type. For example, the hero's main desire is to continually demonstrate his or her value, and worthiness through brave actions. His or her core desire is being good at things,

---

10. Freud.

11. Carl Jung (1961). The well-worn MBTI (personality testing) is based on Jung's notions of the inner world, the sub conscious formed during sensitive periods and critical events in childhood.

achieving and demonstrating mastery and excellence in everything her or she does. His or her core fear is being viewed as weak or a quitter. His or her choices in relationships, jobs and schooling is first and foremost to look like he or she is all together and very good at what they do. He or she looks for the next adventure in large measure to continue to serve his or her ego interests of being a hero.

Alfred Adler

In Adler's theory[12], overt behaviors serve a primary mandate, to compensate for an innate inferiority complex. We are born with an inferiority complex, a personality inclination of not being good enough. Our behaviors, even in early childhood, are chosen to compensate for this sense that we are not good enough. For a person in early adulthood, the ego continues the work of compensation. For example, the young man or woman may experience the first of what might be many disintegrations, the breaking apart of that family structure that defined and nurtured them. The young adult chooses behaviors that compensate for the threatening presence of a new reality, independence, and redefinition of what the birth family means. The new reality perhaps includes blame and development of a sense of victimhood, both good compensatory responses.

Sometimes, early adulthood is the time when is complete by being accommodated to. The young adult has negotiated out where he or she fits in the family he left, what this new reintegration means for them, their partners and perhaps even for children to come. The struggle now to reintegrate into a new family is a major sociological challenge. Independence still feels good, but the uncertainties of past family experiences coupled with the risks perceived to be there in a future family create some new anxieties.

Young adults need to experience community of some sort. The hockey team and book club, being part of a staff in a school and working with a team at the food bank on Friday night are more than benign, fun activities. They serve developmental need for belonging with and to others.

Young adults are, as well, negotiating out whether or not to be part of a religious community and under what conditions would they belong to a church body or other system that primarily brokers in religious ideas,

---

12. Alfred Adler (1954); A contemporary of Jung and intellectual giant in his own right.

and from time to time does things together. They want to feel that they are part of something big and transcendent. Singing lousy poetry set to mediocre music in songs in church might have them humming along but singing Amazing Grace will inspire them and keep them showing up to the building on Sundays.

At this age they need to be over and against something, anything, along with others. Climate change, corporate tax slippage, gender and more. Together with other adults they need to be for something. Save the whales, right to life and equity in schools. Above all they need mentors and coaches who will affirm in a critical friend way their personalized intellectual pursuits, ones that speak meaningfully into the internal and external realities these young people are living into and from. They need to spend time in the abstractions but not camp there—the visible expressions of Jesus's way of right relationships.

They need to be mentors themselves, to be leaders now, someplace, somehow with intellectual honesty, contemplation. They need to tell their stories of resolving issues, addressing problems, and answering real questions that have lived and continue to live in their world. They have personalized understandings of the subconscious and the double bind and want to continue to go into both universes, to continue to learn more about these and other worthy subjects for them to investigate.

The ultimate desire is for the young adult to take up life in real, lived in proximity-based community and be a full-on participant with someone else, perhaps a partner in marriage but a soul mate for sure.

When the young adult begins to give in to issues of justice and injustice and begins to want to do more than to ache for the hurt and pain he sees around him, and begins to ask, "What can I do?", then that person is moving comfortably into Jesus's way of being in the world for young adults.

The young adult can be taken in and influenced by a pioneering approach to being in the world. They generally love and want challenge. Many young adults, live day to day in overly psychologized, "settler" type of Jesus follower. I am often asked by my students what can I do, I want to make a difference but do not know how? My advice continues to be for them to take what they enjoy doing and think about ways to leverage it to make a difference. Writers-write; athletes raise money through marathons; thinkers offer ideas, activists march. Actions which nurture right relationships with young adults.

I have listed ten deliberate and planned "actions" that teachers and parents can either organize or put their young men and women into. Each activity has its own purpose and its own objectives, but the overall aim is for the young person to become entrenched into a service mentality, to be in constant love with acting, and by learning what it really means to do God's work as opposed to merely working for God.

Walkabouts

The young person has set out, on his own, to tackle and solve an imposing spiritual or social problem. They may work part-time for a year in a soup kitchen, go to Mexico to help rebuild houses after an earthquake, or go on a two-week retreat of fasting and prayer. The personal meeting of the challenge includes overcoming fear, marshaling all available tools, and not quitting. Keeping a diary helps with reflections later. Whatever walkabout is chosen, the actual activity can be multi-dimensional with multi-outcomes. For some young people I have coached on different walkabouts, the intended outcome was a conscientization, a wakeup call to the similarities and differences, and meaning of both, within peoples of the world. For others it was an anxiety reducer, a desensitization experience while being carefully coached. For others it was to develop competencies in designing and implementing learning experiences in schools that have limited resources, e.g. using school yard materials to teach science.

Short-Term Purposeful Work

The young person can spend a summer working as a housekeeper or nanny for a family working in an international setting. There are dozens of agencies and organizations that sponsor shorter term work and with just a little bit of study and due diligence to assess an organization, a good choice can be made. My son spent time working on an organic farm in Costa Rica. My youngest daughter spent time working in a very poor neighborhood of Santo Domingo. My eldest daughter working at Mully Children's Family. The secret is how each experience continues to provide meaning these many years later. My eldest daughter today says that people are only ever going to be happy when they are serving others. What a legacy, right?

To use a Paulo Freire's term[13] these shorter term projects can 'conscientize' the young person to what would have been hidden to her, e.g. whose interests have you been serving, what have been your lived experiences where you have lacked freedom, and how has language you use kept you from freedom to be your true self. Any learning outcomes will be in the reflection in and on the experience, not in the actual experience itself. Again, we humans are neither hard wired nor soft wired to learn very much from an actual experience, unless that experience is connected to experience dependent or experience expectant synapses. And by early adulthood, it is debatable if the brain offers up enough of these synapses anyway for actual experiences to alone be the teachers they were in earlier more sensitive developmental periods.

Cross-Cultural Work and Study

The young person can go to another country for a summer to learn a language or to work on a farm, or in construction. The purpose is not to be a tourist, but to refine and master skills that can be used later.

Leading a Relationship Enhancing Community Activity

The young person can lead his own passion in his church, school, or community. He can coach the community basketball team, visit the cancer hospital regularly for storytelling, run his local church's children's church, or be campus crusade director at his high school. She needs to see herself as a pastor; a shepherd, leading some group of people to deeper relationships.

---

13. Paulo Freire; Freire's (1921–1997) books "Pedagogy of the Oppressed" and "Conscientization" have been required readings for college students for years. His strong critical realist orientation, ability to communicate how language itself can be oppressive if it serves interests other than those of the good of the learner, and his years of working alongside marginalized people in Brazil and elsewhere are noteworthy. I took a course from him at Boston College during my Ph D studies. I once offered an opinion to him in a lecture he gave to three hundred students. I claimed that the problem with oppression, unjust treatment of people and ongoing issues of violence and poverty all start with the human heart and wrong mindsets. He looked at me, waited for a few seconds and then gently but firmly called me out by saying, "You are naïve." To this day those words have been a heuristic for me, a guide to unlock the meaning of right relationships and how actions preceded thinking, how unjust structures and language need to be called into question for whose interests are being served.

Refining a Skill

It is during the early adulthood years when the opportunities need to be taken up for applying mastered skills so that they can be used to build right relationships. Going further and deeper with music, refining an additional learned language, taking lessons towards certification in coaching, teaching or leading, or developing communication skills are all done with an eye to "How can I change my world for the better." Sometimes I hear an alternative story, that early adulthood is about continuing to develop a base of skills. Self-efficacy, the confidence that the young adult has the competency to be effective, is built on a single or at best two foundations. It remains debatable whether there is a, transferable and single problem-solving skill, or critical thinking skill. Problem-solving skills may be contextual, i.e. what I use to solve a math problem may not be the same problem-solving approach I use to solve an interpersonal problem. Self-efficacy on the other hand may be generalizable, transferable across different activities and one more reason for encouraging young adults to refine skills instead of just learning new ones.

Mentoring

A young person can naturally, in the normal ebb and flow of life, take on the job of mentoring another. By lovingly modeling and teaching another about the Creator and ways a young person is doing what the church has failed to do, and what Jesus explicitly told us to do, i.e. feed the hungry, provide shelter for the homeless, etc. Simply sharing each other's stories is mentoring at its best. Mentoring can be disguised in many forms-from walking quietly alongside someone in their journey through grief to modeling then explaining the disinhibitory effects in one's life of learned experiences.

Being Responsible to a Cause

There is a great deal of difference in being responsible *for* something or someone than being responsible *to* something or someone. In the same way, there is a difference between working for God and doing God's work. Thomas H. Greene, in *Darkness in the Marketplace*, says that Martha, while fixing meals, worked *for* God, while Mary, in worshiping

Christ, was illustrating *doing* God's work.[14] There is a difference. Being responsible for a cause, is different than being responsible to a cause, or to someone or something for that matter. If the Creator has placed an issue, question, or problem in the mind of a young adult, this helps open learning avenues for them. The complexities of life need new thinking and action; how to affirm both choice and life for the unborn, how to discuss intelligently the reasons to avoid that second look at pornography, or how to simply pray meaningfully. Whatever the cause, we are all, I believe, called to be responsible somewhere.

Being a Team Member.

A young adult will have pressures and obstacles to continuing to play community soccer or hockey or participate in a community theatre group; however, they should be encouraged to continue to be part of some group, some team. A choir, a sports team, a marching band, all have inherent potential to offer new possibilities to learn how to learn important life lessons from others. We live in an individualistic culture and need to experience the joys and challenges of once more being part of a group.

Dating

Young people are probably safer rock climbing without a rope, punching Mike Tyson in the nose, or eating raw mushrooms found out in the back yard than they are in entering into our culture's "dating" game that is now described as being polyamorous. Once upon a time, long, long ago, in a land far away, I would ask a girl out to a dance. I would walk her home, say good night, and thank you. How quaint. I am quite sure that I too, as a healthy 17-year old, had a sexual thought every seven seconds. But there were fences put up in our Catholic upbringing that made some common sense. G.K. Chesterton put it best by proposing not to remove a fence until you know why it was put up in the first place.[15] Young adults might seriously consider the idea of dating one on one when full and committed partnership is intended. Otherwise, why bother with one on one dating, really?

14. Green, *Darkness in the Marketplace*.
15. Chesterton, *The Thing*.

Praying and Reading.

Young adults are ready for and habitually could have "active" quiet times, without a device in hand or computer game to entertain. In the strategies and tactics described throughout this book, minds-on reflection is the place of learning, where connections are made. Time and opportunity to do so could be encouraged into a young adult's day.

Conclusion

> O My God? When will it please Thee to grant me the favor of living always in that union of my will with Thy heavenly will? Where saying nothing all is said and all is done by leaving all to Thee; where we achieve much by surrendering evermore to Thy will and yet are relieved of all toil since we place everything in Thy care and are concerned only to trust wholly in Thee . . . So that, by the habitual inclination of my heart, I may constantly Repeat: "Thy will be done!" Yes, my God, yes to whatever may please Thee. May all Thy holy wishes be fulfilled, I renounce mine which are blind, Perverse and corrupted by that despicable ego, the mortal enemy of Thy Grace, Thy perfect love, Thy glory and my sanctification."[16]

This book has one main theme, a big idea, an essential concept, that the goal of teaching young people is for them to develop right relationships. Not all at once, but experiences of successive approximations of right relationships, with the Creator, others, themselves and the created and natural order.

Teaching young people requires a systematic plan that is based on who children are becoming at different ages. Young people are living in an idea-contaminated, relationship-challenged world; where the distinction between truth and lies, right from wrong are more blurred than ever before. Parenting tasks are many; but teaching young people to develop right relationships first, then pursue the truth and what is right regarding relationships is the main task. Guiding children through their lived experiences of frustrations, anxieties and the good, bad, and ugly of relationships, is the biggest challenge of a teacher.

---

16. De Caussade, *Abandonment to Divine Providence*.

Study Guide

THIS STUDY GUIDE IS the accompaniment to a eight-part video series titled Old Ideas, New Practices. This series is intended for use by teachers, parents, and pastors in their design of educational programs in homes and church. Each video in the series takes an old idea understood as true and important by Christians for a long time, e.g., the centrality of the mind in transformation (Romans 12:1–2) and describes some new possibilities for new practices in Christian education based on that old idea. For example, this series considers new practices in creating new mindsets and guiding learner concept formation, and, one video in this series proposes, from a brain and behavior point of view, the science of how minds are renewed, something that has rarely, if ever, been considered in Christian education. Each video proposes new practices in Christian education from the foundation of an old idea.

The big idea in doing a series described as "new practices based on old ideas" does not begin with the premise that old practices in Christian education are wrong. The premise is that many old practices are simply not good enough. Coloring pictures of baby Jesus in the crib is not wrong for children to do. It is just not good enough to meet the child's developmental and spiritual need for competency development, transcendence, and identity formation—a sense of being identified and loved personally by a triune God. Many current church related activities intended to be educational for children, youth, and adults for that matter, simply do not align with what we know about brain and behavior, or the importance of neighborhood based community groups and mindsets in the nurture of faith. Pizza nights for youth on Friday night are not good enough for the youth formation of and influence by important concepts and schema. Marriage seminars alone are not good enough in building perseverance and resilience, and certainly fall short in teaching couples about contributing to marriage savers—communities that last, ones that have been taken in and inspired by the bigness and truthfulness of the Christian story and its vision for people. The new practices described in this video series just might be the answer to the shortcomings in current educational practices in our churches.

This eight-part series and the study guide will give you an opportunity to consider new possibilities and the future in Christian education in your churches, homes, and community. Discuss this issue with your home group, church education team and pastor, to name a few. Two final comments. I am not advocating a complete deconstruction of what we do today in Christian education; I am advocating something that is called the "adjacent possible."[1] My proposal underlying each video in this series is that we take what we currently practice in Christian education and build it out, modify, add to it, and take risks in doing so.

Also, you will not read in this study guide or see in the videos what is commonly included on the topic of Christian education. Do not expect to read or see the use of isolated Scriptures leading the way, mentioned first in each video. That would simply lead to proof-texting. Instead, look carefully to see the Scripture play a far deeper and more profound role in educational practices—pouring meaning into our lived experiences as learners. I propose, for example, that we teach the story of Exodus first through guiding learners to understand their own experience of exodus. You might be tempted to quickly decide to go no further with this video series and claim, "Where is Jesus? Where is the Bible?" I believe that your practice of the practices proposed in this video series will lead you to conclude that Jesus and the Bible are, in fact, woven deeply into the new practices. You know the story of the boy in the Sunday school class who was asked to describe a picture of a diesel freight train. He replied, "Well, it looks like a train, but it must be Jesus." Read deeply and better, take up the practices, deeply, as they are described in this video series. You will indeed then see Jesus and the Scriptures. As CS Lewis once wrote, "The universe rings true wherever you fairly test it."[2] If it looks like a truth from psychology or sociology in this study, then it just might be, well, true. And, of course, if it is true somewhere, it is true everywhere.[3]

---

1. Kauffman, *Where Good Ideas Come From*, referred to by Diamandis and Kotler, *Abundance*, 236.
2. Lewis, *Surprised by Joy*.
3. Rohr, "Truth is One."

Study Guide

Let us begin this study where we should start—at the end. What is the reason for Christian education anyway? Why bother? Is it to maneuver people, love them, try to convince them with Christian concepts, so that they will make a decision for Jesus? Is it to teach them about the seven habits of being an effective person? The virtues of a Christian person? How to follow the rule and regulations in Scripture? Are these the ends of Christian education, the goals and intended outcomes? Frankly, I hope not. Why? These have all been tried and found wanting in the long run. These and other old practices may continue to be legitimate desires for most parents and teachers. But each are illegitimate goals. Each of them is suspect for many reasons and should not be the core reason for Christian education, and certainly not an essential goal of Christian education.

Ask yourself this question first, "What is the big idea of Jesus teaching?" Or, if you prefer the language of English language arts, "What was, and arguably still is, his central theme?" Let us start there, at the end, the point of it all, as Jesus taught us in and through everything He taught, did, gave evidence to and confirmed.

The kingdom of God is a particular way of being in the world that comes about through right relationships with God, each other, ourselves and the created (cities, neighborhoods) and natural order. When we take up and practice the teachings of Jesus, it produces right relationships.

If this sounds like a tautology, you are not reading it right. If this sounds all too easy, then you are not reading it right either. The kingdom of God is ontological. "Being" means more than thinking and doing. "Being" is at the far end of complexity—the simplicity that is at the far end of intellectual, moral, and of course, spiritual conversion. "Being" is the end, the intended outcome of our Christian education. The means to the end are behaving and thinking, practices and mindsets, influences of models of virtue and character, heavy lifting of dealing with deep wounds and imagining new possibilities for ourselves, each other, the world and our hand in hand walk with God. The kingdom of God is both the end and the beginning, the source of our ideas for the new practices of old ideas in Christian education and the outcome of our new practices.

Every topic, suggested learning activity, strategy, tactic, logistic or relationship builder is designed to be a heuristic, a guide that leads children and youth, as well as adults, to take up the practices and teachings of Jesus. Over time, they will be participants in the kingdom of God through right relationships. With the end in mind, the reign or kingdom of God being the essence of Christian education, the goal and outcome, the means and strategy for real life, let us move on to Session #1.

Session #1

Insanity is continuing to do the same thing repeatedly and expecting different results.

—A. EINSTEIN

Topic Title: Old Ideas, New Practices

Introduction to Session: The first session is designed for you to begin the fun but important work of imagining new possibilities, new futures for Christian religious education in your home, church, and community. This session is light on content but heavy on sharing your stories and lived experiences, and trusting that, as Paula D'Arcy says, "God comes to us disguised as our lives"[1] Get ready to imagine . . .

Big Idea: The most effective education programs for developing habits of character, virtue, faith (trust in God), and security and significance in young people are rarely found in our churches. They are developed, over time, in right relationships as they are experienced in loving contexts in homes, K to 12 schools, community sport and athletic programs, boys' and girls' clubs, service oriented agencies, and intentional communities where families do life together. It is time for us to reimagine what we do in education programs in churches, to be architects of learning experiences that are engaging, life changing, and faith nurturing. In this first session, we will together travel intellectually through old ideas and together re-imagine new practices based on these old ideas.

---

1. D'Arcy, *Gift of the Red Bird*.

Old ideas, New Practices: https://drive.google.com/open?id=1zx4Bocu ZOSDZzc3-ThG1rnZf8ZHhCvLA

Final Study Guide Activity for Session 1

Now what? What is an adjacent possible, a possible new future, a potentially better possibility for your church and its practices in Christian education?

Notes

_____
_____
_____
_____

Session #2

It is a good idea to be yourself, because everyone else is already taken.

—OSCAR WILDE

Topic Title: Development: From False Self to True Self

Introduction to Session: This second session is designed to guide you to re-engage with some of your past experiences. This session asks you to remember one or two experiences that might have contributed to what the early social psychologists called "the separation of the self from the 'I' (true self) to the 'me' (presenting self)." William Glasser's looking glass theory of self-concept[1] might be a good advance organizer for you to consider as you begin this session. His theory is generally summed up in I am not who I think I am; I am not who you think I am; I am who I think you think I am. The purpose in doing this introspection activity is to put you on high alert, to avoid making the same mistakes with your children, to following along the same decision ruts and grooves laid down in your sensitive years. And, of course, the purpose includes making the same good decisions also laid down in your own life, during your own sensitive periods of time.

Before you begin this session, referring to you personally, ask yourself two questions. "Who is the 'self' Christ died for?" and, "Does it matter to God that I am on a journey towards my true self?" Get ready for some personal analyses of how in the world you came to present yourself the way you did.

---

1. William Glasser. (1981). *Glasser is best known for his writing on choice therapy*

Big Idea: Thomas Merton writes that we spend the first half of our lives putting our ladders up against the wall of pleasing people, getting ahead financially, seeking security and significance through accomplishments and so on, only to find out that there is nothing up there.[2] We have put our ladders up against the wrong wall.

Our lack of forgiveness for a past hurt, a deep wound and desire for revenge, for a rejection that we carry alone, our desire to please people to keep us safe from further hurt, are all rungs on the wrong ladder. What then are the right rungs? What does the right wall look like?

Positioning Question: How can I guide people in my family, community, and church in their spiritual development, so that they put their ladders up against the right walls? What might a right wall look like in my family?

Study Guide Activity #1

Complete the stem

> I appear to be__but really I am_____
> My child appears to be_____but really she/he is_____

How in the world did this happen? (The answer will almost always be a dichotomy, a separation of self between appearance and real.)

Usually a self-concept schema takes events, circumstances, and an ecology (family, school, church) that contributes inadvertently to the separation of self. For example, developing a predisposition to be dishonest with our children is quite easy to do. Be angry and upset at them for not doing what you believe that they should do; in particular, be honest in telling you that they have not done what you expect them to do, and after a few expressions of your anger any self-respecting, intelligent child will lie to keep themselves safe from your future anger. Agreed?

Study Guide Activity #2

In the ecology we call family, what is my unique contribution to my children's spiritual formation? Choose one and explain how it contributes to your child's development.

---

2. Thomas Merton's actual quote is: "People may spend their whole lives climbing the ladder of success only to find, once they reach the top, that the ladder is leaning against the wrong wall" (no original source found).

scripture memorization_____
love and acceptance_____
modeling_____
rules and guidelines_____
stories_____
other_____

Study Guide Activity #3

Watch the video. The Ecology of Human Development: https://drive.google.com/open?id=1QZ20io_Q7cO9JDqvKOpbnlzV3k_iFvmF

The often go-to Scripture for parents is Proverbs 22:6 (KJV). "Train up a child in the way he should go; and when he is old, he will not depart from it." In the hands and mind of a person shaped by short-sighted and wrong-headed ideas of punishment, training, and what is the way a child should go, this Scripture just may be the most dangerous one for children. Hitting children has been justified using this Scripture as proof. However, the original language for training was far closer to teaching or guiding than it was to some boot camp idea of training . . . in the way they should go" was far closer to "given their bent, their predispositions, their personalities . . ." than it was to some abstraction or system of platonic shadows. The genius of the Scripture is that it rings true if properly understood. If a child is guided or taught, given who they are, based on who they truly are—an image bearer of God, a masterpiece created in Christ Jesus for good works that He has prepared in advance for them to do (Ephesians, 2:10), then good outcomes are inevitable.

Study Guide Activity #4

In what way does the Scripture and your understanding of who your child(ren) is call you forward to one change, one adjacent possibility, one new way of being in your family?

Study Guide Activity #5

Personal Manifesto: Create a set of promises, or commitments, regarding changes you promise to make in your ecology, your family, church, or community. Two categories, guiding or teaching your children and studying your children like you would a book, then discern who they are, really, and how to guide them in that way of their personality, bent, and predispositions.

Notes

_____
_____
_____
_____

Session #3

... to see eternity in a second and the universe in a grain of sand.
—WILLIAM BLAKE

Topic Title: Nurturing: Tending to the inner world of the learner

Introduction to the Session: This third session claims that understanding first, then aligning learning experiences to the psychological and developmental needs of children, is mission critical for teachers and parents. For example, children are concrete operational thinkers. This does not mean that they need concrete experiences to learn, though that is not a bad idea. They make sense of new experiences, messages, words, behaviors of others, etc., through and only through, their own lived, concrete experiences. The concept of family is understood through their lived experience of their own family.

Big Idea: Teaching the story of the exodus makes no sense unless taught through the experience of understanding their own inner exodus. To teach the principle of "who of you who worry can add a year to his life" is best taught by looking closely with children at their experience of wasted worrying. This perspective is about a teacher being intentional and deliberate in aiding and sustaining the personal well-being of the student—the psychological, developmental, and spiritual health of a child.

Positioning Question: Is it your job as a parent to first and foremost teach your children the Scriptures? Is your job first to be concerned with or focused on the inner world and psychological well-being of your children? The answer is, yes!

The dichotomy in thinking in the question posed has long been a problem in Christian education and raising children. We end up thinking in either/or categories about children's Christian education, often because we are unsure, perhaps a bit desperate, and lost on this landscape called parenting that we feel the need for certainty that answers seem able to give. For you and me to be over and against a Christian education that uses Scriptures primarily to teach seems to come largely from past experiences growing up, when the Scriptures were misused and misapplied, often boring you to death. We know a lot more today about children making meaning and how important their concrete lived experiences are in making their meaning of the Scriptures than we have ever applied to most church education. On the other hand, being over and against education in churches focused on the inner world of children seems to come from a misunderstanding of how children make meaning and construct conceptual frameworks and schema. Frankly, it demonstrates just how important the inner world is of a child to understanding the Scriptures.

Study Guide Activity #1

Watch the video. Anthropology: https://drive.google.com/open?id=1cU3Pg966I2zaUs_oqY566OfFanSdEVYg

Choose one idea from the video that you agree with. Why? What assumptions, beliefs, theories about children or past experiences give rise to your agreement?

Choose one idea from the video that you disagree with. Why? Again, discuss why you might disagree with the idea.

So what? Now what? What inner work do you need to do to be that model of virtue and character for your children?

Study Guide Activity #2

Develop a lesson plan concept for your children, a paragraph in which you describe how you would teach an important principle to them based on a Scripture or set of Scriptures (that represent a theme) and in which you intentionally consider your child's deepest needs for security and significance. Try it out.

Notes

Session #4

We learn the right behavior by being trained in the presence of models of virtue and character.

—WILLIAM KIRKPATRICK

Topic Title: Apprenticeship: When is it okay to be the sage on the stage ... maybe?

Introduction to the Session: The apprenticeship perspective is about the enculturation of an individual with the larger contexts and settings in which the person finds himself or herself. Enculturation is through a progressive, mutual accommodation of the person with the expectations, theories, values, assumptions, behaviors, and beliefs of the contexts we find ourselves (e.g. marriage, families, work, culture). Your future role to consider in this session is to consider being more of a coach than a lecturer with your children.

Big Idea: This session is an invitation to move away from being the deliverer of information, a broker of abstractions, a big dump truck dumping loads of ought to, should and have to into your little dump trucks (a.k.a. children). The big idea of this session is that apprenticeship and all its manifestations and expressions—to coach, mentor, demonstrate and inspire through story and modeling—are very effective if done right. Besides, you are not that endlessly fascinating anyway as a deliverer of information.

Positioning Question: Telling people what to do, how to do it, and what they should know and how to apply it, is not apprenticeship, good coaching, or effective mentoring. If not, then what does good apprenticeship look like? What are the possibilities for good apprenticeship programs in our churches and education programs?

Study Guide Activity #1

Draw a concept map with "apprenticeship" in the middle with branches leading off to the following: expressions of apprenticeship that my family is ready to take up; strategies that I know my children appreciate and respond to; tactics that I have used at work or with others, ones that I enjoyed; logistics, or ways to organize my family and is commitment to being coached; and, relationships, how I can motivate and inspire my family. The outcome? Your family's manifesto, and the beginning of a strategic plan for apprenticeship.

Concept Map

Study Guide Activity #2

Identify an apprenticeship program that you have experienced personally or know something about conceptually. You might consider Registered Apprenticeship Programs in high schools, internship programs in medicine and law schools, teacher induction programs in school districts, or training programs in businesses and trades. You might also choose to identify programs like Scouts and Guides (which are largely apprenticeship based).

What strategies, tactics, logistics, and relationship builders were evident? Add what you and a partner have identified to your concept map.

Study Guide Activity #3

Videos: TED Talk: Grit-Angela Duckworth *https://www.youtube.com/watch?v=H14bBuluwB8*

TED Talk: Fake it until you make it-Amy Cuddy https://www.youtube.com/watch?v=RVmMeMcGcoY

Conclusions: So what? Now what?

Draw one conclusion and one implication for your emerging apprenticeship program in your family.

Final Study Guide Activity for Session 4

Resilient kids have more social capital (parents, coaches, mentors, friends, advisors, teachers) than young people who have less social capital. What might be one implication for the Christian education of children based on this notion of social capital?

Notes

_____
_____
_____
_____

Session #5

I could become a Christian if I ever met one.

—GANDHI

They will have to sing better songs for me if I am going to believe in their Savior; his followers will have to look more redeemed.

—FRIEDRICH NIETZSCHE

Topic Title: Social Reform: Whose interests are being served?

Introduction to the Session: Then iceberg concept useful reminder, that most of what exists in the mind is below the level of consciousness.

Big Idea: The social reform perspective is about the uncovering of the assumptions and values, beliefs, and theories that give rise to power and control. The core question is, "Whose interests are being served, and why, by the decisions made in a church, home or community?" The ideal of social reform is the change of unjust structures, the bringing about of justice and shalom.

Positioning Question: Choose one activity in your church, preaching, children's programs, mission overseas, for example, then ask and answer the question, "Whose interests are being served by the approach used to enact this activity the way it is in my church?"

Study Guide Activity #1

Is there another possibility for the activity you chose? If so, what might a scenario look like for that new possibility? If not, why not?

Study Guide Activity #2

Videos: Scenario Building: https://drive.google.com/open?id=1tjptVeLYrJnCTUU8mD_oTNfRd3XY3RDy

Study Guide Activity #3

The video you watched talked about scenario design. The premise of the "adjacent possible" or taking what is already there rather than throwing it out, deconstructing it entirely, is much more effective. It is better to create or design a better expression of it through a systematic and intentional set of pedagogic movements. The goal is a better expression of some aspect of education in your context.

Following the pattern of scenario design, reform some aspect of education in your church. Try to contain your scenario to a two-paragraph expression.

Final Study Guide Activity for Session 5

So what? Now what? Problems have been addressed and perhaps solved from your initial scenario. What does the solution look like? (Here think of an artefact, a visible expression of the solution, not a concept, principle, or theological idea. These are all important but now you want to present an actual, on the ground, visible expression of your solution.

Notes

_____
_____
_____

Session #6

Life with all its yield of joy and woe, hope and fear,
is just our chance of the prize of learning love.

—E. B. BROWNING

Topic Title: Brain and behavior: What comes first, and does it matter?

Introduction to the Session: There is an art to teaching based on how the brain functions. Some of what we discuss and consider in this topic will surprise you and some of what we take up will leave you saying, "Well, of course that makes sense." But, for now, the idea to lead the way into this study is this: the brain is an adaptive system. It responds and develops through actions, behaviors, emotions, and more. This is how God made it and maybe, just maybe, we need to design and implement learning experiences accordingly.

Big Idea: We don't think our way into new ways of acting; we act our way into new ways of thinking (Parker Palmer)

Positioning Question: What do Pioneer Girls and Boys Clubs, AWANA, the girl's church basketball team, one-week camp out with others, and Scouts all have in common?

Study Guide Activity #1

Can you guess what these and other programs have in common? How is the brain implicated and why?

Would you be willing to give in and suspend disbelief for just a short period of time and consider that similar, behavioral, action oriented and minds-on programs could be more effective for a child's faith formation than Bible memorization and doing catechism question and answer activities?

Study Guide Activity #2

View the video: Brain and behavior: https://drive.google.com/open?id=1CLJ9jy43KSaT6nNIE3AxTNysZmQBgo4y

Study Guide Activity #2

What one idea in the video for you is most worth investigating further?

Go back to Session #1 and read again William Kirkpatrick's quote about training of children. Has your opinion changed regarding his quote?

Study Guide Activity #3

Project-based learning, problem-based learning and inquiry are powerful brain developers in part because the brain adapts to the behaviors, emotions, activities, and decisions made by youth in particular but adults as well, in completing a project, solving a problem, or inquiring into real issues and questions. A brief description of project-based learning is found in Chapter 5.

Final Study Guide Activity for Session 6

Parker Palmer wrote that we do not always think our way into new ways of acting; we act our way into new ways of thinking. Really? Do you agree? Do you have a lived experience of the truthfulness of this notion?

Notes
_____
_____
_____
_____

Session #7

A father's protection is more important than a mother's love for the healthy psychological development of a child.

—SIGMUND FREUD

Topic Title: Psychoanalytic: The influence of the subconscious in learning

Introduction to the Session: The psychoanalytic perspective is a family of distinct but not separate set of ideas about how the subconscious influences learning. The perspective and our work in it will raise important questions about change and what can change in people, influence early experiences on present behavior, addictions and more. Deep wounds that remain unhealed, patterns of behaving that are hurtful to you and others and another way to look at how we come to understand what we understand, and more, are taken up in this study.

Big Idea: The ruts and grooves laid down in our lives are what we are pulled down onto when threatened or in a state of unease. Jesus's particular way of being, e.g., forgiveness, no worry, prayer for others, the beatitudes described (not prescribed) in Scriptures is hard won. Some conditions better than other ones need to be set up in Christian education so that the way of Jesus can be practiced and have its way into our lives.

Positioning question: CS Lewis claims that our behavior today follows along ruts and grooves laid down in our minds during formative, sensitive time periods when experiencing difficulties. How would you describe your widest and deepest "rut and groove" on which your behavior travels when you feel threatened or anxious, frustrated, or angry?

Study Guide Activity #1

Does the video call into question an assumption, belief, value, or theory that you have depended on in your child raising or teaching?

    Mind-sets and Group Dynamics: https://drive.google.com/open?id=1Mhu9Vg27lhGWEUGVcCY9ujoUHacwb5t8

    What will you choose to do now?

Study Guide Activity #2

You and I will respond in most situations, if not all situations, that have emotions (anxiety, frustration, anger, anticipation, etc.) attached to the circumstance of the situation (e.g., disagreement with a spouse). Our behaviors follow along ruts and grooves laid down in our lives during sensitive periods in our lives, when we were in anxiety provoking situations. The important question for us here is can we change? Will we and our students always be pulled down into these ruts and grooves when we are threatened? Should we teachers be about the business of trying to lay down better ruts and grooves in our students' minds? Smoothing out old and negative ruts and grooves?

    What can change? What would a change mean for your well-being and happiness?

Final Study Guide Activity

Watch the TED talk video. Why you think you're right—even if you're wrong | Julia Galef—YouTube

    So what? Now what?

Notes

_____
_____
_____

Session #8

I won't care how much you know until I know how much you care.
—UNKNOWN

Topic Title: Community: a visible expression of that particular way of being in the world

Introduction to the Session: This session provides teachers with an opportunity to extrapolate from what is known about communities that last and re-imagine the attributes and characteristics of those communities into our families, churches, and neighborhoods.

Big Idea: Community is built when people gather around a great idea. Communities are sustained when they see themselves as transcendent, being against something, being for something, used as symbols, and are physically close. We will examine how to transfer some heady ideas about community and its formation and sustainability into new church education practices.

Positioning Question: Community by this definition then is not the building you use on Sunday mornings to sing songs and listen to someone speak, the small group you meet with once a month, the yoga group you see once a week. What is it? What one condition above all others would you want to extrapolate and practice in your family, church, or neighborhood?

Study Guide Activity #1

Does my statement above annoy you? Trouble you? Inspire you? Why?

Study Guide Activity #2

Watch the video: Communities that Last: https://drive.google.com/open?id=1TdIS5-yARHnoTiLqsJHwlUbiKh5Sa4kv

Study Guide Activity #3

What one idea from the video will you take forward and design into your church education program?

Final Study Guide Activity

Build your reimagined church program by drawing principles and practices of communities that last into your design of your reimagined program for Christian education.

Notes

_____
_____
_____
_____

Glossary

Adaptive styles and learning

The adaptive style learning theory model comes from an experiential theory and model of learning developed by Kolb (1984) and based on the seminal contributions of John Dewey, Kurt Lewin, and Jean Piaget. It is a practical self-assessment instrument that can help us assess our unique learning preferences and responses to problems, issues, and questions, followed by learning more about how we solve problems, address issues, and answer questions in everyday life. In Kolb's experiential model, learning is viewed as a continually recurring problem-solving process in the four-stage cycle. Concrete experiences are followed by reflective observations that lead to the formulation of abstract concepts and generalizations that lead to active experimentation to test the hypotheses that have been developed. This is an ongoing process and may be entered anywhere in the cycle.

Anomaly

An idea or action that is different than what might be expected or considered normal. Paradigm shifts, changes in a person's or culture's accepted rules or methods, can be attributed to an anomaly, as with the case of Einstein's theories that changed the way scientists view time and space (now known to be relative and not absolute).

Attention

An idea or action that is different than what is expected or considered normal. Paradigm shifts, changes in a person's or culture's accepted rules or methods, can be attributed to an anomaly, as with the case of Einstein's theories that changed the way scientists view time and space (now known to be relative and not absolute).

Glossary

Assessment

Gathering information about information about student learning to make decisions about that learning. The most common decision is to make a judgment or evaluation of the worth or value of student learning (assessment of learning). However, other decisions may include to diagnose gaps in student learning, determine students' prior understandings before embarking on an instructional course of action, making curricular and course modifications from information gathered. We call this 'assessment for learning.' Finally, teachers may deploy tactics of gathering information about student learning that require students to re-enter or re-engage with a topic, idea, concept of skill. We call this assessment as learning

Authentic assessment

Gathering information about student learning through student's visibly expressing learning through a presentation, project, portfolio, debate, theater or artistic expression. Essays, term papers, answers to questions, test are not included as means of authentic assessment

Authentic

Synonyms include words like real and genuine. Antonyms include words like false, fake, and disingenuous.

Assimilation and accommodation

Assimilation is one part of Jean Piaget's adaptation process, a cognitive activity in which new information is perceived, interpreted then incorporated into an existing concept or schema. People will modify an experience often to make it 'incorporable' and meaningful. The other half of Piaget's adaptation process is accommodation, again a cognitive based process in which concepts and schema are changed because of the influence of the new information. Both processes work together, often quickly and almost always in the presence of actual experiences. These processes would be the minds-on part of learning. One more interesting piece of Jean Piaget's larger idea is that of equilibration, borrowed from his work as a biologist, to explain the mind's movement some sort of balance between the two process and seeking out of some idea that removes any cognitive dissonance or confusion.

Augustine (354–430)

Christian bishop and theologian who helped create modern Christian thought through some of his works like Confessions and The City of God.

Banking teaching

A metaphor used by Paulo Freire to describe instruction instructional practices oriented to simply depositing information into a person, like one would deposit money into a bank. Learning is a re-creation of experience, an active event of pouring meaning into the leftovers of experiences we call memories.

Beatitudes

Found in Matthew and are descriptions of the relationships between two 'ways of being' in the world, e.g. peacemakers and being called children of God. The beatitudes serve as reminders to us that so much of scripture needs to be read as descriptive not prescriptive. The beatitudes are descriptions of what the kingdom of God could look like.

Bernard Lonergan (1904–1984)

A Canadian, Jesuit priest, philosopher and author of Method in Theology and Insight. His work has been very influential, so much so that he is considered by many to have been one of the best theological thinkers in the twentieth century. Lonergan institutes have been established in North America, devoted to the study of his writing and its application to teaching and learning. Lonergan's thinking is largely concerned with questions of epistemology and how we humans come to 'know what we know.' He offered us a 'method' in theological thinking-beginning with being attentive to the data of our lives, the experiences that gave rise to what we are paying attention to, including the bias that might keep us from being fully attentive and aware, then understanding, judging and acting on what we have come to .

Bloom's Taxonomy

A useful and well-worn framework, and old idea (originated in 1955) for questioning, designing learning outcomes and describing how we might 'come to know' in increasingly sophisticated ways-recall, comprehension, application, analyses, synthesis, and evaluation.

Case study

When used as a problem-based learning strategy, this is the process of inquiring or researching into the 'narrative' of the case (story lines) towards the goals of detailed consideration regarding development of a particular person, group, or situation over a period of time, in particular noting how the person or group addressed an issue, answered a question or addressed a problem. Through a sequence of intentional andragogic movements students can describe, analyze and/or evaluate an instance of something used to solve a problem, address an issue, or answer a question. The outcome of case study is a student's enhanced competency to deduce and illustrate a thesis or principle that may be generalizable or extrapolatable to their world.

Catechisms

The formal summaries of Christian beliefs and practices, for children and adults. Often structured in a question and answer format. Catechisms sprouted up within various sects and Christian denominations, largely to capture the doctrinal distinctives in the denomination. For some time, Catholics used the Baltimore Catechism (ending its use in the 1960s) The Reformed Catechism, Geneva Catechism and many other variations have been deployed.

Catechumenate

An organized time of Christian formation and education regarding baptism as a rite of passage into the church, into all the formal and informal practices associated with Christian life.

Circle of Courage

Presents four developmental needs of children and youth-Belonging, Mastery, Independence and Generosity-usually in the form of a native medicine wheel. You would find the principles and practices of from the Circle of Courage in well over 100 books, articles, curricular programs for schools and agencies that work with young people. Two of my children attended a High School with many of its practices drawn directly from the Circle of Courage. Their lives were changed in this school and its practices.

Glossary

Churchill ('never quit')

The story goes that shortly after the end of the second world war Winston Churchill, the Prime Minister of The United Kingdom, was asked to speak at Harvard. The expectant audience filled the auditorium to hear the man who inspired and motivated a country and its allies during a very dark and troubled time in history. He stood up, waited a few seconds, then said, 'Never, ever, ever, ever quit.' The sat down. That was it, the entire speech. After a few seconds, the audience stood as if one person and gave him a standing ovation.

C.S. Lewis (1898–1963)

Well known and read author of some of the most cogent apologetics to be written in the 20th century. He had a winsome ability to argue persuasively and logically for the truthfulness of Christianity. Many people claim to have had their faith built on his writings and ideas, and I am one of them. His life story is well worth a read to understand the genesis of his remarkable, intelligent faith in God and Christ.

Chuck Colson (1931–2012)

Watergate co-conspirator, write and convert to Christianity later in his life. He worked with prisoners in a ministry that has persisted and continues to offer mercy and hope to prisoners, a new practice of love and mercy nested in a unlikely and ostensibly unattractive place.

Circular Reasoning

A type of reasoning people use, either consciously or sub consciously, that proves what they set out to prove, regardless of logic, evidence or what has been previously known, Sometimes referred to as revolving door thinking, circular reasoning is evidenced by ending up in one's reasoning where one started, at the very the assumptions, theories, values, and beliefs that one was unlikely to permit being changed by virtue of the evidence to the contrary of one's original reasoning.

David Elkind (1931-present)

Author whose books were for years required reading in university and teacher colleges of education. He writes along a line of reasoning shared by others such as Goodman (Growing up Absurd), that young people's developmental psychological realities need to be taken into consideration when designing teaching and learning experiences. Pushing children too fast to soon interrupts their normal development. Good reads of Elkind's include The Hurried Child, Miseducation and All Grown Up and No Place to Go.

David Pawson (1930-)

British writer and pastor who proposed in his book A Normal Christian Birth that was is most wrong with Christians today is that they have had a poor spiritual birth; they have started wrong and needed a 'normal' Christian birth that included repentance, baptism and more than just 'praying the sinners prayer.'

Didache

The Didache or the Teaching of the Twelve Apostles was discovered in a monastery in 1873 and published in 1883. Originally published in the first century A.D., the first English translation came out in 1884. Despite the claims by some scholars that the Didache is a questionable document for its source and purpose it remains the earliest, post-scripture written document we have that represents ideas about early Christianity. Other copies of the Didache, other than the one found in Constantinople, have been found in Egypt, leading some scholars to accept the veracity of the Didache. Regardless, from the Didache we get a snapshot, an image from the past that emphasized behaving and being, not right ideas in Christianity, at the center of the Christian life.

Design Thinking

A problem-based learning strategy that intends for a student to develop, over time and through a series of well-planned instructional activities, a prototype or visible expression of a solution to a problem, one that is eventually tested in the world that the student works or serves.

Glossary

Direct Instruction

Any form of teaching in which the content is deemed more important than the learning of that content, the learner is passive and the teacher active, meaning is concluded to reside in what is being transmitted directly. Any form of teaching, including lecture, video, power point presentations, reading, modeling in which the teacher 'delivers' information and the learner receives it. It has continued to be the main teaching method despite evidence that transfer of learning and transfer of training are quite low, particularly when the teacher does not design conditions that would assist the earner to make sense of the delivered information.

Double Bind

The concept that a learner experiences disjunction and confusion when being told he is loved while his mother spanks him. Either there is something wrong with his mother, a perception that does not fit well with him given the spanking, or this something wrong with him, which seems to be the more likely conclusion. At a more philosophical level, we want to believe God is love and are told that God is indeed love; but pain, suffering and evil exist. Either there is something wrong with God, or something wrong with me, and my perceptions of pain and evil. The double bind is a close cousin to Keirkegaard's notion of paradox-that we want to discover and know God and to do that we need to use our minds. However, God is unknowable through the mind. How then can I discover and understand the undiscoverable and unknowable.

Expectations

Ideas one has that serve as predictors of what one will experience or see in another person or situation.

Faith

Typically thought of as a mental construct that exists despite evidence to the contrary or no ostensible evidence. Faith in the Christian tradition includes an element of trust, a dependency on some larger good will from a divinity to persons.

Donald Kraybill (1946-present)

A writer and thinker best known for his academic work and study on the Anabaptist tradition and the Amish. His writing is also popular in non-academic circles. His book titled The Upside-Down Kingdom was widely popular and much read. His core idea in this book is that if we today were to take the best normal, taken for granted thinking about a topic, any topic, and turn it on its head, upside-down, there we would find the ideas of the kingdom of God.

Edward Schillebeeckx (1914–2009)

Dominican priest, influential in Vatican 2 and controversial theologian, particularly for his views on the literal resurrection of Jesus.

Elizabeth Elliot (1926–2015)

A popular writer and speaker, the author of Passion and Purity, in which she made a strong argument for an old idea, sexual expression to be within the marriage relationship. Today, this view is considered quaint and hardly relevant to the times we live in, but a sober second read might not be a bad idea.

Enlightenment (explanation regarding influence in Christianity)

An 18th century philosophical and intellectual shift towards the importance of progress, individual determination, liberty, and reason, in political, church and individual life. One driving cause, arguably, or effect as some have claimed, was the separation of church and state. During this period Descarte coined his famous phrase, "I think, therefore I am." Kant was trying to reconcile faith and reason. The period saw the emergence of a feminist philosophy, e.g. Mary Wollstonecraft based on reason and that women should be treated as rational beings. The period saw notion of rationalism rise to prominence and some feel that this was the beginning of the erosion of Christianity as a force to be reckoned with.

Erik Erikson (1902–1994)

The grandfather of the theory of identity and its formation over time, in stages and throughout a lifespan. A life-crises is characteristic of each stage of a person's identity development. For example, young children, aged 6–12 are resolving the life crises of competency vs inferiority. The resolution of this crises is along a continuum and rarely to one end of a spectrum or the other. In other words, young children develop an identify towards competency provided they get 'good' at activities like making friends, sports, school, and other activities. If, however, they do not experience success experiences they develop their identity towards inferiority. Erikson proposed 8 life crises, each with a resolution and identity development outcome along a continuum.

Feminist consciousness

An awareness-raising of the political and social causes and conditions that have oppressed women. Attention is paid to language used as well as to hidden curricular practices, in workplaces and schools, the oppress girls and women. Surprising to some that snapshots of feminist consciousness can be seen in 19th century letters and literature, and not surprising is the full-on emergence and entrenchment of feminist consciousness in the U.S. in the 1960s

Foundational pedagogy

Children, aged 5–11 approximately, do give evidence of patterns, developmentally and psychologically, across time and culture. For example, egocentric generosity (being recognized and acknowledged for doing good), stereotyping (drawing stereotypical conclusions, sweeping generalizations and often ethnocentric statements; concrete operational thinking (my family is what families are); competency motivation (getting good at something-repeating it often-from building lego models to playing computer games); learned control (need to learn deferred gratification-eat your vegetables before eating your desert); handling fears-('be 'brave but careful' when climbing that tree or making a new friend); predictability (security and significance tied directly to routines, safety and expected responses from parents, friends and teachers); autonomy (freedom to explore, make mistakes, have down time); take subjective responsibility (I was wrong, it was my fault, how can I make it right); discuss anomalies (why are some people homeless); develop pro-social behaviors (e.g. being kind works for good for everyone involved).

Gamification

The use of online games for teaching and learning purposes and ends. An old idea using games to teach, but a new practice using online platforms to do so.

Gary Colwell

Retired professor of Philosophy at Concordia University of Edmonton.

G. K. Chesterton (1874–1936)

Poet, writer, theologian, and literary and art critic, skilled at turning a complex idea into a succinct, proverb-like point e.g. 'The most important truth is what things are.' A convert to Catholicism he loved debates that had a religious element; he regularly debated George Bernard Shaw about matters of faith and God. He was a regular on BBC giving talks that were widely listened to. He was the typical absent-minded genius. One story goes that he would regularly telegraph his wife to tell her where was, then to ask her 'where should I be?" To which she would reply, 'home.'

Gnosticism

A religious ideology established in the first and second century AD that says the world is created by a lesser divine being that sparked the human soul. The underlying premise of Gnosticism is that there is secret body of knowledge available to some but not all.

Goals

The ends intended from a program or instruction. Disguised often as desires, or objectives. An old idea that has shown up in new practices in education like universal design and backward design for learning.

Habituation

A form of learning in which a response to a stimulus decreases after repeated presentations of that stimulus. For example, children can become habituated when exposed to repeated threats of punishment, time out, or removal of some positive reinforcer, particularly if a parent does not follow through with the consequence. Habituation is best understood by another theory called drive theory, behaviors that are learned when *a drive is reduced by the choice of behavior. Experiencing a threatening situation and perhaps by ignoring the cause of the threat, the effect of the threat is reduced. Children' learn' to stop responding to a stimulus when it is no longer biologically relevant. Habituation usually refers to a reduction in behaviors, rather than behaviors acquired through conditioning.*

Parents and teachers do well to consider the relationship 'consequences' of environments (homes, classrooms) that are loaded with aversive stimuli like threats, warnings, fear creation and excessively difficult tasks, ones beyond the capacity and therefore motivation of young people. It is important to design tasks within the range of 50/50.

Hans Kung (1928-)

Swiss born theologian, Catholic and controversial writer who regularly called into question papal infallibility, clergy abuse, commonalities in world religions and death with dignity.

Harold Morris

Author of Twice Pardoned, Beyond the Barriers, Overcoming Hard times— many faith-based books. He began writing in 1984 after being diagnosed with terminal cancer.

Henry David Thoreau (1817–1862)

He wrote on a variety of topics, from philosophy to natural history. He had an ability to pay attention closely to the messages that nature offered and the meaning that nature offered up for how people ought to live.

Hidden curriculum

The hidden curriculum is the unplanned, unintentional outcomes of young peoples' learning experience in homes and schools. Ask a young person what they learned in school today? Ask yourself what you learned in school (or your home for that matter). Did you learn how to survive? Please people to keep yourself secure and significant? Study for trivial pursuit type examinations? Change the world? Young people learn much from their interpretations of messages sent to them from teachers, parents, and peers, and sadly, the outcomes can often be negative.

Inquiry

Perhaps the oldest 'idea' in this book new legitimized into new practices of problem-based learning, characterized by students being open to wonder and puzzlement and coming to know and understand the world through addressing their wonder and puzzlement. Inquiry is a stance that pervades all aspects of life and is essential to the way in which knowledge is created. Inquiry is based on the belief that understanding is constructed in the process of people working and conversing together as they pose and solve the problems, make discoveries and rigorously testing the discoveries that arise in the course of shared activity.

Jean Piaget (1896–1980)

A biologist who contributed some important early understandings of children's and youth's cognitive development. A stage theorist who proposed that children progress through four stages that are invariant and sequential, but not universally connected to specific ages. Generally, with exceptions, children progress through stages, from sensori-motor (0–2 years), psycho-motor (2–6 years), concrete operational (6–11) and onto formal operation thinking. Piaget contributed a language that still is valid today-including schema, assimilation, accommodation, and equilibration. His theory generally however has been called into question and is less persuasive than more recent cognitive psychologists such as Alberta bandura and Lev Vygotsky. Piaget's claims remain evocative however, for example, claiming that 'We can teach any subject, to any child, at any age in any intellectually honest fashion.'

John and Paula Sandford

Husband and wife team who founded Elijah House and ran it for twenty years, offering people opportunities to think deeply into the conscious and subconscious causes of people's experiencing of discontent and lack of freedom. Their flagship book is Healing the Wounded Spirit. Paula Sandford died in 2012.

Josh McDowell (1939-)

Christian apologist and public speaker, author OF Evidence Which Demands a Verdict and More than a Carpenter. Old ideas based on logic and rationalism, ostensibly requiring new practices that would be persuasive to young people.

J.I Packer (1926–2020)

Once name by Time magazine as one of the top 25 evangelicals in America. His book Knowing God *is hailed as a classic.*

Jurgen Moltmann (1926–)

Theologian and writer who wrote Theology of Hope *and other books to express his view that God suffers with us as well as rejoices with us when we suffer and rejoice. He was influenced by Hegel and the notion of the dialectic yet remained strongly reformed in his theology. He was also strong oriented to liberation theology. His personal background is quite fascinating. It includes joining the German army in 1944, surrendering to the first British soldier he saw then spending the rest of the war in prison. He remained deeply troubled by Auschwitz and Germany's treatment of Jews and others, as evidenced in his writing.*

John Fischer (1947–)

A musician, public speaker and writer, author of Real Christians Don't Dance and other books that have helped people recognize what is important and what is not in Christianity, an old idea that arguably needs revisiting often.

John Hus (1369–1415)

Czech theologian and philosopher who outlined his reform of the church in his book De Ecclesia. He was later burned at the stake as a heretic and his followers launched a civil war against the Holy Roman Empire.

John Comenius (1592–1670)

Moravian philosopher who is considered the father of modern education.

Johann Herbart (1776–1841)

German philosopher who founded pedagogy as an academic discipline. His concept stemmed from logic, metaphysics, and the analysis of experience.

Leo Tolstoy (1828–1910)

The author of War and Peace, Anna Karina and other classics, Tolstoy is considered one of the most influential writers of the 19th century. He was a philosopher, writer and critic of religious rituals, the latter contributed to his excommunication from the church in 1901. He was critiqued as a moralist but ironically had personal sexual struggles and a very troubled marriage. He was praised as brilliant writer and wise philosopher. His contributions continue today to be in his thoughtful critique of surface religiosity and proposals for new ways of thinking about a person's relationships, in particular with God and the social order-a strong pacifist who saw lots wrong with war and violence.

Lombardian

German people who invaded Italy in 568 and created the region known as Lombardy which means "money lender."

Martin Marty (1928-)

Author of dozens of books and articles on various topics but best known for his writings on trends in religion and cultural influences on these trends. He was ordained Lutheran minister. He wrote in a compelling narrative style. He tells the story of catching his son stealing from him and that he responded not with anger or punishment but with tears and sadness. His son says that his father's response here was a turning point in his life.

Manicheanism

A religion that taught about the struggle between a good spiritual world of light and an evil material world of darkness. It was founded in Persia in the third century AD and spread into the Roman Empire and Asia, lasting until the 13th century.

Martin Luther (1483–1546)

Arguably the most significant, if not one of the most significant persons in the Reformation. Today, the evangelical and reformed perspective includes that salvation is not earned by good deeds but only received as a free gift of God's grace.

Memory-architecture

Human memory architecture is one way of conceiving memory-sensory memory-less than 1 second; short term memory (active and working memory with 20–30 second life span, in which data (sights, sounds, language read or heard) must be actively engaged with (tactics of engagement include generalizing, abstracting, using acronyms, making some connection with previous learned experiences without which no long-term memory is possible, the storage of information that simply will need a trigger or association to be brought back up into the short term, active or working memory to do its work of engaging with new experiences. Much more information is needed, and this book is not designed to include more than a brief snapshot of memory.

Metaphor

A literary construct that describes something in terms that enlarge or diminishes the thing it describes. Jesus s as the good shepherd is metaphorical.

Mind

The activities of thinking. These activities include recall, comprehending and analyzing to more complex activities like hypothesizing and synthesizing. The mind is not a noun, it is a verb.

Moravian Church

One of the oldest Protestant religions of all, founded in 1457 in Bohemia.

Neoplatonists

Platonic philosophy established in the third century AD that went against Hellenistic thought. The essence of Plato's ideas remained alive and well in Neoplatonism. Some old ideas just do not die out.

Other messiahs in Jesus's time

Jesus entered human history at a time that was rife with messiahs. Jesus was likely thought to be just another messiah until he begins to teach an unusual message (e.g. deliberately leaves out the last line from Isaiah's prophecy (61:1–2) and challenging the mind set of God's agenda of vengeance; present unusual opportunities for his gang to see differently and just enough (the transfiguration(Matthew 16:18)) and sets in motion in his teachings that emphasized an entirely different mind-set about everything important, including people's relationship with God, self, others and the created and natural order. His resurrection sealed the deal that He was indeed different.

Paradigm

An accepted and acceptable pattern of thinking about the nature of the world and its elements. Often used in science to explain and encompass the evidence, for example evolution is now paradigmatic.

Paradigm shift

When an anomaly causes a disjuncture in the accepted pattern of thinking about the world and its elements.

Parker Palmer (1939-)

Author of The Courage to Teach and To Know as we Are Known. *His writing is often characterized by themes of personal identity, authentic self-hood, and development of a true self, particularly for teachers.*

Pelagianism

The belief that original sin did not taint human nature and people can still distinguish between good and evil without divine intervention.

PhD (University of Alberta, 1983–1987)

My dissertation title was "The meaning of Christian religious education: An interpretation." My academic interest was in the lived experience of young people in their Christian religious education, and how language expressed this experience. I was surprised as I engaged in an ethnographic study with two fifteen-year old young people as well as three years of study of religious education experiences found in case studies and research. My research themes included young people's expression of the importance of personal growth guiding their learning agenda, their acknowledged need for community, and desire for meaningful learning experience.

Paulo Freire (1921–1997)

His books Pedagogy of the Oppressed *and* Conscientization *have been required readings for college students for years. His strong critical realist orientation, ability to communicate how language itself can be oppressive if it serves interests other than those of the 'good' for the learner and his years of working alongside marginalized people in Brazil and elsewhere are noteworthy. I took a course from him at Boston College during my Ph D studies. I once offered an opinion to him in a lecture he gave to three hundred students. I claimed that the problem with oppression, unjust treatment of people and ongoing issues of violence and poverty all start with the 'human heart' and wrong mindsets. He looked at me, waited for a few seconds and then gently but firmly called me out by saying, "You are naïve." To this day those words have been a heuristic for me, a guide to unlock the meaning of right relationships and how actions preceded thinking, how unjust structures and language need to be called into question for 'whose interests are being served.'*

Principle

A guiding idea of a teaching practice. For example, one guiding idea or principles of the practice of inquiry as teaching strategy is that children are naturally cur

Problem-based learning

Learner centered andragogy in which the student learns about a topic through solving a problem, addressing an issue, or answering a question that 'lives' in their world. Through the formal and intentionally designed learning movements or phases, the learner reflects deeply about the problem and 'reasons' (thinks systematically) through to solutions to the problem, ways to address the issue and answers to the question.

Reflective Action

Pouring meaning into a behavior, action, decision, or way of solving problems, addressing issues, or answering questions. Reflection can occur during or after an action. Another example of an old idea that has morphed into new educational practices.

Reformation

A sixteenth century opposition to the Catholic practices of indulgences, papal infallibility and authority and political influence in Germany and elsewhere. Often marked as the key turning point in theology. Spawned the counter-reformation and arguably both movements are still in process today.

Robert Bellah (1927–2013)

Sociologist whose interests included the influence of individualization in American life and culture- common good vs individualism-and the emergent self-centeredness in American life.

Robert Jacks (1943–2014)

Australian author of Rules to Live By, and Just Say the Word!

R.C. Sproule (1939–2017)

Founder of Ligonier Ministries, author, and apologist for the concept of the holiness of God. He was a proponent for reformed theology. In my D Min studies at Reformed Theological Seminary (unfinished) I would 'listen in' on conversations he would have with truth-seeking students. To a student who asked him 'where do aborted babies go' he responded with the traditional reformed line that we all deserve God's punishment, but some people will 'receive' God's mercy and get to heaven. That statement from Sproule was the beginning of a theological turning point for me

Samuel Clemens

The author of Huckleberry Finn and Tom Sawyer, humorist, and speaker. Quotes include, 'Don't let your schooling interfere with your education,' and "I have had a lot of bad experiences in my life, and some of them have actually happened."

Scaffold

A metaphor used by Lev Vygotsky to describe some activity or declarative knowledge that makes additional learning more likely to occur. The best teachers scaffold learning. Using titles is a scaffold, as is learning to ride a bike with pedals so kids sense and develop balance first is another example of a scaffold. Knowing that 2 groups of 4 objects results in 8 objects is a scaffold to multiplication. Not every scaffold is effective and in fact may be problematic. Water wings used to teach swimming confounds and conflicts with learning to swim because the prime movers in swimming are the arms and are now impeded in doing their task. Physical punishment like spanking is another lousy scaffold because the hidden curriculum outcome includes decisions tinged with avoidance and performance, fear, and worry.

Scenario thinking

A problem-based learning strategy that intends for students to develop a strategic plan, business plan, terms of reference or any organization statement used in planning and implementation. Scenarios are developed over time through a series of well-designed instructional activities designed to be responses to issues, answers to questions and solutions to problems that live in the student's world.

Scholasticism

Thomas Aquinas is often credited with the creation of this theory that offers the idea that one must follow the traditional standards of doctrine and thinking in order to understand correctly matters of religion.

Screwtape Letters (1942)

Lovely little classic book, a satire written by C.S. Lewis depicting a conversation between two demons-a wise, senior mentor devil and a junior 'up and comer' demon. He wrote the book for J.R.R. Tolkien.

Self Concept

Metaphorically, the pictures hung in the galleries of our minds, often hierarchical with one picture taking the prominent place (physical appearance becoming most prominent on date night) depending on context and circumstances. However, self-concept tends to be stable and may contribute over many years to how one feels about or values one's self (self-esteem). Self-preoccupations, particularly physical ones in adolescence, can be strong interferers with learning. A person's self-concept is developmental, iterative and strongly influenced by external events and circumstances, contrary to a common belief that it is primarily genetic.

Set Induction

A tactic designed to draw a learner emotionally and cognitively into a teaching learning act about to come. My Grade 7 teacher used memorable set induction for me and others, in turning over a full glass of water on a table, after creating enough surface tension with a simple sheet of paper over the top of the glass. I was hooked, engaged, and had to find out how he did it.

Shared praxis

Christian religious education by shared praxis can be described as a group of Christians sharing in dialogue their critical reflection on present action in light of the Christian Story and its Vision toward the end of lived Christian faith (ongoing conversion; personal and communal transformation). Thomas Groome, Christian Religious Education, 1981.

Shifts in attendance/participation in church

The Barna Group has studied trends, shifts in practices and the health of the church in North America. In their seven-year study, Church Attendance Trends Around the Country, ending in April,2016, they found that increasing numbers of North American evangelical Christians, while maintaining strong allegiance to Jesus and Christian principles, are less prone to identify church attendance as a priority. In Canada, Dr. Reginald Bibby, University of Lethbridge, in extensive data collected since the early 1980's, found similar trends to be the case in Canada). Dr. Joel Thiessen, in his current book, The Meaning of Sunday (2018) has focused on trends within the evangelical community, particularly on the reasons given for Christian practices of church attendance to have devolved to Christmas, Easter and life events like weddings and funerals.

Somen Das

His paper, An enquiry into the paradigm shifts in contemporary ethical theological thinking: A religio-cultural critique, *offers a perspective on paradigm shifts from an eastern worldview perspective.*

Thomas Groome (1945–)

Currently a faculty member at Boston College. He is an author, former priest and strong supporter for women included in the Catholic priesthood.

His book, Christian Religious Education *is now considered to be a classic and important foundational text for use for teaching young people. I studied with Thomas Groome at Boston College and to this day remain strongly influenced by his interpretations of praxis, how people learn, the role and place of scripture and his clear and evocative style and content of teaching.*

Thomas Kuhn (1922–1996)

His book Scientific Revolutions *poured new meaning into the word paradigm and popularized the notion of paradigm shifts. One of his core notions is that anomalies are at the heart of shifts in paradigms. Shifts in paradigms occur when accumulated evidence-anomalies- no longer supports a current theory or practice.*

Thomas Aquinas (1225–1274)

A Catholic priest and one of the top thinkers of Scholasticism. He came up with natural law theory, which states that the first principle of human action is based on reason

Virtues Project

A Canadian originated program designed to systematically develop daily practices of virtues, one at a time. An award-winning program that has been deployed in schools, families, schools, churches, and workplaces. The program includes five strategies-speak the language of virtues, use teachable moments to teach, set clear boundaries, honor the spirit and offer companying.

Zeitgeist

A German word that refers to the spirit of an age or time-period. More comprehensive that than a paradigm or philosophy. The concept includes a set of guiding ideas that implicitly guides human endeavors in economics, politics, and education. A zeitgeist encompasses cultural aspects of an age; it can be discerned in art and music, as well as what is chosen to research in academic areas like psychology and sociology. It is woven deeply into people's psyches and their assumptions, beliefs, values, and theories. The current zeitgeist in western countries is arguably one characterized by individualism and liberal democratic values of progress, rights and self-determination.

Bibliography

Adler, Alfred. *Understanding Human Nature: The psychology of personality.* 7th Impression. Allen & Unwin, 1954.
Adler, Mortimer Jerome. *Six Great Ideas.* New York: Macmillan, 1981.
Barna, George. *Trends: The Truth About a Post Truth Society.* Baker, 2018.
Bellah, Robert. "Civil Religion in America." *Daedalus* 96, no. 1 (Winter 1967) 1–21.
Bronfenbrenner, Urie. "Bronfenbrenner's Ecological Systems Theory of Development: Definition & Examples." Study.com. April 02, 2013. Accessed September 07, 2020. https://study.com/academy/lesson/bronfenbrenners-ecological-systems-theory-of-development-definition-examples.html.
Bibby, Reginald. *Emerging Generation.* Toronto, Canada: Irwin, 1985.
Bloom, Benjamin, et al. *Taxonomy of Educational Objectives: The Classification of Educational Goals.* Handbook 1, *Cognitive Domain.* New York: McKay, 1956.
Buechner, Frederick. *Wishful Thinking: A Theological ABC.* New York: HarperOne, 1993.
———. *The Final Beast.* New York: Atheneum, 1965.
Chesterton, G. K. *What's Wrong With the World.* Scotts Valley, CA: Pantianos Classics, 2016.
———. *What's Wrong With the World.* Scotts Valley, CA: CreateSpace, 2017.
———. *The Thing: Why I Am A Catholic.* New York: Dodd, Mead and Company, 1930.
Crabb, Larry. *Effective Biblical Counselling: A Model for Helping Caring Christians Become Capable Counsellors.* Grand Rapids, MI: Zondervan, 1977.
———. *Encouragement: The Key to Success.* New York: Zondervan, 1990.
Craig, Marian B. "My Opportunity." *Follow the Lamb,* November 11, 2013, http://www.followthelamb.net/.
D'Arcy, Paula. *Gift of the Red Bird: The Story of a Divine Encounter.* Chestnut Ridge, NY: Crossroad Publishing, 2002.
Das, Somen. "An Enquiry into the Paradigm Shifts in Contemporary Ethical Theological Thinking: A Religious-cultural Critique." *Indian Journal of Theology* 36.2 (1994) 14–26.
De Caussade, Jean-Pierre. *Abandonment to Divine Providence.* Overland Park, KS: Digireads, 2005.
Diamandis, Peter H., and Steven Kotler. *Abundance: The Future Is Better than You Think.* New York: Free Press, 2012.
Dewey, John. *Experience and Education.* New York: Kappa Delta Pi, 1938.
Dobson, James. Interview with Ted Bundy. *Focus on The Family Films,* 1989.

Elliot, Elisabeth. *Passion and Purity: Learning to Bring Your Love Life Under Christ's Control.* 2nd ed. Ada, MI: Revell, 2013.

Erikson, Erik. *Identity Youth and Crisis.* New York: Norton, 1968.

Elkind, David. *All Grown Up and No Place to Go: Teenagers in Crisis.* Boston, MA: Da Capo Press, 1998.

Fischer, John. *Real Christians Don't Dance.* Bloomington, MN: Bethany House Publishers, 1990.

Fowler, James. *Stages of Faith: The Psychology of Human Development.* New York: HarperOne, 1995.

Freud, Sigmund. *Collected Works of Sigmund Freud: Three Contributions to the Theory of Sex, and Dream Psychology.* Charleston, SC: BiblioBazaar, 2007.

Freire, Paulo. *Pedagogy of the Oppressed.* 30th Anniversary Edition, New York: Continuum, 2005.

Gardner, Howard. *Frames of Mind: The Theory of Multiple Intelligences.* New York: Basic, 2003.

Gilligan, Carol. *In a Different Voice: Psychological Theory and Women's Development.* Reprint, Cambridge, MA: Harvard University Press, 1982.

Glasser, William. *Stations of the Mind.* New York: HarperCollins, 1981.

Goodman, Paul. *Growing Up Absurd: Problems of Youth in the Organized Society.* New York: Random House, 1960.

Green, Thomas. *Darkness in the Marketplace: The Christian at Prayer in the World.* Notre Dame: Ave Maria, 1984.

Gregory of Nyssa. "A Quote by Gregory of Nyssa." Goodreads. Accessed September 07, 2020. https://www.goodreads.com/quotes/485600-concepts-create-idols-only-wonder-comprehends-anything-people-kill-one#:~:text="Concepts create idols; only wonder comprehends anything. us fall to our knees.".

Groome, Thomas. *Christian Religious Education: Sharing Our Story and Vision.* San Francisco: HarperCollins, 1980.

Harris, Maria. "The Original Vision: Children and Religious Experience." In *Family Ministry*, edited by Gloria Durka and Joanmarie Smith, 56–79. Minneapolis: Winston, 1980.

Jacks, Robert, and Betty Jacks. *Your Home a Lighthouse: How to Host an Evangelistic Bible Study.* Carol Stream, IL: NavPress, Inc., 1987.

Jung, Carl. *The Collected Works of Carl Jung.* Vol 4, *Freud and Psychoanalysis.* Edited and translated by Gerhard Adler and R. F. C. Hull. Bollingen Series 20. Princeton: Princeton University Press, 1961.

Rudyard Kipling, "If," in *Rewards and Fairies* (New York, Charles Scribner's Sons, 1910), 200–201.

Know.u, Kevin. "Don't Let Your Schooling Interfere with Your Education." Master Intelligence Economique Et Stratégies Compétitives. March 06, 2018. https://master-iesc-angers.com/dont-let-your-schooling-interfere-with-your-education/.

Kraybill, Donald. *The Upside-Down Kingdom.* Harrisonburg, VA: Herald, 1978.

Kuhn, Thomas. "Paradigms and Sociology." *The British Journal of Sociology* 26, no. 3 (September 1975) 354–59.

Kuhn, Thomas. *The Structure of Scientific Revolution.* Chicago: University of Chicago Press, 1962.

Küng, Hans. *Christianity Essence, History and Future.* New York: Continuum International, 1999.

Bibliography

Lewis, C. S. "Answers to Questions on Christianity." In *God in the Dock: Essays on Theology and Ethics*, edited by Walter Hooper, 22–30. Grand Rapids, MI: Eerdmans, 1972.

———. *The Last Battle: The Chronicles of Narnia*. New York: HarperCollins, 2007.

———. *Mere Christianity*. New York: HarperCollins, 1952.

———. *Miracles*. New York: HarperOne, 2015.

———. *The Problem of Pain*. New York: HarperOne, 2015.

———. *The Screwtape Letters*. New York: HarperOne, 2015.

———. *Surprised by Joy: The Shape of My Early Life*. New York: Harper One, 2017.

———. "We Have No Right to Happiness Anyway." *Saturday Evening Post*. December 21, 1963.

Lonergan, Bernard. *Method in Theology*. 2nd ed. Toronto: University of Toronto Press, 1990.

Marcia, James. *Ego Identity: A Handbook for Psychosocial Research*. New York: Springer, 1993.

Means, Richard K. *Methodology in Education*. Foundations of Education Series. Columbus, OH: Merrill, 1968.

Morris, Harold. "Twice Pardoned, Part I—An Ex-Con Talks to Teens." Interview by Dr. James Dobson. *Focus on The Family: Part I and II VHS series*, 1987.

Muggeridge, Malcolm. "Malcolm Muggeridge Quotes." BrainyQuote.com, BrainyMedia Inc, 2020. https://www.brainyquote.com/quotes/malcolm_muggeridge_162600, accessed July 22, 2020.

O'Donohue, John. *Anam Cara: A Book of Celtic Wisdom*. 1st ed. New York: Harper Perennial, 1998.

Papalia, Diane E., et al. "Physical and Cognitive Development in Adolescence." In *Human Development*, 352–87. 11th ed. Boston: McGraw, 2009.

Parton, Dolly. "Dolly Parton Quote." AZ Quotes.com, Wind and Fly LTD, 2020. Accessed July 16, 2020. https://www.azquotes.com/quote/349668.

Pawson, David. *The Normal Christian Birth*. London: Hodder & Stoughton, 1987.

Piaget, Jean. *The Construction of Reality in the Child*. London: Routledge and Kegan Paul, 1954.

Power, F. Clark, and Ann Higgins. *Lawrence Kohlberg's Approach to Moral Education*. N.p.: Columbia University, 1991.

Rohr, Richard. *Immortal Diamond: The Search for Our True Self*. San Francisco: Jossey-Bass, 2016.

———. "Truth Is One." *The Perennial Tradition Daily Devotional*, November 22, 2016. https://cac.org/truth-is-one-2016-11-22/.

Sandford, John, and Paula Sandford. *The Transformation of the Inner Man*. Tulsa, OK: Victory, 1982.

Sproul, R. C. *The Holiness of God Video Series*. Orlando: Ligonier Ministries, 1986.

Thoreau, Henry David. *Walden*. Penguin Classics 13. London: Penguin, 2016.

Tolstoy, Leo. *The Kingdom of God Is Within You*. New York: Dover, 2006. (translated by Constance Garnett)

Whitehead, Alfred North. *The Aims of Education and Other Essays*. New York: New American Library, 1961.

Wiggins, Grant, and Jay McTighe. *Understanding by Design*. Alexandria, VA: ASCD, 2005.

Index

A.N. Whitehead, 1, 109
Abstractions, 33, 45, 49, 92, 93, 99, 126, 132, 135 155
Accidente, 33
Adjacent possible, 162
Adolescence, 63, 83, 99, 125–27, 136–37, 149–50
Advanced organizer, 65, 103, 108
Alexander Solzhenitsyn, 29–30
Alfred Adler, 152, 154–56
Anecdotal record, 138
Anomalies, 12, 23–24, 29, 30, 187, 202
Apprenticeship, 174–75
Archetypes, 121, 153
Architect, 5–6
Assessment, 142, 188
Augustine, 35–36, 189
Autogenous, 77

Banking teaching, 59–60, 189
Barna Group, 206
Beatitudes, 19, 60, 98, 182, 189
Beliefs, 23, 32, 33, 98, 151
Bernard Lonergan, 13, 111–13, 189
Big idea, vii, 3–4, 8–9, 11–12, 17, 22–24, 29, 31, 32, 35, 36, 37, 39, 40, 41, 42, 43, 53, 126, 140, 160
Blog, 145
Brain, 19, 31, 46, 52, 125–26, 157, 161
Brainstorming, 83–84
Buzz session, 85

C.S. Lewis, 5, 14, 17, 34, 50, 55, 61, 71, 90, 119, 124, 135, 162, 191, 205
Capturing attention, 105

Carl Jung, 152, 153–54
Carol Gilligan, 151, 152
Case study, 117, 190
Catechisms, 40–41, 60, 63, 190
Catechumenate, 18, 32–33, 36, 190
Christian (as an adjective), 20–21
Christian religious experience, 15, 31–32, 63, 190
Christian schools, 15–16, 63, 91, 161–64
Christian story, 110–11
Chuck Colson, 134, 191
Church, 25–27, 32, 38, 39, 64–65, 74, 133–36, 157
Church attendance, 25, 206
Circle of Courage, 54, 89, 190
Coaching, 139
Cognitive dissonance, 25, 27
Cognitive perspective, 149–50
Collection/Portfolios, 121
Colloquium, 118–19
Committees, 84
Community, 23, 26, 32–35, 36, 37, 74, 122–23, 154, 157
Competency, 8–9, 49–50, 53
Competency precedes confidence, 53
Concepts, 20, 27, 60–61, 96–98, 108 161
Conditions of learning, 70, 78, 80, 101
Conference, 138
Conservation, 36–37, 40, 152
Conversion, 52, 111, 128, 132–33, 163
Counseling, 138–39
Creeds, 36, 60
Cross-cultural, 136, 157
Culture, 26, 95, 132–33, 159
Current events, 145

213

Curricular focus, 14, 54
Curriculum of being, xxii

David Elkind, 99, 192
David Pawson, 54, 192
Debate, 117–18, 119
Decision-making theology, 34
Declarative knowledge, 204
Deconstruct, 40, 162
Deductive method, 42
Design thinking, 115–16, 144, 192
Developmental phases, 8, 10
Developmental stages, 77
Dialectic, 111, 192
Didache, 31, 192
Differentiated instruction, 19
Direct instruction, 19, 100, 101–2 104, 108, 109, 193
Discussion, 119, 120, 140
Disequilibrium, 98, 112, 113
Disinhibitory effect, 54, 60, 158
Disruptive, 6, 25, 52
Donald Kraybill, 13, 194
Double bind, 27, 155, 193
Drama, 87
Drill, 139

Education, 14–16, 30, 40, 42–43, 45, 161–64
Edward Schillebeeckx, 24, 194
Elizabeth Browning xxii, 179
Elisabeth Elliot, 124, 194
Emilio Reggio, 42
Emotional predispositions, 67–68
Enlightenment, 24, 43, 194
Epistemology, 24, 189
Equity, 9, 155
Erik Erikson, 49, 92, 148, 152, 194–95
Executive control functioning, 20, 51, 92, 116–17
Exodus, 8, 35–36, 43, 121, 162
Expectations, 23–24, 78–79, 82–83, 193
Exploration, 68, 127

Faith xiii, 33, 36–38, 110, 151–52, 193
Faith development perspective, 151–52
Family, 26, 43–44, 84, 87, 154, 156, 175
Feedback, 78–79

Food chain of knowledge representations, 27, 28, 33
Formalized religion, 17
Forum, 119–20
Foundation, 8, 46, 49–60, 62–66, 68, 70–71, 75, 82–83, 93, 152, 158, 195
Frederik Buechner, xiii, 127
Freedom, viii, 81, 95, 98, 126, 157
Freud, 152–53, 182
Friendship, 8, 18, 32, 61–62, 80, 148
Fundamentalist, 27, 99

G.K. Chesterton, viii, 14, 159, 196
Gamification, 73, 86, 196
Gnosticism, 35, 196
Goals, 72, 163, 196
God's will, 91
Graphing, 143
Greenhouse, 69
Group, 32, 39, 85, 140, 159

Habits, 71, 73, 128, 130–31
Habitus, 40
Hans Kung, 24, 197
Harold Morris, 74, 197
Henry David Thoreau, 127, 197
Hidden curriculum, 12, 15, 53, 69, 85, 197
Horace Bushnell, 42
Howard Gardner, 150

Identity vs role confusion, 92, 116
Image, 22, 68, 96–97, 129
Imagine, 22, 94–95, 133–34
Inclusive, 16, 74, 92, 134
Inferiority, 8–9, 49, 148, 154, 195
Inherent contradictions, 33
Inner emotional life, 66
Inner vows, 128
Insight generating, 101, 111
Integrate, 107, 154, 63–64, 76
Integration, 63–64, 84, 149, 154
Intelligence, 113, 150
Interview, 139–40
Intimacy vs isolation, 9, 46, 95, 125, 127, 149
Inventory, 122

Index

Iterative, 6, 13, 52, 74

J.I. Packer, 16, 199
James Fowler, 151, 152
Jean Piaget, 49–50, 60, 109, 149–50, 187, 188, 198
Jewish system of education, 30
Joel Thiessen, 25, 206
Johann Herbart, 41, 199
John 14:29, 18, 72
John Comenius, 40, 42 199
John Dewey, 42, 43, 187
John O'Donohue, 68, 91
Jurgen Moltmann, 24, 199
Justice, ix, 9, 95, 113, 119, 148, 151, 155

Kingdom of God, 3–5, 11–14, 20, 28–29, 42, 44, 52–53, 75, 96, 98, 137, 163–64, 189

Larry Crabb, 55, 61
Lawrence Kohlberg, 150–51, 152
Lectures, 140
Leo Tolstoy, 13, 200
life crises, 8, 148–49, 194–95
Liturgies, 32, 35, 36
Lived experience, vii, 12, 69, 91, 96, 202
Logistics, 7, 46, 94, 120
Luke 17:21, 13

Maker space, 142
Malcolm Muggeridge, 136
Mapping, 143
Maria Harris, 56
Maria Montessori, 42
Martin Luther, 17, 39–40, 200
Matthew 25:1–23, 19, 72
Matthew 7:23, 12
Maxine Greene, 141
Meditating, 131
Memories, 22–23, 46, 50, 68
Memory, 22, 50–52, 108 201
Mentoring, 126, 158
Mentorship, 115, 128, 132
Metaphor, 5, 12, 20, 201
Metaphysical, 38
Mindset, 7, 20, 25–26, 51, 75, 93, 95, 161

Minds-on teaching, 6
Misconceptions, 108–9
Misdirection, 91
Mock-up, 144
Model, 29, 73–74, 93, 121, 132, 144, 158
Moral perspective, 150–51
Mortimer Adler, ix, 9
Motivation, 70–71
Mutual accommodation, 28, 174
Mystagogy, 33

Narrative, 36, 65, 150
Natural development, 66
Negative reinforcers, 5
Neo-platonist, 35
Nurturing, 14, 22, 39, 41, 42–43, 93, 136

Online resources, 122
Ontological, 16, 20, 29, 53, 163
Open ended inquiry, 88
Operationalized, 29, 34
Oral report, 122

Pageant-Maker Faire, 86–87
Panel discussion, 120
Paradigm, 13, 17–18, 23–25, 28, 32, 38, 39, 96, 133, 202, 207
Paradigm shifts, 12, 15, 17–18, 22–44, 187, 202, 207
Parker Palmer, 7, 31, 179, 180, 202
Paul Goodman, 99, 137, 192
Paulo Freire, 16, 157, 189, 203
Peacemaker, 14, 60, 92, 96, 189
Pedagogic reason, 19
Prerequisite skill, 81–82
Personality, 99, 152–53
Platonic, 37–38, 126, 168, 201
Play, 32, 85, 86, 87, 162
Political, 19, 22, 27, 28, 30, 39
Poster, 142, 144–45
Predicting, 80, 86, 106
Presentation, 105, 108, 122, 140, 143,
Principles, 57–59, 91–101, 105, 107, 109, 117, 139, 203
Problem-based learning, 84–85, 115–16, 203
Proceduralize, 93, 99, 101
Project, 115–16, 123, 142

Projection, 87–88, 152
Propinquity, 34, 74
Protestant Reformation, 17–18, 25, 29, 35, 39–40, 204
Psychoanalytic perspective, 152
Psychological, 7, 9, 46, 77, 91, 92, 93, 105, 116
Psycho-social perspective, 148–49
Purpose, 11, 45, 80, 83, 91, 104, 119, 156–57

Questionnaire, 123

R.C. Sproule, 204
Readiness, 78–79, 81, 82
Reason, 11, 27–28, 38, 191, 194
Reclamation project, 22, 28, 34, 37, 40
Reflective action, 109, 203
Regenerate, 22–23, 27, 28, 32, 33, 36
Reginald Bibby, 25, 134, 206
Responsible, 13, 38, 115, 137, 158–59
Review, 33, 138, 141
Rhymes and Songs, 88
Robert Bellah, 27, 204
Robert Jacks, 64, 204
Role playing, 85
Romans 14:17, 13
Rudyard Kipling, 81

Samuel Clemens, 134, 204
Sandfords (John and Paula), 128, 198
Scaffolding, 43
Scenario building, 118
Scholasticism, 37, 38, 205, 207
Sects, 30, 40, 190
Self regulatory strategies, 92, 108, 116–17
Self worth, 55
Self-appraisal, 123, 124
Semantic Knowledge, 20, 41, 59, 108
Set Induction, 103, 206

Short term work, 156–57
Skill, 50–52, 53, 73, 78–81, 158, 188
Social construction, 34, 35, 93, 98, 100
Social reform perspective, 177
Sociological, 22, 27, 154
State-church relationship, 37
Story telling, 65
Strategies, ix, 7, 9–10, 54, 68, 83, 89, 100–102, 116–17, 160, 175
Subconscious, 55, 148, 152–53, 155
Survey, 120–21
SWOT, 114
Synthesize, 76, 99, 111

T.S. Eliot, 76
Tableau, 88
Tactics, 7, 83, 114, 116, 117, 134
Team, 60, 159
Theological paradigm, 25
Theologies, 12
Thomas Aquinas, 37–39, 205, 207
Thomas Groome, 16, 62, 70, 109–11, 206
Thomas Merton, xiv, 168
Training, 58, 71–72, 169
Transaction, 3
Transcendent, 17, 96, 155, 184
Transfer, 117, 158, 193
Truth, 14, 16, 43, 49, 64, 65, 67, 76, 96–99, 110–11, 135, 160, 162

Unfamiliar from the familiar, 50, 77, 102–3

Values, 23, 73, 95, 121
Virtues Project, 54, 89, 207

Walkabouts, 156
William Glasser, 167
Wisdom, 13, 31, 37, 38, 42, 113
Workshop, 120

www.ingramcontent.com/pod-product-compliance
Lightning Source LLC
Chambersburg PA
CBHW060601230426
43670CB00011B/1925